SPECIAL TEACHING FOR
SPECIAL CHILDREN?

INCLUSIVE EDUCATION

Series Editors:

Gary Thomas, Chair in Education, Leeds University, and
Christine O'Hanlon, School of Education, University of East Anglia.

The movement towards inclusive education is gathering momentum throughout the world. But how is it realized in practice? The volumes within this series will examine the arguments for inclusive schools and the evidence for the success of inclusion. The intention behind the series is to fuse a discussion about the ideals behind inclusion with the pictures of inclusion in practice. The aim is to straddle the theory/practice divide, keeping in mind the strong social and political principles behind the move to inclusion while observing and noting the practical challenges to be met.

Current and forthcoming titles:

SPECIAL TEACHING FOR SPECIAL CHILDREN?

Pedagogies for inclusion

Ann Lewis and Brahm Norwich

Open University Press

Open University Press
McGraw-Hill Education
McGraw-Hill House
Shoppenhangers Road
Maidenhead
Berkshire
England
SL6 2QL

email: enquiries@openup.co.uk
world wide web: www.openup.co.uk

and Two Penn Plaza, New York, NY 10121-2289, USA

First published 2005

A catalogue record of this book is available from the British Library

ISBN 0 335 21405 3 (pb)   0 335 21406 1 (hb)

Library of Congress Cataloging-in-Publication Data
CIP data has been applied for

Typeset by RefineCatch Limited, Bungay, Suffolk
Printed in the UK by MPG Books Ltd, Bodmin, Cornwall

Acknowledgements

Our thanks to Lin Walsh for her tolerance and efficiency in working good-humouredly on the manuscript and keeping track of all the minutiae associated with this project.

We are also grateful to the British Educational Research Association (BERA) who funded the review (1999–2000) which evolved into the collaborative venture described here.

Finally, our thanks to the National Association for Special Educational Needs (NASEN) which, in inviting each of us to speak in 1998 at a seminar on SEN policy, provided the kernel for the development of ideas aired there.

Contents

Contributors

Paul Cooper, Professor of Education, Centre for Innovation in Raising Educational Achievement, University of Leicester, UK.

Graeme Douglas, Research Fellow, School of Education, University of Birmingham, Birmingham, UK.

Alan Dyson, Professor of Education, Faculty of Education, University of Manchester, UK.

Felicity Fletcher-Cambell, Principal Research Officer, Department of Professional and Curriculum Studies, NFER, UK. UK National Coordinator, European Agency for Development in Special Needs Education.

Susan Gregory, Consultant, previously Senior Lecturer in Hearing Impairment, School of Education, University of Birmingham, UK.

Liz Hodges, Lecturer, School of Education, University of Birmingham, Birmingham, UK.

Rita Jordan, Professor in Autism Studies, School of Education, University of Birmingham, Birmingham, UK.

Ann Lewis, Professor of Special Education and Educational Psychology, School of Education, University of Birmingham, Birmingham, UK.

Mike McLinden, Lecturer, School of Education, University of Birmingham, Birmingham, UK.

Deirdre Martin, Senior Lecturer, School of Education, University of Birmingham, Birmingham, UK.

Olga Miller, Course Leader, Disabilities of Sight, Institute of Education, University of London, London, UK.

Brahm Norwich, Professor of Educational Psychology and Special Educational Needs, School of Education and Lifelong Learning, University of Exeter, Exeter, UK.

Tim O'Brien, Consultant in the area of EBD, UK.

Jill Porter, School of Education, University of Birmingham, Birmingham, UK.

Madeleine Portwood, Senior Educational Psychologist, Durham LEA; Dyspraxia Foundation Trustee, Chair of the Education Committee, UK.

Gavin Reid, Senior Lecturer, Faculty of Education, University of Edinburgh, Edinburgh, UK.

Jean Ware, Director of Special Education, St Patrick's College, Dublin, Ireland.

Jennifer Wishart, Professor of Special Education, Moray House School of Education, University of Edinburgh, Scotland, UK.

Series editors' preface

'Inclusion' has become something of an international buzzword. It is difficult to trace its provenance or the growth in its use over the last two decades, but what is certain is that it is now *de rigeur* for policy documents, mission statements and political speeches. It has become a slogan – almost obligatory in the discourse of all right-thinking people.

The problem about the sloganising of 'inclusion' is that the word has become often merely a filler in the conversation. People can talk about 'inclusion' without really thinking about what they mean, merely to add a progressive gloss to what they are saying. Politicians who talk casually about the need for a more inclusive society know that they will be seen as open-minded and enlightened, and will be confident in the knowledge that all sorts of difficult practical questions can be circumvented. And if this happens, if there is insufficient thought about the nitty gritty mechanics, those who do work hard for inclusion can easily be dismissed as peddling empty promises.

This series is dedicated to examining in detail some of the ideas lying behind inclusive education. Inclusion, much more than 'integration' or 'mainstreaming', is embedded in a range of contexts – political and social as well as psychological and educational – and our aim in this series is to make some examination of these contexts. In providing a forum for discussion and critique we hope to help provide the basis for a wider intellectual and practical foundation for more inclusive practice in schools and elsewhere.

In noting that inclusive education is about more than simply 'integration', it is important to stress that inclusive education is really about extending the comprehensive ideal in education. Those who talk about it are therefore less concerned with children's supposed 'special educational needs' (and it is becoming increasingly difficult meaningfully to define what such needs are) and more concerned with developing an education system in which equity is striven for and diversity is welcomed. To aim for such developments is surely uncontentious; what is more controversial is the means by which this is done. There are many and varied ways of helping to develop more inclusive schools and the books of this series – and in particular this book edited by Ann Lewis and Brahm Norwich – examine some of these. While one focus in this has to be on the place and role of the special school, it is by no means the only focus: the thinking and practice which go on inside and outside schools may do much to exclude or marginalise children. The authors of this series try to give serious attention to such thinking and practice.

The books in this series therefore examine a range of matters: the knowledge of special education; the frames of analysis which have given legitimacy to such knowledge; the changing political mood which inspires a move to inclusion. In the context of all this, they also examine some new developments in inclusive thinking and practice inside and outside schools.

Special Teaching for Special Children?: Pedagogies for Inclusion tackles the controversial issue of whether there are particular teaching approaches that suit children with particular learning needs. Some researchers have claimed that there are few if any special approaches that have been shown to be more effective than others for children with difficulties. It is also claimed that the supposed existence of such approaches further marginalizes and excludes children with difficulties. However, there are patently better and worse ways of teaching children who have discrete and identifiable difficulties – for example, methods for children with restricted vision and hearing – and if this is the case the argument can be extended to children with more complex or less easily identifiable difficulties. It is essential for teachers to have the evidence available to them on the effectiveness and practical use of such methods if inclusion is to succeed.

It is sometimes argued that mainstream teachers do not have available to them the skills necessary for teaching children with specific or complex difficulties. What this book demonstrates is that there are avenues that can be followed and methods that can be tried – in short, special pedagogies – that may help teachers and their assistants to include the broadest possible range of children in their classes. Ann Lewis and Brahm Norwich are expert in the field of special pedagogy and they and their contributors have made an important contribution to this series in this book.

Gary Thomas
Christine O'Hanlon
Series Editors

Preface

This book reflects a collaborative project in which the exchange of ideas and materials between contributors has been far greater than in a conventional 'edited' book. This integrated approach was evident from an early stage when the draft chapter 1 was circulated to all contributors for comment. It was also the focus of a seminar to explore with contributors the underlying ideas and rationale. Our summaries are inserted after each chapter to reference this initial framework to key points from the chapter. As writing progressed, contributors exchanged draft material and attended a seminar to explore initial positions, thus strengthening the dialogue across chapters. The summaries scaffold the final chapter, which was also circulated in draft to contributors. This approach reflects an ethos suited to the times, the field, the issue and the expertise.

The challenge to contributors was to present, defend and critique a conceptual analysis of the specificity or otherwise of teaching used with particular special educational needs learner groups. One justification for this approach is in the importance of sustaining and increasing the professionalization of teachers and related professionals specializing in special needs. This is vital in a climate in which there is a tendency for special educational needs (SEN) to be marginalized, or subsumed, and to be the focus of apology rather than intellectual curiosity. The range of staff working, in schools and other settings, with children identified as having special educational needs has broadened over the past decade to include groups (e.g. teaching assistants) without (usually) extensive specialized training related to SEN. Thus there are strong pressures to produce practical tips for these workers and while there is a place for these, without also a sound conceptual base the worker has no systematic and coherent basis for discerning the relative value of a plethora of tips and packages. Leaders in schools, researchers and policy-makers need robust reference points.

The genesis of this book was in papers given in response to a major UK government discussion document on provision for pupils with special educational needs (Lewis 1998; Norwich 1998) and our subsequent review, sponsored by the British Educational Research Association, on 'SEN pedagogy' (Lewis and Norwich 2000; Norwich and Lewis 2001). The ensuing development of ideas has been informed by responses to our dissemination of the review to practitioners, policy-makers and researchers. This background illustrates the power of small, grass roots initiatives in developing ideas and practice over time, giving space for reflection, the evolution of ideas and the reference point of an intellectual not a political agenda, fostering a conceptual integrity.

Universities have a vital role to play in informing, shaping and critiquing public policy. The latter is the focus of lively debate internationally, as is illustrated in responses to Jacoby's *The Last Intellectuals* (2000), Posner's *Public Intellectuals* (2001) and O'Neil's *A Question of Trust* (2002). The area of special educational needs is strongly politicized and we contend that academics in this field should be engaging with policy-makers at regional, national and international levels. The basis for this engagement has to be a sharply focused critique, a strong research base, imagination and intellectual independence. This rationale underpins the approach here as reflected in individual chapters and the book's conclusions.

References

DfEE (1997) *Excellence for All Children: Meeting SEN*. London: DfEE.

Jacoby, R. (2000) *The Last Intellectuals*. New York: Basic Books.

Lewis, A. (1998) Effective teaching and learning for pupils with SEN, in K. Wedell (ed.) *Future Policy for SEN*. Tamworth: NASEN.

Lewis, A. and Norwich, B. (2000) *Mapping a Special Educational Needs Pedagogy*. Exeter: University of Exeter and University of Warwick.

Norwich, B. (1998) Aims and principles, in K. Wedell (ed.) *Future Policy for SEN*. Tamworth: NASEN.

Norwich, B. and Lewis, A. (2001) A critical review of evidence concerning teaching strategies for pupils with special educational needs, *British Educational Research Journal*, 27(3): 313–29.

O'Neil, O. (2002) *A Question of Trust*. BBC Reith Lectures (http://www.bbc.co.uk/radio4/reith2002/).

Posner, R. A. (2001) *Public Intellectuals*. Cambridge, MA: Harvard University Press.

cial children?

1978) severe, moderate, mild and specific learning
n 'categories of special educational needs' (DFES
ations. However, they reflect administrative, place-
ation decision-making and not necessarily categories
cs that have pedagogic relevance (see, for example,
n the fuzziness of the 'MLD group').
vance of categories of cognitive learning difficulties
n their association with other kinds of difficulties, e.g.
otional, behavioural. However, it may be that more
es, perhaps some still to be identified, are more pedagogic-
ample, work in psychoneurology might point to particular
rns as being (a) distinctive to a sub-group with learning dif-
ied to specific intervention or types of pedagogic strategy.
vork in the 'learning styles' tradition could conceivably point
t of categorization of learners ('wholists', 'serialists' etc.) and
much more closely to effective pedagogic strategies than do
upings (Read 1998). This is not to argue for those categories
ut to highlight the possibility that categorization of learners may
ally helpful even though the delimiting of the categories may yet
he general differences position could be held within a more or less
n stance, but it would have implications for teacher training
nique differences position, pedagogic decisions and strategies are
only by common and individual needs. Unique differences are in the
d, with common pedagogic needs more in the background. General
eeds are not recognized. This is a position which assumes that while
ers are in one general sense the same, they are also all different. This
that particular pedagogic strategies are relevant or effective for all
irrespective of social background, ethnicity, gender and disability. Dif-
es between individuals are accommodated within this position, not in
ct groups or sub-groups, but in terms of the uniqueness of individual
ls and their dependence on the social context. Yet, for this to be so, com-
n pedagogic needs have to be considered in terms of principles that are
neral and flexible enough to enable wide individual variations to be possible
ithin a common framework. Those who favour a strong inclusive position to
he education of pupils with difficulties or disabilities adopt this view (Bull and
Solity 1987; Ainscow 1991). Indeed, it would be rather odd to claim a common
pedagogy but still argue for separate schooling.

Critique of evidence

In our systematic and evidence-based review we set out to subject the above
assumption concerning the validity of a broadly common curriculum for all
pupils to critical scrutiny. We addressed the question: can differences between
learners (by particular special educational needs group) be identified *and* sys
tematically linked with learners' needs for differential teaching? Generi
teaching effectiveness studies have assumed that what works with most pupil

CHAPTER ONE

How specialized is teaching pupils with disabilities and difficulties?
Brahm Norwich and Ann Lewis

Introduction and background

This book is about one of the most basic and perplexing questions in the
education of learners with disabilities and difficulties: how specialized is the
teaching of this group? The question is challenging because, on one hand, it
calls for a thorough analysis of 'teaching', and, on the other, it requires clarity
about how we conceptualize differences in the area of what we call disability
and difficulties (or special educational needs).

The book is timely given the current context of education policy and practice, both in the UK and abroad. In the USA, the UK and more widely, there are
centrally prescribed curricula which are supposed to be inclusive of those with
disabilities and difficulties. For example, in the USA the requirements of the
IDEA Amendments of 1997 state that pupils with disabilities:

Must be given the opportunity to progress in the same general curriculum
taught to all other students in the public educational system . . . in order
for their involvement to be meaningful, and for the expectation of progress to be realistic, the curriculum must be made accessible to the students. In terms of learning, universal design means the design of
instructional materials and activities that allows the learning goals to be
achievable by individuals with wide differences in their abilities to see,
hear, speak, move, read, write, understand English, attend, organize,
engage, and remember. Universal design for learning is achieved by means
of flexible curricular materials and activities that provide alternatives for
students with disparities in abilities and backgrounds

(Orkwis and McLane 1998)

Such statements reiterate the need for universalizing curricula but stop short of clarifying the nature, rationale and evidence base for particular modifications. Such questions have been sidelined by the very powerful concerns with school-level, not teaching-level, changes required in fostering inclusion. In line with this, an extensive UK government-commissioned review concerning provision for pupils with special educational needs (Dockrell *et al.* 2002) was given a remit reflecting this preoccupation with school, not teaching, level, modifications. The relevance of this book to the current interest in inclusive education and schooling is that it goes beyond the usual focus on school level accommodations for the diversity of learners. If inclusion is about increasing the participation of all learners in mainstream schools, then it must go beyond general questions of the presence of children with special educational needs in such schools, and their social and learning participation. We need to address questions of classroom teaching and curriculum in considering inclusion and inclusive practices. This is the focus of this book.

This book arose from an extensive review and critique of research into teaching approaches used with pupils with different forms of learning difficulties: low attainment, moderate, specific, severe and profound learning difficulties (Lewis and Norwich 2000, 2001; Norwich and Lewis 2001). Our review addressed two questions that are central to fostering effective inclusion:

- First, can differences between learners (by particular special educational needs group) be identified *and* systematically linked with learners' needs for differential teaching? Many studies have addressed only the first part of this question.
- Second, what are the key criteria for identifying pedagogically useful learner groups?

The conventional special educational needs groupings may not be valid or useful when planning pedagogic strategies. However, even if this is so, there may still be valid groupings of learners to identify as the base for differential pedagogy (see below for discussion of this term). In asking whether pupils with learning difficulties require distinct kinds of pedagogic strategies, we were not asking about whether these pupils need distinct curriculum objectives. We were asking whether they need distinct kinds of teaching to learn the same content as others without learning difficulties. These are important points as questions about distinct or special pedagogies are also part of wider questions about whether pupils with learning difficulties need distinct educational provision. Distinct provision includes pedagogic strategies but also curriculum objectives, the setting for learning and time availability. We recognized then that some pupils with learning difficulties take part in programmes that have distinctive and different curriculum goals (such as the fostering of augmentative or facilitated communication). This was a different focus from our question concerning differential pedagogies to reach the same curriculum goals.

Gen[...]
differe[...]
position[...]

Figure 1.1   Pedagogic[...]

Conceptual framewo[...]

At the start of that review we[...]
Norwich (1996), which focused[...]
gogy. Three broad kinds of pedago[...]
pedagogic needs common to all lea[...]
to groups of learners and pedagogic[...]
assumed that pedagogic decisions can[...]
and that there are two relevant contras[...]
be identified using this three-dimension[...]
difference and the *unique differences* positi[...]

An explanation is required of why these[...]
forms of need were selected. There are in fact se[...]
these three kinds of needs. Four of these invo[...]
specific and unique; common and specific; speci[...]
needs only) and two unique needs (common and[...]
needs alone). One involves common needs alone. Th[...]
versions of the general and unique differences position[...]
We consider that possible positions need to recognize w[...]
viduals as well as what is common to all. Therefore all[...]
three forms of need that do not include these two forms[...]
leaves the two combinations that we have called the un[...]
position (common and unique needs) and the general differ[...]
(common, specific and unique needs).

Figure 1.1 shows that pedagogic decisions and strategies are i[...]
both positions by needs that are common to all learners as well as[...]
are unique to individuals. However, in the *general differences*[...]
pedagogy is also informed by needs that are specific or distinctive to a[...]
that shares common characteristics. In this position the specific needs[...]
sub-group of those with disabilities and difficulties are in the foregrou[...]
needs that are common to all and unique to individuals, though importan[...]
are more in the background. It is a view favoured by those who recognize[...]
general categories as relevant to pedagogic decisions and strategies, as in the[...]
research tradition of those who have sought aptitude × treatment interactions[...]
(Cronbach and Snow 1977). The historical and current groupings of learners[...]
(e.g. Schonell's three broad types of 'backward' pupils, the 1944 Act's eleven

CHAPTER ONE

How specialized is teaching pupils with disabilities and difficulties?

Brahm Norwich and Ann Lewis

Introduction and background

This book is about one of the most basic and perplexing questions in the education of learners with disabilities and difficulties: how specialized is the teaching of this group? The question is challenging because, on one hand, it calls for a thorough analysis of 'teaching', and, on the other, it requires clarity about how we conceptualize differences in the area of what we call disability and difficulties (or special educational needs).

The book is timely given the current context of education policy and practice, both in the UK and abroad. In the USA, the UK and more widely, there are centrally prescribed curricula which are supposed to be inclusive of those with disabilities and difficulties. For example, in the USA the requirements of the IDEA Amendments of 1997 state that pupils with disabilities:

> Must be given the opportunity to progress in the same general curriculum taught to all other students in the public educational system . . . in order for their involvement to be meaningful, and for the expectation of progress to be realistic, the curriculum must be made accessible to the students. In terms of learning, universal design means the design of instructional materials and activities that allows the learning goals to be achievable by individuals with wide differences in their abilities to see, hear, speak, move, read, write, understand English, attend, organize, engage, and remember. Universal design for learning is achieved by means of flexible curricular materials and activities that provide alternatives for students with disparities in abilities and backgrounds
>
> (Orkwis and McLane 1998)

Such statements reiterate the need for universalizing curricula but stop short of clarifying the nature, rationale and evidence base for particular modifications. Such questions have been sidelined by the very powerful concerns with school-level, not teaching-level, changes required in fostering inclusion. In line with this, an extensive UK government-commissioned review concerning provision for pupils with special educational needs (Dockrell *et al.* 2002) was given a remit reflecting this preoccupation with school, not teaching, level, modifications. The relevance of this book to the current interest in inclusive education and schooling is that it goes beyond the usual focus on school level accommodations for the diversity of learners. If inclusion is about increasing the participation of all learners in mainstream schools, then it must go beyond general questions of the presence of children with special educational needs in such schools, and their social and learning participation. We need to address questions of classroom teaching and curriculum in considering inclusion and inclusive practices. This is the focus of this book.

This book arose from an extensive review and critique of research into teaching approaches used with pupils with different forms of learning difficulties: low attainment, moderate, specific, severe and profound learning difficulties (Lewis and Norwich 2000, 2001; Norwich and Lewis 2001). Our review addressed two questions that are central to fostering effective inclusion:

- First, can differences between learners (by particular special educational needs group) be identified *and* systematically linked with learners' needs for differential teaching? Many studies have addressed only the first part of this question.
- Second, what are the key criteria for identifying pedagogically useful learner groups?

The conventional special educational needs groupings may not be valid or useful when planning pedagogic strategies. However, even if this is so, there may still be valid groupings of learners to identify as the base for differential pedagogy (see below for discussion of this term). In asking whether pupils with learning difficulties require distinct kinds of pedagogic strategies, we were not asking about whether these pupils need distinct curriculum objectives. We were asking whether they need distinct kinds of teaching to learn the same content as others without learning difficulties. These are important points as questions about distinct or special pedagogies are also part of wider questions about whether pupils with learning difficulties need distinct educational provision. Distinct provision includes pedagogic strategies but also curriculum objectives, the setting for learning and time availability. We recognized then that some pupils with learning difficulties take part in programmes that have distinctive and different curriculum goals (such as the fostering of augmentative or facilitated communication). This was a different focus from our question concerning differential pedagogies to reach the same curriculum goals.

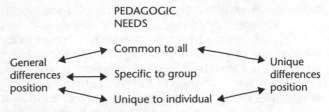

Figure 1.1   Pedagogic positions: general versus unique difference positions

Conceptual framework

At the start of that review we formulated a conceptual framework, based on Norwich (1996), which focused on the commonality–differentiation of pedagogy. Three broad kinds of pedagogic need can be identified in this framework: pedagogic needs common to all learners; pedagogic needs specific or distinct to groups of learners and pedagogic needs unique to individual learners. We assumed that pedagogic decisions can be influenced by all three kinds of needs and that there are two relevant contrasting positions to 'difference' that can be identified using this three-dimensional view about needs: the **general difference** and the **unique differences** positions (see Figure 1.1).

An explanation is required of why these two combinations of the three forms of need were selected. There are in fact seven distinct ways of combining these three kinds of needs. Four of these involve specific needs (common, specific and unique; common and specific; specific and unique; and specific needs only) and two unique needs (common and unique needs, and unique needs alone). One involves common needs alone. This leaves us with the two versions of the general and unique differences positions, shown in Figure 1.1. We consider that possible positions need to recognize what is unique to individuals as well as what is common to all. Therefore all combinations of the three forms of need that do not include these two forms are omitted. This leaves the two combinations that we have called the unique differences position (common and unique needs) and the general differences position (common, specific and unique needs).

Figure 1.1 shows that pedagogic decisions and strategies are informed in both positions by needs that are common to all learners as well as needs that are unique to individuals. However, in the **general differences** position pedagogy is also informed by needs that are specific or distinctive to a group that shares common characteristics. In this position the specific needs of a sub-group of those with disabilities and difficulties are in the foreground; needs that are common to all and unique to individuals, though important, are more in the background. It is a view favoured by those who recognize general categories as relevant to pedagogic decisions and strategies, as in the research tradition of those who have sought aptitude × treatment interactions (Cronbach and Snow 1977). The historical and current groupings of learners (e.g. Schonell's three broad types of 'backward' pupils, the 1944 Act's eleven categories, Warnock's (DES 1978) severe, moderate, mild and specific learning difficulties and the eleven 'categories of special educational needs' (DFES 2003)) are such classifications. However, they reflect administrative, place-ment and resource allocation decision-making and not necessarily categories of learner characteristics that have pedagogic relevance (see, for example, Crowther *et al.* (1998) on the fuzziness of the 'MLD group').

The pedagogic relevance of categories of cognitive learning difficulties might also depend on their association with other kinds of difficulties, e.g. sensory, motor, emotional, behavioural. However, it may be that more appropriate categories, perhaps some still to be identified, are more pedagogic-ally relevant. For example, work in psychoneurology might point to particular neurological patterns as being (a) distinctive to a sub-group with learning dif-ficulties and (b) tied to specific intervention or types of pedagogic strategy. Similarly, some work in the 'learning styles' tradition could conceivably point to a different sort of categorization of learners ('wholists', 'serialists' etc.) and one that related much more closely to effective pedagogic strategies than do the current groupings (Read 1998). This is not to argue for those categories specifically, but to highlight the possibility that categorization of learners may be pedagogically helpful even though the delimiting of the categories may yet be unclear. The general differences position could be held within a more or less pro-inclusion stance, but it would have implications for teacher training

In the *unique differences* position, pedagogic decisions and strategies are informed only by common and individual needs. Unique differences are in the foreground, with common pedagogic needs more in the background. General specific needs are not recognized. This is a position which assumes that while all learners are in one general sense the same, they are also all different. This means that particular pedagogic strategies are relevant or effective for all pupils, irrespective of social background, ethnicity, gender and disability. Dif-ferences between individuals are accommodated within this position, not in distinct groups or sub-groups, but in terms of the uniqueness of individual needs and their dependence on the social context. Yet, for this to be so, com-mon pedagogic needs have to be considered in terms of principles that are general and flexible enough to enable wide individual variations to be possible within a common framework. Those who favour a strong inclusive position to the education of pupils with difficulties or disabilities adopt this view (Bull and Solity 1987; Ainscow 1991). Indeed, it would be rather odd to claim a common pedagogy but still argue for separate schooling.

Critique of evidence

In our systematic and evidence-based review we set out to subject the above assumption concerning the validity of a broadly common curriculum for all pupils to critical scrutiny. We addressed the question: can differences between learners (by particular special educational needs group) be identified *and* sys-tematically linked with learners' needs for differential teaching? Generic teaching effectiveness studies have assumed that what works with most pupils would also work for all pupils. However, little direct evidence for this position has been presented in the literature in relation to various areas of learning difficulties. Similarly, some papers by specialists in the special needs or inclusion areas make calls, which are also mostly unsubstantiated by empirical evidence, for what we called the unique differences position. This rejects pedagogic strategies distinctive to pupils with special educational needs and accepts that there are common pedagogic principles which are relevant to the unique differences between all pupils, including those considered to be designated as having special educational needs. This position is qualified in our review by some recognition of the need for more intense and focused teaching for those with special educational needs.

In our review we have found a trend away from special needs-specific pedagogies that emerged in various ways and for the various forms of learning difficulties. Where we found relevant empirical evidence, this tended to support the unique differences position, as did more general position pieces and general studies of teaching effectiveness, which were not based on empirical evidence. We recognized that the lack of evidence in our review to support special needs-specific pedagogies might be surprising, as there is a persistent sense that special education means special pedagogy to many teachers and researchers. We argued then, and still contend now, that in not finding these distinctive pedagogies we can take one of two positions. We can hold on to the hunch that such special pedagogies do exist in these areas of learning difficulties and that the research is failing to identify them, but will do in time. One option here is to consider that teaching decisions may, in theory, still come to be based on distinctive pedagogies for these forms of learning difficulties, but that the bases of the general groups to which they apply have not yet been identified. More pedagogically relevant groups may be identified in terms of learning process, such as learning styles (Read 1998), than in terms of the general definitions (e.g. MLD, SpLD). The other option is that specific pedagogic strategies apply to other areas of disabilities and difficulties. If what we have called the *general differences* position to teaching pupils with special educational needs is to be maintained, then it is likely to be along these lines. It is this line of argument that gave rise to the current book.

'High density' teaching: Continua of pedagogic strategies

In our initial review, based on various studies, we concluded that the notion of *continua of teaching approaches* would be useful to capture the appropriateness of more intensive and explicit teaching for pupils with different patterns and degrees of learning difficulties. This notion helps to distinguish between the 'normal' adaptations in class teaching for most pupils and the greater degree of adaptations required for those with more significant learning difficulties. These are adaptations to common teaching approaches, and have been called specialized adaptations or 'high density' teaching. Such a position has significant implications for fostering inclusive practice, for preparing teachers and for more exceptional forms of teaching.

The position we have developed was also consistent with other research, which shows how pupils with different kinds of learning difficulties are not provided for adequately in general class teaching. From this review we suggested that there are several facets of teaching where additional emphasis on common teaching approaches is required depending on the individual learning needs of those with learning difficulties (see Table 1.1).

In proposing the notion of continua of teaching approaches we are not suggesting that practical instances of teaching at distant points on the continua do not look distinct or different. However, teaching that emphasizes high levels of practice to mastery, more examples of a concept, more error-free learning, more bottom-up phonological approaches to literacy, for instance, is not qualitatively different from teaching that involves less emphasis on these approaches. There is a tendency to want to split the continua into distinct types, especially for programmes of teaching of pupils at the ends of the continua of attainments. This tendency is reinforced by the historical separation of pupils with significant difficulties and disabilities in separate settings and schools. There can also be professional and parental interests to see the teaching that goes on in these separate settings as distinctive. However, in advocating a position that assumes continua of common pedagogic strategies based on unique individual differences, we are not ignoring the possibility that teaching geared to pupils with learning difficulties might be inappropriate for average or high attaining pupils. We are questioning the way of representing teaching approaches as dichotomies, e.g. error-free versus trial and error.

Table 1.1 Provisional framework of continua of pedagogic strategies

Examples of pedagogic strategies	*Continua of strategies for perceived attainment levels*	
	High intensity	*Low intensity*
Provide opportunities for transfer	Explicit and teacher-led	Autonomous (pupil-led)
Shape task structure	Small discrete steps, short-term objectives emphasized	Larger steps, longer-term goals emphasized
Provide examples to learn concepts	Many and varied, but maximal difference on single criterion stressed	Few examples provided
Provision of practice to achieve mastery	Extensive and varied	Little
Provision of task-linked feedback	Immediate, frequent, explicit, focused, extrinsic	Deferred, moving to self-evaluation
Checking for preparedness for the next stage of learning	Explicit and frequent, teacher monitoring emphasized	Fleeting (by the teacher), self-monitoring stressed

Framework for this book

In this book we move from the conclusion of our earlier review to broaden the focus to a range of 'SEN' groups (see Figure 1.2). Arguably, even assuming that our conclusion was valid for pupils with general learning difficulties, it does not necessarily hold for other groups of pupils with special educational needs.

Parameters and key concepts

Pedagogy

We have taken pedagogy to mean the broad cluster of decisions and actions taken in classroom settings that aim to promote school learning (encompassing pedagogic strategies and, more narrowly, teaching actions). Alexander (2000) and Bennett (1999) discuss, in slightly different ways, the multifactoral nature of pedagogy (organization, discourse and values in Alexander's typology) and (particularly in Bennett's model) highlight the interactions between pedagogical and learning processes. Both slightly under-play the 'real world' context of pedagogical decisions. The teacher is having to respond to many organizational, learning and personal demands; the implementation of an idealized model of effective pedagogy is thus mediated by many other demands and considerations. Effective pedagogy is an ideal that the practicalities of classroom life may threaten or, perhaps, foster in unpredictable ways.

We are also aware that in focusing on pedagogy there can be a tendency to ignore that teaching is a concrete activity taking place in particular contexts. This can lead to the separation of the actions to promote learning from curriculum aims and objectives (what kind of learning?) and from those being taught (who is learning?). So, in asking whether pupils with special educational needs require distinct kinds of pedagogic strategies, we are not asking whether pupils with special educational needs require distinct curriculum objectives. We are asking whether they need distinct kinds of teaching to learn the same content as others without special educational needs. These are important

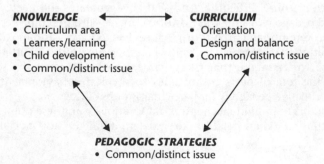

KNOWLEDGE ←——————→ CURRICULUM
- Curriculum area
- Learners/learning
- Child development
- Common/distinct issue

- Orientation
- Design and balance
- Common/distinct issue

PEDAGOGIC STRATEGIES
- Common/distinct issue

Figure 1.2 Teaching framework for book

points, as questions about distinct or special pedagogies are only part of wider questions of whether pupils with special educational needs require distinct educational provision. Distinct provision includes pedagogic strategies but also curriculum objectives, the setting for learning and time availability. We recognize that some pupils with special educational needs take part in pro-grammes that have distinctive and different curricular goals (such as the foster-ing of augmentative or facilitated communication). This is a different focus from our question concerning differential pedagogies to reach the same cur-ricular goals. Clarity about what is meant by pedagogy and curriculum is important in this book.

Our interpretation of pedagogy excludes:

1 Secondary matters such as budget considerations and staffing issues (e.g. whether these pupils are taught by support assistants or teachers).
2 Issues about placement (notably 'segregated' or 'integrated'), as we have taken the position that placement decisions are of secondary relevance compared with what constitutes effective pedagogy regardless of placement.
3 Teaching actions, as narrowly conceived, such as routinely being present in the room before pupils enter for a lesson.
4 The labelling or identification of pupils with learning difficulties (e.g. speci-fication of differences between pupils with mild or moderate learning difficulties).

Area of learning

This book sets out to examine effective pedagogy in generic terms; that is, we are interested in evidence about effective pedagogic strategies across curricular subjects. However, to keep this manageable within the wordage constraints for each chapter, the evidence base has been confined to literacy and/or communication, as applicable.

Cultural context

There is an argument (e.g. see contributors to Daniels 2000) that the personal/ social dimension of classroom interactions is distinctively difficult for many pupils with learning difficulties and that this generates the need for a more specialized pedagogy. While this position concurs with much professional dis-course, we were not able in our original review to locate studies categorically demonstrating that a particular group of learners are uniquely different in this way. Some writers argue that the organizational culture of the school (for example, the role of peers or attitudes to atypical behaviours) is a critical feature of effective pedagogy for particular groups of learners.

Contributors to individual chapters draw variously on these points as well as broader cultural issues relating to gender, ethnicity and social class, as appropriate.

Setting

We have focused on pedagogy in the school setting (primary and secondary school age groups) and have excluded home, nursery, further and adult education. This has been done on the grounds of manageability, although we are also not aware of relevant major studies of effective pedagogy in settings outside compulsory schooling.

Orientation of this book

We, in response to others' comments and discussions about our review, posit the view that we need to conceptualize pedagogic strategies (the focus of our review) in relation to a wider model of teaching. This needs to incorporate strategies in relation to knowledge about teaching and knowledge about the curriculum, as well as knowledge about learners. This conceptual model assumes that teaching is about how teachers and others help the school learning process, what strategies and skills they deploy in the process. However, the model is based on an appreciation that teaching needs to be contextualized within curriculum and knowledge assumptions.

In the way that pedagogic strategies may be common for some pupils with special educational needs but not for others, so it may be that the knowledge base required for teaching may be common for some but not other pupils with special educational needs. This teaching knowledge base has been seen to require both knowledge of the curriculum subject area, e.g. mathematics or personal and social skills, and knowledge of the learning process and the learners to be taught. It is possible that what is specialist about teaching exceptional children might be the teachers' knowledge rather than, or as well as, their pedagogic strategies and skills. In the case of pupils with unusual or special educational needs this may depend on specific knowledge about different forms of learning difficulties and the processes by which these pupils learn. So, although pedagogic strategies are not assumed in our framework to be special or distinct for children with learning difficulties, there may be specific knowledge about pupils in the exceptional range that is required to apply common strategies (Lewis and Norwich 2000).

Historically the educational or teaching process has been seen in various ways, reflecting wider policy and social influences. Prior to the establishment of the National Curriculum in the UK, teaching was seen from a curriculum studies perspective (Lawton 1975; Reynolds and Skilbeck 1976). This positioned teaching as strongly linked to wider philosophical and social decisions about what was worth learning, how curricula were to be designed and what functions they served. Thus the place of teaching, as the how of the process, depended on wider assumptions about the purposes of education. Where the curriculum was cast as a process towards wider educational and developmental aims, a process model, the what and how of teaching were seen as strongly interlinked. Teaching embodied the purposes of education and what was to be learned.

A contrasting assumption was that the curriculum was about the content of what was to be learned and this could be distinguished from the means of supporting the learning of this content, a product or objectives model. The design of the national curriculum in the UK (as elsewhere) reflects the latter model, with its primary focus on content in subject areas and on the content to be learned as separable from the teaching to support the learning process. This orientation to curriculum design lends itself to asking what are the optimal or more effective forms of teaching to achieve specified learning goals or outcomes.

The focus on pedagogic strategies in our initial review and the concept of continua of pedagogic strategies reflect the contemporary assumptions about common curriculum content (in an inclusive centrally prescribed curriculum), which can be separated from the teaching means to support attainment of curriculum targets. This interrelationship between pedagogic strategies and curriculum orientation is also critical to the central question about specialist teaching in this book. We assumed in our review of teaching children with various forms of learning difficulties that teaching is in relation to the core areas of curriculum of English and mathematics. However, the teaching framework for this book assumes that as we widen the range and severity of special educational needs under consideration, what constitutes 'core' in the curriculum might change.

Reference to the contested nature of what is common

This leads to the question of what we mean when we say that there is a common curriculum for all or an inclusive curriculum. It is useful to distinguish here between levels and aspects of what we refer to in talking about the curriculum. Four distinct but related aspects can be identified:

1 General principles and aims for a school curriculum.
2 Areas of worthwhile learning (whether structured in terms of subjects or not) with their goals and general objectives.
3 More specific programmes of study with their objectives.
4 Pedagogic or teaching practices.

We can achieve greater clarity over the curriculum commonality or difference issues by considering various options of commonality and difference for these four aspects. However, we need to emphasize that this is a schematic framework that would not map simply on to the different dimensions and facets of real world actual curriculum programmes.

Of the five schematic options illustrated in Table 1.2, options 1 and 5 represent complete commonality and difference. Neither option is advocated in debates and decisions about curriculum as either viable or socially desirable. Option 2 represents a tendency towards greater commonality where differentiation is at the pedagogic strategy level, and this could be a difference of degree in continua of common strategies or a difference of kind. The National Curriculum in its original 1988 version reflected elements of option 2

Table 1.2 Different options for clarifying the curriculum commonality–difference issue

Option	Aims/principles	Areas of learning	Programme objectives	Pedagogic strategies
1	Common	Common	Common	Common
2	Common	Common	Common	Continua of common strategies or different strategies
3	Common	Common	Different	Different
4	Common	Different	Different	Different
5	Different	Different	Different	Different

Source: based on Norwich (1991).

more than the other options. Options 3 and 4, by contrast, represent a greater tendency towards differentiation in more structural levels of the curriculum. Not only is pedagogy different but programme objectives and areas of learning might be different for some pupils with special educational needs. For them commonality is preserved at the level of general aims and principles, such as those embodied in the Inclusive Statement in the English National Curriculum of 2000:

1 Setting suitable learning challenges.
2 Responding to pupils' diverse learning needs.
3 Overcoming potential barriers to learning.

Another facet of the commonality–difference question in relation to pedagogic strategies in a curriculum context is the nature of curriculum goals when they are different for some pupils with special educational needs. This refers to design options 3 and 4 in Table 1.2, where some areas of learning and/or programme objectives may be different for some pupils. There is a tradition in special education in which what is special about special education is the specialized nature of the areas of learning and the programme objectives within these areas. Specialized areas and objectives have tended to focus on the learner's difficulties either to circumvent them or to reduce them fully or to some extent. These programmes might not be constructed within a discourse of curriculum planning and may not be presented as educational interventions, even though they involve teaching/instruction and learning processes. This is at the uncertain interface between teaching and therapeutic interventions that are learning based.

Table 1.3 illustrates three broad kinds of specialized programmes depending on the kinds of goals: accepting, circumventing or reducing functional difficulties. Recognizing this variety of goals and programmes does not imply any acceptance that the programmes are effective or viable. The point of this analysis is to broaden notions of curriculum scope beyond the traditional focus on basic educational skills or core subject areas. It also elaborates on the possible kinds of differentiation or adaptation of pedagogic strategies that

Table 1.3 Hypothesized relationships between curriculum specialization and pedagogic adaptations

	Curriculum areas and programme objectives		
	Common to all	*Specialized for some*	
Pedagogic adaptations	A. That accept learners' perceived strengths and difficulties (possible target group(s) in parentheses)	B. That aim to circumvent perceived difficulties	C. That aim to reduce perceived difficulties (possible means in parentheses)
	Adapt instructional presentation and learner response modes (sensory and motor impairments)	Learn alternative communication/ mobility access systems (sign systems, spatial orientation, Braille etc.)	Reduce difficulty/ disability (instrumental enrichment for cognitive disabilities); self-control programmes for ADHD etc.)
	Adapt level of learning objectives (cognitive disabilities)		Restore function (reading recovery for literacy difficulties)
	Adapt social emotional climate and relationships of teaching-learning (emotional and behaviour difficulties)		

would be found in curriculum design option 2 (see table 1.2, p. 11). Where there are common principles, areas of learning and programmes objectives (option 2), and pedagogic strategies are assumed to need adaptation, these might be of three kinds, following the analysis of the Warnock Report (DES 1978). As Table 1.3 shows, these are adaptations of instructions presentation and response modes, of level of learning objectives and of social–emotional climate and relationships in teaching.

So, teaching has been conceptualized in this book as involving the interaction of pedagogic strategies, curriculum and teachers' knowledge. The issue of commonality–specialization arises in each element, along with other important aspects. Teachers' knowledge is about the curriculum area and the learners and learning processes. Issues about curriculum models – process versus product models – and balance between areas for learning are also relevant to the commonality–specialization issue. The framework makes it possible to conceptualize the variety and complexity of specialized goals where these may be judged to be effective and viable. It also addresses the grey area where conventional school teaching interfaces with therapeutic interventions that are learning based.

Format of the book

The structure of the book is based on the various special needs groups for whom a case might or might not be made for 'SEN-specific' pedagogic strategies reflecting a specialized knowledge base in the context of specialised curriculum. The purpose of the book is to subject to critical review possible claims about the nature, role and extent of specialization in teaching children and young people with a range of special educational needs. These reviews and critiques are by leading workers within each of the identified fields. The chapters contain in-depth specialist knowledge as well as a robust critique of that material. Each chapter addresses the general questions posed in the book, and outlined in more detail in this chapter, by focusing on pedagogic strategies in their interactions with teaching knowledge and curriculum design. This includes:

1 Defining and describing the focal pupil group, including prevalence data.
2 Commenting critically on the group category or categories and their relationships with other groups.
3 Discussing pedagogic strategies in relation to:
   (a) Communication/literacy area of learning.
   (b) Other relevant curriculum design issues and/or curriculum areas.
   (c) The *unique difference* versus group *difference* positions in relation to a and b.
   (d) The origins of these approaches.
   (e) Underlying principles of the teaching/learning strategies.
   (f) Critique of empirical evaluation evidence of the pedagogic strategies.
   (g) Overall evaluations of teaching practices.
4 Discussing teaching knowledge claims for the focal pupil group as common or distinct.
5 Placing this within an international context.
6 Identifying the potential for research and development in the field.

We have provided chapter summaries following each chapter to help the reader through the material and pave the way for our concluding discussion (Chapter 16).

References

Ainscow, M. (1991) *Effective Schools for All*. London: Fulton.
Alexander, R. J. (2000) *Culture and Pedagogy: International Comparisons in Primary Education*. Oxford: Blackwell.
Bennett, N. (1999) Research on teaching–learning processes. Theory into practice: practice into theory. Eighteenth Vernon-Wall lecture. British Psychological Society.

Bull, S. and Solity, J. (1987) *Classroom Management: Principles to Practice*. London: Croom Helm.

Carpenter, B. (1997) The interface between the curriculum and the Code, *British Journal of Special Education*, 24(1): 18–20.

Cronbach, L. J. and Snow, R. E. (1977) *Aptitudes and Instructional Methods: A Handbook for Research on Interactions*. New York: Irvington Publishers.

Crowther, D., Dyson, A. and Millward, A. (1998) *Costs and Outcomes for Pupils with Moderate Learning Difficulties in Special and Mainstream Schools*. Research Report RR89. London: DfEE.

Daniels, H. (ed) (2000) *Special Education Re-formed: Beyond Rhetoric?* London: Falmer.

DES (1978) *Special Educational Needs (The Warnock Report)*. London: HMSO

DfES (2003) *Data Collection by Type of Special Educational Needs*. London: HMSO.

Dockrell, J., Peacey, N. and Lunt, I. (2002) *Literature Review: Meeting the Needs of Children with Special Educational Needs*. London: Audit Commission.

Fish, J. (1989) *What Is Special Education?* Milton Keynes: Open University Press.

Lawton, D. (1975) *Class, Culture and the Curriculum*. London: Routledge and Kegan Paul.

Lewis, A. and Norwich, B. (2000) Is there a distinctive special educational needs pedagogy?, in *Specialist Teaching for Special Educational Needs*. Tamworth: NASEN.

Lewis, A. and Norwich, B. (2001) A critical review of systematic evidence concerning distinctive pedagogies for pupils with difficulties in learning, *Journal of Research in Special Educational Needs*, 1(1): 1–13.

Norwich, B. (1991) *Reappraising Special Needs Education*. London: Cassell.

Norwich, B. (1996) Special needs education, inclusive education or just education for all?, Inaugural lecture, Institute of Education, University of London.

Norwich, B. and Lewis, A. (2001) A critical review of evidence concerning pedagogic strategies for pupils with special educational needs, *British Educational Research Journal*, 27(3): 313–29.

Orkwis, R. and McLane, K. (1998) A curriculum every student can use: design principles for student access. *ERIC/OSEP Topical Brief*. Reston, VA: ERIC/OSEP Special Project.

Read, G. (1998) Promoting inclusion through learning style, in C. Tilstone, L. Florian and R. Rose (eds) *Promoting Inclusive Practice*. London: Routledge.

Reynolds, J. and Skilbeck, M. (1976) *Culture and the Classroom*. London: Open Books.

CHAPTER TWO

Deafness

Susan Gregory

For children, a major impact of deafness is on the ability to acquire, use and overhear spoken language and this has significant consequences for education. However, deaf pupils constitute a diverse group. As well as general factors relating to gender, ethnicity, socio-economic status and family structure, there are specific factors relating to personality, cognition and other abilities. They also differ with respect to their deafness, which can vary depending on the extent of the hearing loss, the type of hearing loss, whether the loss is permanent or fluctuating, whether it is bilateral or unilateral and whether it is congenital or acquired at a later age.

For the purpose of this chapter, attention is focused on those with permanent bilateral loss of a moderate degree or greater, which is an average hearing loss of greater then 40 dB in the better ear. The conventional classifications for this group are profoundly deaf, severely deaf or moderately deaf (British Association of Teachers of the Deaf 1997). It is estimated that 53 per cent of deaf pupils have a moderate loss, 21 per cent a severe loss and 25 per cent a profound loss (Fortnum *et al.* 2002). It would be possible to include in this chapter the group with lesser, acquired, unilateral or fluctuating losses. However, it is almost always assumed that unless there are additional difficulties (or particular severity such as that associated with acquired hearing loss due to meningitis) these pupils will cope in mainstream education with little or no support and share the same approach and follow the same curriculum as hearing pupils.

In 1998, in a survey of provision for deaf and hearing-impaired pupils in England, the number of pupils notified was 12,063, of whom 30 per cent had an additional disability in that they were educated in special provision other than that intended for deaf children. Seventy-five percent of the total, or 89 per cent of those without additional disabilities, were being educated in mainstream schools (BATOD 2000).

A specialist knowledge base

The need for a particular pedagogy for this specific and distinct group has generally been seen as a function of the particular characteristics of deaf children, the main ones being the need for audiological support, and factors relating to language development, communication and pattern of cognitive abilities. These are usually described by reference to the knowledge, skills and understanding required by teachers of deaf pupils. In Europe there have been specialist teachers of the deaf since at least the eighteenth century and a discrete qualification has existed in the UK since 1885.

Major elements of the skills perceived as needed by teachers of the deaf are competence in the assessment of hearing loss plus an understanding of, and ability to explain, audiograms and the numerical representations of hearing loss. Teachers of the deaf need to understand the effect of losses of different degrees and in different frequencies. Some pupils will have an equivalent loss across the frequencies needed to hear speech, while others will have greater losses in some frequencies compared with others, greater losses in the higher frequencies being particularly common.

Various types of technological support can be given to deaf pupils, the main ones being hearing aids, both digital and analogue. Cochlear implantation is a surgical intervention that improves the ability to hear and requires special understanding about the nature and effects of the implant. Teachers also need skill in understanding and managing the acoustic environment in order to optimize the conditions for learning and teaching. In addition to understanding issues of audiology and technology, teachers of the deaf need to be able to communicate about hearing loss, technological support and environmental modifications to parents, other teachers and pupils.

The inability to hear, or to hear as well as others, results in difficulties in acquiring spoken language and a need for extra attention to be given to language acquisition. Deaf pupils differ from those with speech and language difficulties (see Chapter 8) as deafness is not a difficulty with language acquisition itself and virtually all deaf children can easily acquire sign language. Some deaf children acquire and use sign language as a first or preferred language. Deafness can mean that deaf pupils may have a comparatively small spoken language vocabulary and have difficulty with some syntactical constructions that can be taken for granted with hearing pupils. In addition, some, but not all, deaf pupils may find one-to-one interaction using speech problematic, and their deafness will mean that many will find interacting in group situations difficult.

Additional consequences of deafness can include a limited access to incidental knowledge, which is typically acquired through taking part in, or overhearing, general conversation as well as through incidental learning from the media. This has parallels with the situation for visually impaired pupils (see Chapter 3). There can be difficulties in developing literacy skills, due to limited access to sound and/or spoken language. This will, of course, vary for different deaf children. Moreover, deaf pupils who use sign language may not experience difficulties in the same areas as other deaf children, although there are other issues for this group.

It is thus suggested that teachers need an understanding of how to facilitate language development, whether it be spoken or involving the use of signs. Teaching deaf pupils or supporting those being taught in mainstream classrooms also requires an understanding of gaps in knowledge that can occur, and an ability to understand the need to compensate for these in the educational context. The need to create and maintain a social context for learning, where easy access to spoken language cannot be taken for granted, is also important.

In the UK, deaf pupils are subsumed under the general category of those with learning difficulties. It on this basis that they are given statements of special educational need. However, this is in itself controversial, as deafness does not lead to difficulties in learning *per se*, and the non-verbal IQ of deaf people shows the same average intelligence and range of cognitive abilities as for hearing people (Braden 1994; Maller 2003). However, there can be a discrepancy between language and cognitive ability that needs to be recognized in the education of deaf pupils.

The debate about the cognitive abilities of deaf pupils has a long history (see, for example, Marschark 2003) but current thinking suggests that deaf pupils may function differently in some areas, but that different functioning does not necessarily mean deficit functioning. While short-term memory and sequential learning may be particular areas of difficulty, a number of studies have demonstrated that deaf students who use sign language have enhanced visual spatial functioning in some domains.

There is a clear assumption in the publications on deaf education that deaf children require specialist teachers and this has been seen as self-evident. This is independent of whether deaf children are seen as learning in a similar way to hearing children or perceived as needing different approaches. However, there has been little research that has examined the pedagogical basis of deaf education or the interventions of teachers of the deaf and evaluated their effectiveness, although a number of surveys of parents would endorse the value of the contribution of specialist teachers (see, for example, Powers *et al.* 1999).

Teaching deaf pupils

A main focus of research in deaf education has been the characteristics of deaf learners and their attainments. This often includes discussion as to why attainments are low in particular curriculum areas. There is also a significant body of work that has compared different language and communication approaches to the education of deaf pupils. In the past, publications in deaf education have focused to a large extent on debates on methodology, some taking a theoretical perspective and some comparing how deaf children perform in the various approaches. However, such research studies are almost inevitably flawed because selection for the different approaches is not random. This means that the groups of children in each approach cannot be compared.

Language and communication is the critical issue for the education of deaf pupils. There are a number of educational approaches to take account of the difficulty that deaf pupils have with acquiring and using spoken language. A consideration of distinctive pedagogies differs somewhat for approaches based on English and approaches based on British Sign Language (BSL) as well as English (sign bilingual approaches). English-based approaches usually emphasize the similarity between the education of deaf pupils and others, and follow the same curriculum with the same aims. The involvement of BSL, one of the family of sign languages, with its own lexicon and syntax, creates particular issues for education. While working towards the same goals, it acknowledges the need for a different classroom practice, using a different approach to achieve the same ends. It also recognizes the Deaf community, that group of deaf people who see themselves as a linguistic and cultural minority group rather than a disabled group. Sign bilingual approaches encourage the involvement of deaf as well as hearing people, and a recognition of the culture of deaf people (Gregory 1993).

English-based approaches usually assume a similar pattern of development as for hearing pupils but with the possibility of some delay. Different degrees of classroom adaptations are suggested in order to accommodate these pupils. For example, with audiological support it may be assumed that with adequate hearing aids and the use of radio aids in the classroom, the pupils will cope with little additional support. However, it may be that class teachers need to adapt their practice: for example, always facing the class when talking, providing visual support for learning and perhaps providing handouts for lessons (Watson *et al.* 1999). For some pupils withdrawal from some lessons may be necessary and/or the provision of communication support in the classroom may be necessary. While this may meet curriculum needs, it has consequences for social needs and peer group learning (Edwards and Messer 1987).

Sign bilingualism is based on the idea that, as deaf children have difficulty in accessing spoken language, they should be given the opportunity to acquire sign language to give them a rich language for access to the curriculum and as the basis for the development of English (or their appropriate language). The relative use of the two languages (such as English and BSL) differs in different programmes but an essential feature is that each language is recognized as distinct and used differently. There are several reasons for this: two languages are involved, because English is often taught as a second language, and because BSL, like other sign languages, does not have a written form, this approach emphasizes the different needs of deaf children in particular ways with implications for pedagogy.

While the goals of education for English- and sign-based approaches are for the most part similar, they differ in social aspects. Sign bilingual approaches emphasize pupil self-esteem, the valuing of deafness and sign language, and a recognition of the unique and distinctive deaf culture (Pickersgill and Gregory 1998). English-based approaches see participation and integration into the hearing world as paramount.

The dominant educational approach to the education of deaf children is based on speaking and listening. This is achieved by exploiting the child's hearing through the use of effective and appropriate hearing aids (or a cochlear implant), through developing listening skills and providing a facilitative environment for the development of spoken language. This is known as the aural–oral approach, although it takes a number of different forms (Watson 1998). The proportion of children being educated using this approach is 68 per cent (Fortnum *et al.* 2002).

A further English-based approach uses signs from BSL together with spoken English. Critically, this is thus an English- rather than BSL-based approach. It is generally known as Sign Supported English (SSE) and retains English word order while providing extra information about the communication in addition to speech. It is difficult to state how many pupils are educated using SSE as they are subsumed within the category of 'total communication', which is used with 27 per cent of pupils, of whom some will be using SSE.

A small proportion of children (3 per cent) are educated through a specifically sign bilingual approach, although the group probably involves a larger proportion of pupils than this as some children in total communication programmes will be using BSL within their education.

Literacy

Literacy is a topic that receives the most attention of all curriculum areas in deaf education. Much of the published research confirms that deaf children are behind in their reading and writing compared with hearing pupils. The landmark study was probably that of Conrad (1979), who tested all deaf school leavers (aged 16 years) and found a median reading age of nine years. Later studies have been smaller in scale but have basically confirmed a significant delay, although with some suggestion that it is less now than in 1979 (Powers *et al.* 1998).

The literature contains extensive discussion as to why deaf children should perform badly in reading, together with suggestions for improving reading skills. The reasons suggested for poor performance can be seen in top-down as well as bottom-up skills. Both limited language competence and poorer understanding of the nature of story are seen as making it difficult to predict the next word or phrase. However, word building skills can also be limited by poor phonological awareness.

A study that looked at teaching reading was that of Wood and his colleagues (1986). One of the team, Pat Howarth, recorded deaf children reading to their teacher at school. She then identified hearing pupils in other schools who were reading the same reading book and recorded them too. The study showed that, on average, deaf children were interrupted more frequently than hearing children, and that many more breaks with hearing children included an element of praise than did those for deaf children. Interruptions for hearing children were most often to clarify phoneme–grapheme correspondence, and it was assumed that the child knew the words and syntactic structures, whereas for deaf children the stops were to teach the meanings of words. Thus reading for deaf children also involved language teaching, while the necessary language ability could be assumed for hearing children. The reading rate for deaf children was 20 words per minute compared with 64 words per minute for hearing children. Based on this study, the team concluded that the experience of learning to read is very different for deaf and for hearing children, and that the teacher performs a different function.

Gregory (1998), in a study of the writing of sign bilingual pupils, suggests that the errors they make often relate to the character of BSL grammar and that teachers, rather than seeing these as a problem, could use them for a contrastive analysis in developing written English skills (see Chapter 3 concerning Braille readers). Swanwick (1999), in her comparison of deaf children writing from a BSL story and a language neutral source (a sequence of pictures), endorsed this conclusion, but also suggested that a strong first language such as BSL could facilitate writing skills in the second language, English.

Reading is a particularly useful area to examine in the context of this chapter, as it is an area where deaf children have considerable difficulty but it is also an area where there are a range of teacher aspirations. These range from getting deaf children to function as much like hearing pupils as possible to accepting that deaf children are different and require different approaches. Proponents of oral methods suggest that this provides the best approach to literacy because of its similarity to the learning process for hearing pupils. Watson (1998: 99–100) suggests that 'natural auralists believe that it [oralism] represents the best opportunity for deaf pupils to learn literacy in a way similar to hearing children'. However, from a sign bilingual perspective, Knight and Swanwick (2002: 78) suggest a model that accepts difference and looks at 'the process of literacy development from a bilingual perspective and explores the notion that sign bilingual children approach the learning of literacy with established sign language skills through which English language skills can be mediated'.

Mathematics

Deaf pupils are behind their hearing counterparts in mathematics, although the delay is not as great as for literacy skills. Studies vary in the extent to which they see deaf children as functioning differently mathematically. Wood *et al.* (1986), looking at mathematics performance for a large number of deaf school leavers in oral settings, found that although they were delayed by an average of three years, their pattern of mistakes was similar to that of hearing pupils. They found the same problems difficult and they made similar errors. Thus pupils did not seem to be using different strategies. However, other studies have found systematic errors in the performance of deaf pupils that can be related, in particular, to the language used in presenting the problems. For example, Pau (1995) found a relationship between reading competence in deaf pupils and their ability to solve mathematical problems. He suggested that problems were easier if the data and the unknown factors were presented in problems in the order in which they were used, and thus the presentation was critical.

Sign bilingual approaches present particular issues for mathematics. As with many curriculum areas, the necessary sign vocabulary does not exist. This is not because BSL is unable to address such mathematical concepts: like any living language it has the potential to evolve and develop. However, the suppression of sign languages until the 1980s has meant that they were only used in a limited context, within the Deaf community, and use in educational settings was rare.

A more basic issue is related to mathematical thinking in sign itself, which may be different. Nunes and Moreno (1998), in a study of mathematical development of deaf pupils, showed that in the early stages of computation, signing and counting may be confusing for deaf children because of the similarities in use of the fingers. However, sign language may also confer advantages because, as a visual–spatial language, it conveys much more information about mathematical concepts such as size and shape in the ways in which problems are presented.

Language and interaction

A small number of studies have looked at classroom interaction in English-based approaches. An influential study was that by Wood *et al.* (1986), which looked at teachers' contribution in classroom interactions in oral settings. They found that the higher the level of teacher control in interaction – for example, asking closed questions that demand a particular response – the less the child's contribution to the dialogue. They found that teachers could change their style and become less controlling, gaining greater responses from pupils. Based on their findings, they suggested that deaf children's difficulties might be exacerbated by teachers who were over-controlling. The group repeated this study with pupils using SSE with similar findings.

Other studies have looked at the interaction of deaf pupils specifically in mainstream classes. Gregory and Bishop (1989) looked at the strategies the deaf pupils and teachers employed to maintain the interaction. Pupils would repeat the last phrase they heard or use standard answers, while teachers would pretend to understand when they had not, or, in response to a patently wrong answer, pretend the child was 'teasing' them. These strategies probably function well with hearing children in maintaining interaction but can be counterproductive for deaf pupils. Hopwood and Gallaway (1999) used a similar approach (but with only one child) and suggested that when there is a major discrepancy between the deaf child's linguistic ability and that of the rest of the class, the pupil is severely limited in what they can gather from the lesson. The pupil in this case received essential support by being withdrawn from some lessons for extra tuition by a teacher of the deaf.

There are fewer studies of the interaction of sign bilingual children in the classroom. However, Knight and Swanwick (2002), looking at interaction in classrooms, have analysed the nature of the demands made of pupils in sign bilingual programmes. Observations of classroom interactions demonstrated that adults working with sign bilingual pupils switch between English and BSL with little formal marking, often to maintain communication and interest. They comment: 'Learning English in a bilingual context requires the pupils to move automatically across languages and modes unless the languages are kept strictly separate, and we have so far seen that this is not practical' (*ibid.*: 74). Thus, in addition to a knowledge of sign language itself, teachers have to be skilled in the differential use of two languages in the classroom.

How different is the teaching of deaf children? The unique differences versus group (general) difference position

In terms of the distinctiveness of the group of deaf pupils, opinions differ, from those who minimize any difference and point to overriding similarities of deaf and hearing children, to those who see deaf children as significantly different and requiring different educational procedures. At one level this is inevitable because of the heterogeneity of the group. Children with lesser losses can be significantly assisted by hearing aids such that they can cope in mainstream classrooms, although they may be disadvantaged by poor acoustics, noisy environments or working in large and lively groups. English-based approaches exemplify a unique differences position in that they point to a whole range of different provision to meet educational need. These include adaptations that can be seen as benefiting all pupils, such as good acoustics and attention to visual as well as spoken representations of ideas, or special provision such as communication support in the classroom and withdrawal.

Although numerically the numbers of deaf children being educated through a sign bilingual approach are small, they are an important group because they constitute a clear example of a group difference position. Deaf pupils learning through sign require a different pedagogy in order to achieve some of the same goals. They require the use of sign in the classroom, some modified and specially developed materials and a recognition of different ways of teaching subjects using a visual spatial language, sign language, compared with a linear oral language, spoken language. In order to achieve a classroom where they are can participate fully they require the presence of other deaf children and deaf adults, in recognition that the classroom is a social context for learning, not simply a teacher–pupil learning situation.

Of course the position is not this clear cut. Where significant changes are made for pupils using English, such as the introduction of a communication support assistant in the classroom, issues similar to those for sign bilingual pupils arise. While the pupils are not using a different language, their access to English in the classroom situation may be limited, which raises questions about the extent of their participation with other pupils as well as the teacher, and their own learning style, which may be more visually based. The distinction introduced between the two groups may not be as robust as may appear, and deaf children have both group and unique needs. Thus there is a tension between the two positions in considering the pedagogical needs of deaf pupils.

Potential for research and development in this field

The account of research given in this chapter makes it clear that the majority of the research in deaf education looks at pupil differences in language, in learning ability and in access to classroom discourse etc. Relatively little attention is paid to differences in classroom practice or what happens when additional support is given. The studies reported here that do focus on classroom activity would seem to demonstrate that to be an effective teacher of deaf pupils, special knowledge and skills are necessary. This would suggest a need for further research that looks at classroom strategies and, in particular, what constitutes good classroom practice.

Deaf education is undergoing rapid changes. The development of cochlear implantation means that in developed countries significant numbers of profoundly deaf children will receive implants and thus are likely to function more as severely deaf pupils, resulting in a greater move towards more aural–oral approaches. Newborn screening for deafness, resulting in intervention starting at an earlier age, will also have an impact. However, by contrast, the recognition of sign languages as full languages and the beginning of bilingual education has focused attention on the use of sign language in deaf education. This has been more marked in countries with a flexible attitude to language learning in general and thus the Scandinavian countries tend to be leaders in this area, while English-speaking countries lag behind.

The role of teacher of the deaf is also changing, as more deaf pupils are educated in mainstream schools. For pupils educated through an aural–oral approach, there is a shift from teaching groups of children to supporting pupils in mainstream, and often this is done by working with mainstream teachers and schools rather than individual pupils. It could therefore be argued that for this group the specialist skills required are not necessarily in terms of classroom practice but relate to the management of the learning environment for deaf pupils.

For sign bilingual pupils the situation may be different. Where education is predominantly in sign language, effective teaching will need to be in groups, whether they be in specialist or mainstream schools. However, the aspiration of the approach is that older pupils will be educated in their appropriate mainstream schools through the use of interpreters, and it may be that here too the skill of the specialist teacher will be in supporting the learning environment, including interpreters and skills in learning through interpreters, rather than direct teaching.

There emerges an argument for both a unique difference and a general difference position with respect to deaf pupils, but developments in the management of deafness together with changes in educational policy mean this situation is fluid rather than fixed.

Summary

Nature of the group

- Heterogeneity of the group, including by social, emotional, cognitive and familial differences, as well as degree of hearing loss.
- Criterion for definition: permanent bilateral hearing loss of moderate, severe or profound degree (excludes here children with lesser, acquired, unilateral or fluctuating hearing loss).

Pedagogy

- Weak research base through absence of randomized allocation of pupils to methods.
- Distinction between approaches based on English, sign-supported English, sign bilingual approaches.
- English-based approaches reflect delayed, rather than different, perspective.

Curriculum

- Distinction between approaches based on English, Sign-Supported English and sign bilingual approaches.
- Deaf culture and self-esteem are highly significant for sign bilingual approaches.
- In contrast, aural–oral approaches (based on English) stress the development of speaking and listening skills.
- Conflicting evidence about mathematics and deaf pupils as same/different, regarding error strategies, compared with hearing peers.
- Classroom culture/organization as enabling or otherwise (e.g. noise control).

Knowledge

- Assessment of hearing loss.
- Differential impact of varying degrees and frequencies of hearing loss.
- Technological support (including cochlear implants).
- Impact of deafness on communication/language and access to information.
- Relationship between cognition and deafness.
- Consequences of deafness for literacy.

Unique versus general differences position as pedagogic base

- Deaf pupils may function differently in some areas but different functioning does not mean deficit functioning.
- Sharp differences of view concerning deaf culture (with repercussions for knowledge, curriculum and pedagogy). Advocacy of BSL reflects a strong 'general differences' position.
- Modifications to classroom environment may benefit all pupils, e.g. noise reduction (i.e. direction of change from special as benefiting all), reflecting a unique differences position.

- Concludes that both individual and general differences positions are needed (compare Chapter 6 on macro/micro levels of strategies).

Notable aspects introduced

- Disability culture as impacting on pedagogy.
- Polarization/diversity of teacher beliefs about deafness/difference and hence appropriate curricula/pedagogies.

Visual impairment

*Graeme Douglas and
Mike McLinden*

Definition and description of visual impairment

Visual impairment is a broad term that describes a wide continuum of loss in visual function. There are many aspects of visual function, e.g. visual acuity (ability to resolve detail), accommodation (ability to focus), field of vision (area which can be seen), colour vision and adaptability to light. It follows therefore that there are many causes, types and severities of visual impairment. The definition used by the World Health Organization (WHO) to describe the degree of visual impairment is based mainly on an assessment of the individual's ability to resolve fine detail (i.e. visual acuity) using standardized methods (e.g. the Snellen chart). Thus, a visual acuity of between < 6/18 and 3/60 after correction in both eyes is described as *low vision*, and < 3/60 as *blind*, although people with better acuity can also be described as having a visual impairment if they show an appreciable loss of visual field. Importantly, the majority of individuals with a visual impairment, including those classified as 'blind', do have some residual vision that can be optimized in order to undertake daily tasks and activities. In the UK the legal terms used to classify visual impairment are *blind* and *partially sighted*, and the legal registration as either is similar to those defined by WHO (though not exactly the same).

For those children who have residual vision, it is widely acknowledged that medical descriptions of visual impairment (based on a clinical assessment of visual function) do not provide an accurate indication of how the child is able to use their vision for functional activities – or *functional vision*. In educational terms, therefore, it is necessary for a functional assessment of vision – that is, the extent to which one can use vision to complete activities (Corn and Koenig 1996) – to be undertaken to complement the information provided from a clinical assessment. A detailed functional visual assessment, usually undertaken by a teacher with specialist training in this area (e.g. Qualified Teacher of the Visually Impaired or QTVI) will include an assessment of how the child is able to use vision for 'distant' activities (e.g. to read writing on a white board) as well as 'near' activities (e.g. reading different size fonts, interpreting pictures). For many children with more severe and complex needs, it will not be possible to undertake an accurate assessment of their visual function (e.g. standard methods used to record visual acuity) and there will be a greater reliance on information gleaned from functional visual assessments.

Visual impairment has a range of causes, which may be broadly classified as hereditary, congenital (acquired at or around the time of birth), adventitious (e.g. the result of an accident) or disease or age-related. Some conditions affect the eye itself (i.e. ocular visual impairment such as a cataract), while others are the result of damage to the optic pathways (e.g. optic atrophy). Further, a significant number of children with physical disabilities and complex learning difficulties are reported as having cortical visual impairment (i.e. damage to the visual cortex) or, indeed, cerebral visual dysfunctions (damage to processing areas of the brain other than visual cortex) (Buultjens 1997). Prevalence across the world is therefore somewhat difficult to establish because of the variety of causes of visual impairment, and how this differs across country, climate, culture and economic boundaries. Even in relatively developed countries precise comparisons are not possible because of differences in definitions of visual impairment (see Kakazawa *et al.* 2000 for a comparison of the UK and Japan). In the case of the UK, it might be expected that prevalence of visual impairment would be reflected in numbers registered as blind or partially sighted. In terms of children, the few apparent benefits resulting from registration mean that this is not the case. Nevertheless, the Royal National Institute of the Blind (RNIB) has carried out repeated surveys of local education authorities (e.g. Clunies-Ross and Franklin 1997; Keil and Clunies-Ross 2003), the latest of which concludes that in 2002 there were approximately 24,000 children and young people of school age in England, Scotland and Wales (i.e. up to and including the age of 16), a prevalence rate of 2.4 per 1000 (see Table 3.1).

In terms of relationships with other special needs groups, an influential survey by Walker *et al.* (1992) reported that children with a visual impairment do not form a homogeneous group, highlighting in particular the high proportion of children with 'additional' disabilities. Further support comes from the most recent RNIB survey (Keil and Clunies-Ross 2003), which collected data on children with a visual impairment within four broad categories.

Children with a visual impairment and 'additional disabilities' were described as children with sensory, physical and/or mild to moderate learning difficulties (but excluding severe or profound learning difficulties) and who were broadly within the usual developmental range for their age. Children defined as 'multi-disabled visually impaired' (MDVI) were described as having multiple difficulties, which included severe or profound learning difficulties, and who were functioning at early, or very early, stages of development. Children defined as 'deafblind' were described as children with a combination of both visual and hearing impairment of 'sufficient severity to warrant

Table 3.1   Number of blind and partially sighted children in England, Scotland and Wales extrapolated from a population base of 56 per cent (rounded)

Age of pupils	Number of pupils educated within and outside the LEA				
	Visual impairment without additional disabilities	Visual impairment with additional disabilities	Multi-disabled, visually impaired	Deafblind	Total
11–16 (secondary)	4490	1680	2770	150	9090
5–10+ (primary)	5750	2080	3130	140	11,100
Under 5 (early years)	1650	640	1330	50	3670
Total	11,890	4400	7230	340	23,860

Source: Keil and Clunies-Ross (2003).

substantial curriculum intervention/differention' (see Chapter 4). However, this category excludes children with hearing impairment and severe or profound learning difficulties, who are categorized as 'MDVI' for the purposes of the survey. There is evidence from this survey that some children with visual impairments and additional disabilities (e.g. 'severe' or 'profound' learning difficulties) are reported in categories *other* than visual impairment. Thus, Keil and Clunies-Ross (2003) report that due to the complexity and severity of these disabilities, their visual impairment is not always recognized, thereby adding further support to the view that prevalence figures under-represent the true number of children with a visual impairment (e.g. Webster and Roe 1998; Kirchner and Diament 1999).

Identifying learner needs

Given the heterogeneity in the population reported above, we can briefly consider a question that is key to this chapter, namely in what ways can the learner needs of children with a visual impairment, including those with additional needs, be considered as being distinctive? Of key significance in addressing this question is an understanding of the role of vision in a child's learning experiences, as well as an appreciation of the potential impact of impaired vision on learning and development.

There is general agreement that vision plays a key role in linking different types of sensory information during learning and development. As such, vision is commonly described as a sense that coordinates or *integrates* the information received through the other senses. McLinden and McCall (2002) sum this up concisely, arguing that visual impairment serves to restrict both the *quantity* and the *quality* of information available to a child, thereby reducing their opportunities to acquire accurate *incidental* information through vision. As McCall (1999) notes, in comparison with sighted peers, children with visual impairments arriving at school may have had fewer or limited opportunities to:

- explore their environment;
- learn through incidental and unplanned experiences;
- refine motor skills by observing and copying actions of others.

These reduced opportunities can result in a 'reduction in the information necessary for understanding how the world is organised and how it can be acted upon' (Webster and Roe 1998: 142), and as a consequence, children with visual impairments will have 'fewer ways of observing what others are doing, how individuals deal with situations and events, and what kinds of responses adults tend to give to peers who produce certain kinds of behaviour' (*ibid.*: 143). Further, as Ferrell (2002: 30) notes, a significant reduction in visual information can result in learning that 'occurs too often by chance, and it occurs in discrete, fleeting pieces that cannot easily be combined into concepts'. She highlights, therefore, that learning for children with visual impairments needs to be more deliberate, incorporating 'thoughtful and planned use of the time available to increase the chances for success by mediating an environment that cannot be experienced visually' (*ibid.*: 28).

Curriculum and teacher knowledge

An important distinction made in this book is between curriculum, knowledge and pedagogic strategies (see Figure 1.2). The task of unpicking these aspects of teaching is difficult because these three different aspects are interdependent and consequently each is difficult to discuss without reference to the others. For this reason we spend some time initially considering curriculum and knowledge prior to discussing pedagogic strategies. This, in part, reflects our belief that curriculum and the teacher's knowledge of the learning process underpin decisions about pedagogy – indeed this is where much of the *empirical* is found.

Additional curriculum areas for pupils with a visual impairment

The distinctive needs of children with visual impairments have given rise to a number of curriculum areas that are considered to be either 'over and above' the mainstream curriculum (e.g. Arter *et al.* 1999) or areas that are outside the mainstream teacher's expertise (e.g. Spragg and Stone 1997) and require input from professionals with specialist training (e.g. QTVI, mobility officer). Although these areas have been presented in a variety of ways, they can be captured in the following 'additional' or 'special' (see Mason *et al.* 1997) curriculum areas:

- Mobility and independence (e.g. body and spatial awareness, social and emotional development, travel skills, and independent living skills; see, for example, Pavey *et al.* 2002).
- Maximizing use of residual vision (e.g. developing skills in using low vision aids for close and distance activities; see, for example, Jose 1983).
- Maximizing the use of other senses (e.g. developing listening skills and/or tactual skills; see, for example, Arter 1997; McCall 1997).
- ICT (e.g. developing skills in using specialist ICT to access the curriculum; see, for example, Douglas 2001).
- Literacy development (e.g. through specialist codes such as Braille or Moon,[1] or through print/modified print).

Some of these curriculum areas fall outside the statutory curriculum (National Curriculum in England), and in some cases fall within what the editors call the 'uncertain interface between teaching and therapeutic intervention that are learning based' (Chapter 1: 11). Mobility and independence education is a particular case in point, and it has been argued that the inconsistency of this provision in mainstream schools is in part due to the uncertainty about which agency is responsible for its delivery (e.g. Pavey *et al.* 2002). However, the authors go on to argue that the development of mobility and independence skills is an essential part of education,

> The key objective of mobility and independence provision is to help the child to learn and develop. To fully engage with their education children need to learn how to move from lesson to lesson, navigate around the classroom, handle equipment, navigate around their desk successfully, and communicate successfully with their peers.
>
> (Pavey *et al.* 2002: 10)

A key principle of the additional curriculum is that many children with a visual impairment will require structured teaching to enable them to learn to do tasks that normally sighted children learn without such formal input. This is true for many of the areas of the additional curriculum listed above – whether it be structured mobility, visual training, including the use of low vision aids, or ICT work including specialist access technology. In simple terms, those who teach children with a visual impairment aim to address the issue of reduced quality and quantity of information (or *information access*) by enabling curriculum access through either enhancing visual presentation (e.g. providing a modified picture with appropriate task lighting to a child with low vision) or providing an alternative modality (e.g. providing a verbal and textual description of a picture). Similarly, the additional curriculum seeks to address the same issues by developing the children's concepts and skills that enable them to access information. It follows that different parts of the additional curriculum will be relevant to different children depending upon their needs. Some of the key variables that predict this need are related to the child's vision, and have already been discussed (most obviously, a child with no vision will not benefit from aspects of the additional curriculum concerned with maximizing residual vision). However, the decision as to the amount and type of input required for a given child is usually far more subtle.

While space does not allow a full discussion here, mobility is a useful example of this point. Observation of a person with a severe visual impairment travelling along a route reveals the strategies they use to acquire the information necessary for that journey. This might, for example, involve the use of a cane to gain information about the immediate environment, the use of optical devices to gain information about more distant information such as a sign or bus number and, of course, careful attention to auditory information. The detail of some of these strategies should not be underestimated (e.g. 'squaring off' to ensure walking commences perpendicular to a wall, 'indenting' to ensure the safe crossing of a side street, the use of idiosyncratic 'landmarks' to break up a route into chunks). Similarly, the strain they can put upon the memory of the person adopting them, the limitations of the strategies and the special knowledge of those who are involved in the process of teaching these skills are considerable.

Literacy and visual impairment

Routes to literacy
We have already highlighted the heterogeneity of the population of children with a visual impairment, and this is particularly well illustrated in relation to literacy. Broadly, it is useful to distinguish between three types of student: those who use a formal tactile code (Braille or Moon), those who use print ('low vision readers'; Lamb 1998) and those who do not use either (children with more complex needs). For the purposes of this discussion we focus upon the use of formal literacy codes (in the most part Braille and print, and to some extent Moon). Even this distinction needs qualifying. For example, in discussing the needs of individuals when selecting a literacy medium, Koenig (1998: 56) reports that:

> Some individuals may approach tasks visually at a distance, but prefer tactile methods at near point. Others may clearly be visual learners but have a progressive or unstable eye condition that requires attention to learning non-visual approaches. Still others may be auditory learners, but few professionals would advocate relying solely on audio taped books or live readers as the primary literacy medium.

The heterogeneity within the population suggests, therefore, that within the two broad groups of print and tactile readers we might not expect learners to fall neatly within one category or the other. Indeed, as Koenig (1998) concludes, neither 'legal' nor 'functional' definitions of blindness and visual impairment alone are adequate for selecting appropriate literacy media. Increased emphasis is now being placed on individuals using a combination of media to attain full literacy (e.g. a child who uses an audio book to listen to a novel and Braille to read the menu in a restaurant).

Further, recent case study research exploring the viability of Moon as an alternative embossed code in offering a literacy medium for children unable to access Braille provided evidence for different 'literacy routes' (Douglas *et al.* 2003). This notion of 'literacy routes' is a useful one, and a developed version of this is presented in Table 3.2.

The choice of literacy code is clearly more complex than one might initially expect, but even within each code there are other considerations (which may have an impact upon pedagogic strategies). In the case of Braille, for example, there are issues relating to the selection of grade one and two Braille. This is similarly the case for Moon, and there are decisions about the chosen size of the Moon characters. In the case of print, there are issues of size and style of print used, and the use of low vision aids and lighting. In all cases there are issues related to writing, including the use of ICT.

Our conclusion is that children with a visual impairment follow different routes to literacy. All children with visual impairment must be taught many things that are the same as children with normal sight, e.g. phonological skills, blending, principles of sequence and story, vocabulary. However, they must be taught some different things compared to children with normal vision – sometimes instead of aspects of the mainstream curriculum (e.g. the Braille code instead of the print code), sometimes as well as aspects of the mainstream curriculum (e.g. the efficient use of low vision aids).

Knowledge of the literacy process and performance

Most of the empirical research into the literacy development of children with a visual impairment has focused on reading rather than writing. Two relatively large-scale studies are in the areas of reading test development (Greaney *et al.* 1998; Douglas *et al.* 2002) and focus upon the Neale Analysis of Reading Ability (NARA). The authors aimed to generate norm scores for Braille and print readers respectively. Although both studies paid little attention to the routes to

Table 3.2 Examples of different literacy routes for pupils with a visual impairment

Example route label	Description, including context and features of visually impaired pupil
Route 1	Congenitally blind, tactile reader from outset (primary literacy medium: Braille or Moon). Tactile code as a route to literacy.
Route 2	Adventitiously blind (e.g. during adolescence), print reader initially then transferred to tactile code (primary literacy medium: Braille or Moon). Tactile code as a route through literacy.
Route 3	Congenital visual impairment, predictable prognosis, medium for literacy print *or* tactile code.
Route 4	Congenital visual impairment, uncertain prognosis, medium for literacy print *and* tactile code.

literacy discussed above, they provide broad findings that serve as a useful context for the present discussion.

Douglas *et al.* (2002) tested the reading of 476 children with low vision using an unmodified print version of the NARA. The data showed that the average reading ages for accuracy, comprehension and speed for the sample are generally below their chronological age when the comparison is made with their fully sighted peers. This finding is in keeping with general observations of teachers and existing literature (e.g. Tobin 1993 in terms of speed; Gompel *et al.* 2002 in terms of 'decoding'). It appears that up to the age of approximately seven years, the reading performance of children with low vision is in line with sighted peers but then begins to lag, and the size of this lag increases with age.

Greaney *et al.* (1998) tested the reading of 317 Braille readers using a Braille version of the NARA. Similarly to the study with low vision, the data showed that the average reading ages for accuracy, comprehension and speed for the sample are generally below their chronological age when the comparison is made with their fully sighted peers (and those of low vision readers). Again, the size of the 'lag' increases with age. In the case of Braille, however, there appeared to be a greater lag in terms of reading speed.

These broad findings indicate that there may be developmental implications of the apparent difficulty of access. Traditionally, commentators will often refer to the impact upon speed of access, but results seem to indicate that there is what Douglas *et al.* (2002) call a general 'developmental lag' in reading.

This raises a number of questions. First, bearing in mind the arguments of population heterogeneity, is it valid/useful to look at norms across the population (albeit 'Braille' and 'low vision' sub-groups of that population)? In both cases, the authors see the reading test as merely being a tool in understanding *individual* children's reading. Second, it raises the more subtle question of whether low vision and Braille readers merely lag sighted readers, or differ in other ways (which in the context of this chapter would have implications for *what* is taught, and possibly for *how* it is taught).

In terms of other literature, the case for the differences in Braille reading is relatively well developed (see Chapter 2 concerning a sign bilingual approach). One seemingly obvious, but nevertheless crucial, difference when comparing the reading performance of sighted and tactile readers is that while 'the eye can easily take in a whole word at a glance, the finger can only take in one character at a time' (McCall 1999: 38). This 'letter-by-letter' approach to Braille reading has resulted in the development of reading schemes that are reliant on phonic-based approaches rather than whole-word recognition or 'look and say' methods in the early stages of reading. Differences in reading print and Braille have given rise to what Greaney *et al.* (1998: 24) describe as 'Braille specific errors' in the reading process, and they are supported by Miller (1996: 50), who states that children 'acquire *different* strategies to those which sighted children would use when learning to read print' (our italics).

In part, evidence for these differences is a somewhat obvious consequence of using a different code and more importantly a different sense (i.e. touch rather than sight). Even so, careful observation by researchers and practitioners has generated quite a sophisticated knowledge base of Braille reading, including types of error that are particular to the Braille code (such as reversal, rotation and alignment errors), efficient hand movements and correct posture (e.g. Olson and Mangold 1981; Millar 1997; Greaney *et al.* 1998). We would argue that this is the crucial distinctive knowledge of the child's development and the learning process (see Figure 1.2), which is required by those teaching children Braille.

There has been less research related to low vision readers. In the area of the psychophysics of reading, some research has been carried out investigating the eye movements of low vision readers (usually adults) by Legge and his colleagues. For example, Legge *et al.* (1996) showed that the visual span is smaller and glances between eye movements are longer for low vision readers than for normally sighted readers. One of the few studies to investigate reading errors directly was carried out by Corley and Pring (1993). They examined the reading errors of nine partially sighted children (aged 5:8 to 8:7 years) in detail (repeated testing over a seven-month period). They found that the errors made resembled those of fully sighted children of a younger age, but otherwise there were no categorical differences. Nevertheless, Douglas et al (2004) compared the reading profiles of 25 normally sighted readers (mean age 8 years 8 months) with 25 low vision readers (mean age 10 years 5 months). All the children were tested using the NARA and were matched on the reading accuracy score produced by the test. The purpose of the analysis was to search for differences in the children's reading despite them being matched for overall reading accuracy. A closer analysis of the reading error profile was carried out, which revealed some differences. Low vision readers were more prone to making substitution errors than mispronunciations and the reverse was true for normally sighted readers. Perhaps this is not surprising – it might be expected that a student who is on average two years older and finding it difficult to see the print may be more prone to 'guessing' a semantically appropriate word. While further research is required, the authors propose that subtle differences such as this will clearly inform teachers when considering what they teach.

Pedagogic strategies and visual impairment

Having considered the particular consequences of visual impairment upon the curriculum and the required teacher knowledge of the learning processes of pupils with a visual impairment, we now consider how this *may* affect the pedagogic strategies adopted and the empirical evidence to support this. The focus is upon low vision and Braille readers.

Table 1.1 usefully makes a distinction between pedagogic strategies and continua of those strategies (high and low intensity). However, it does not capture the modification of strategies in terms of *modality* of presentation (enhanced or alternative presentation). We would argue that it is this modification that is often crucial for children with visual impairments. After all, modification of modality of presentation of material is neither more nor less 'intense' – it is just different.

To make this distinction explicit we use the labels of 'macro' and 'micro' strategies. Macro strategies are those at a higher level and are typified by the examples in Table 1.1 (e.g. provision of practice to achieve mastery). Micro strategies are very particular modifications of macro strategies (and subordinate to them). We would argue that these modifications are either the enhanced or the alternative presentation required by children with a visual impairment to access the curriculum. For example, a commonly adopted pedagogic strategy as outlined by the editors is 'Provide examples to learn concepts'. We can think about this in relation to teaching a child about farm animals. The strategy could be applied to Braille readers (e.g. giving a child the opportunity to feel a real horse or a tactile representation of a horse), low vision readers (e.g. an enhanced picture of a horse with verbal description) and normally sighted readers (e.g. a picture of a horse).

Irrespective of micro or macro pedagogic strategies as defined above, relatively little research exists that investigates the *effectiveness* of particular pedagogic strategies for pupils with a visual impairment. In the area of Braille teaching (which is possibly the most extensively researched area of visual impairment education), Rex *et al.* (1996: 131) arrived at an 'unsettling' conclusion that despite an extensive body of literature, relatively little is known about the teaching of reading and writing of braille: 'Therefore some of the common instructional practices in teaching literacy to children who are blind may not be the best possible practices. The truth is, professionals in the field of blindness simply do not know.' Nevertheless, a number of researchers have investigated the efficacy of teaching particular Braille reading skills (e.g. Mangold 1978; Caton *et al.* 1980; Wormsley 1981). At the micro strategy level, then, some of the approaches adopted are very particular to the teaching of tactile codes, e.g. the use of hand-over-hand techniques to demonstrate hand movements, or particularly pertinent because of the lack of access to the visual modality, e.g. verbal descriptions of pictures, the use of tactile pictures, the use of real world sounds. In part, these points are self-evident. However, some micro strategies require the teacher to draw upon a more sophisticated knowledge base as described in preceding sections. The choice of letter introduction in Braille, the introduction of Braille contractions, the correction of errors that are particular to the Braille code – these are all choices of pedagogic strategies that should be considered carefully. A bibliography constructed by Tobin (undated) of over 70 articles describing strategies to teaching Braille demonstrates the practitioner interest in these micro strategies.

The evidence in the case of low vision readers is even more limited. There is some research that demonstrates the importance of strategies involving the modification of print, such as enlarging or reducing (e.g. Keeffe 2001) and the use of magnifiers (e.g. Tobin 1993). Other strategies that are almost universally used but have not been investigated in any great depth are the modification of posture (e.g. bringing text closer) and the use of task lighting. Not surprisingly, studies of this type tend to demonstrate that no single modification suits all, although it is widely accepted that the general principle of print modification (in its broadest sense) is likely to be useful to all low vision readers. In the terms described above, these are distinctive micro pedagogic strategies concerned with enhancement of print.

The concern of these types of strategy is primarily with issues of *access* to text rather than the *teaching* of reading – and it is for this reason that we categorize them as micro rather than macro strategies. There is no evidence of particular approaches to the teaching of reading being more suitable to low vision readers, although emerging evidence of different reading development patterns described above may challenge this position.

Turning our attention to macro strategies, historically it is perhaps this distinction of *access* and *teaching* that is crucial in the field of visual impairment. The traditional focus of research has been upon the former rather than the latter. Importantly, we are using the word 'access' to refer primarily to the modification of presentation, rather than the modification of content. It would seem then that there is little or no evidence that there is a distinct macro pedagogy for children with a visual impairment. At a micro strategy level of teaching we can identify evidence of a group (general) difference position that has its basis in access to the curriculum, and results in specific approaches that must be taken when teaching children with a visual impairment. Nevertheless, it would be an oversimplification to conclude that particular strategies are universally applied to the whole visually impaired population; instead, sub-groups of it can follow different educational routes (e.g. literacy routes). Important factors in making the choice of educational route include the child's severity and type of the visual impairment, as well as the extent of their additional needs.

Perhaps there are three consequences of different micro strategies in this way. First, some presentations are simply less practical than others (e.g. providing real examples or three-dimensional models). Second, different types of presentation have different qualities, and to this extent different levels of access. In the teaching of reading, the specific 'whole word' pedagogical approach is simply not possible in Braille, and may be difficult for children with low vision. Therefore, children with a visual impairment may not share a distinctive pedagogic strategy, but have an inaccessible pedagogic strategy in common. Third, research described above noted that the reduction in access to literacy as a consequence of visual impairment (despite compensatory micro strategies) makes reading slower. Perhaps the greatest implication of this is the reduction in time available for the macro pedagogic strategy of *practice*.

Whether what we have called 'micro' pedagogic strategies are distinct or mere modifications of 'macro' pedagogic strategies is open to debate and interpretation. However, what is clear is that their application is crucial to the education of children with a visual impairment, and those who have responsibility for teaching these children require a developed knowledge of the students' learning processes and their distinct routes through the curriculum.

Summary

Nature of the group

- The distinction between the medically defined degree of visual impairment and functional vision is important.
- There is a heterogeneity of children with visual impairment in relation to (a) differing causes of visual impairment and (b) possible co-occurrence.

Pedagogy

- Learning experiences need to be 'more deliberate' (see 'knowledge' below).
- Structured teaching is needed for certain tasks that other children learn without such formal input or do not need to learn (see 'curriculum' below).
- Modifying the modality of presentation is important – not just a case of high/low intensity of pedagogic strategy.
- Distinctive micro strategies for visually impaired learners may reflect practicality, accessibility and the repercussions of reduced time for practice.
- There is a lack of research on the general effectiveness of particular strategies for learners with visual impairments.

Curriculum

- Various 'curriculum areas' are needed 'over and above' those of the mainstream: mobility and independance, use of residual vision, maximal use of other senses, ICT-related, specialized literacy approaches (e.g. Moon).
- Three contrasting approaches to literacy are illustrative of the need for specialized curriculum/knowledge for learners with visual impairments: tactile (Braille/Moon-supported); print, using residual vision; neither, because both precluded through the learner's complex needs.
- This leads to the concept of different literacy routes (reflecting heterogeneity of the vision impairment group – see above).
- Braille versus print approaches to literacy lead to differences in reading strategies (arising in part from letter by letter versus whole word/phonic decoding).

Knowledge

- Vision coordinates information received.
- Hence visual impairment reduces the reception of information needed to make sense of learning experiences.
- The evidence base relates more to knowledge/curriculum than to pedagogy.

Unique versus general differences position as pedagogic base

- There is little or no evidence for a distinct pedagogy concerning visual impairment at the macro level.
- However, the authors make a case that emphasizes differences in curriculum/required knowledge for learners with a visual impairment that consequently lead to group-oriented and individual pedagogic differences at the micro level.

Notable aspects introduced

- The authors introduce the notion of macro and micro levels of pedagogic strategy; macro strategies being 'higher level' (e.g. provision to practice mastery) and micro strategies being 'very particular modifications of macro strategies'.
- A distinction is made between 'access' and 'teaching'.

Note

1 Braille is a tactile code based upon dots arranged in two by three matrix, forming a braille cell. Grade 2 braille contains 'contractions' which include many common letter clusters (e.g. 'sh', 'ou') represented by a single braille cell (see Greaney *et al.*, 1998). Grade 1 braille does not use contractions. Moon is a tactile code based upon a lined alphabet. (See McLinden and McCall 2002 for further information)

References

Arter, C. A., Mason, H. L., McCall, S., McLinden, M. and Stone, J. (1999) *Children with Visual Impairments in Mainstream Settings*. London: David Fulton.

Buultjens, M. (1997) Functional vision assessment and development in children and young people with multiple disabilities and visual impairment, in H. Mason, S. McCall, C. Arter, M. McLinden and J. Stone (eds) *Visual Impairment Access to Education for Children and Young People*. London: David Fulton.

Caton, H. R., Pester, E. and Bradley, E. J. (1980) *Patterns: The Primary Braille Reading Program*. Louisville, KY: American Printing House for the Blind.

Clunies-Ross, L. and Franklin, A. (1997) Where have all the children gone? An analysis of new statistical data on visual impairment amongst children in England, Scotland, and Wales, *British Journal of Visual Impairment*, 15(2): 48–53.

Corley, G. and Pring, L. (1993) The oral reading errors of partially sighted children, *British Journal of Visual Impairment*, 11(1): 24–7.

Corn, A. L. and Koenig, A. J. (1996) Perspectives on low vision, in A. L. Corn and A. J. Koenig (eds) *Foundations of Low Vision: Clinical and Functional Perspectives*. New York: American Foundation for the Blind.

Douglas, G. (2001) ICT, education, and visual impairment, *British Journal of Educational Technology*, 32(3): 353–64.

Douglas, G., Grimley, M., Hill, E., Long, R. and Tobin, M. J. (2002) The use of the NARA for assessing the reading ability of children with low vision, *British Journal of Visual Impairment*, 20(2): 68–75.

Douglas, G., Grimley, M., McLinden, M., and Watson L. (2004). Reading errors made by children with low vision. *Opthalmic and Physiological Optics*, 24, 4, 319–322.

Douglas, G., McLinden, M. and McCall, S. (2003) Case study – an investigation into the potential of embossed 'dotted' Moon as a production method for children using Moon as a route to literacy. DfES SEN Small Grants Programme TO45. University of Birmingham.

Ferrell, K. (2002) Promises to keep: early education in the United States. *The Educator*, 15(2): 28–33.

Gompel, M., van Bon, W. H. J, Schreuder, R. and Andriaansen, J. J. M. (2002) Reading and spelling competence of Dutch children with low vision, *Journal of Visual Impairment and Blindness*, 96(6): 435–47.

Greaney, J. Hill, E. and Tobin, M. (1998) *Neale Analysis of Reading Ability – University of Birmingham Braille Version*. Windsor: NFER/Nelson and RNIB.

Jose, R. T. (1983). *Understanding Low Vision*. American Foundation for the Blind: New York.

Kakazawa, T., Douglas, G., Kagawa, K. and Mason, H. (2000) Students with visual impairments in special and mainstream schools in Japan: a survey, *Journal of Visual Impairment and Blindness*, 94(4): 218–28.

Keeffe, J. (2001) What size print is best?, *Journal of South Pacific Educators in Vision Impairment*, 2(1): 17–20.

Keil, S. and Clunies-Ross, L. (2003) *Survey of the Educational Provision for Blind and Partially Sighted Children in England, Scotland, and Wales in 2002*. Peterborough: RNIB, Education and Employment Research Department.

Kircher, C. and Diament, S. (1999) Estimates of the number of visually impaired students, their teachers, and orientation and mobility specialists: part 1, *Journal of Visual Impairment and Blindness*, 93: 600–6.

Koenig, A. J. (1998) The literacy of individuals with low vision, in A. L. Corn and A. J. Koenig (eds) *Foundations of Low Vision: Clinical and Functional Perspectives*. New York: American Foundation for the Blind.

Lamb, G. (1998) Communication, in P. Kelley and G. Gale (eds) *Towards Excellence: Effective Education for Students with Vision Impairments*. North Rocks: North Rocks Press.

Legge, G. E., Ahn, S. J., Klitz, T. S. and Luebker, A. (1996) Psychophysics of reading. XVI. The visual span in normal and low vision, *Vision Research*, 37(14): 1999–2009.

McCall, S. (1999) Accessing the curriculum, in C. Arter, H. L. Mason, S. McCall, M. McLinden and J. Stone (eds) *Children with Visual Impairment in Mainstream Settings*. London: David Fulton.

McLinden, M. and McCall, S. (2002) *Learning through Touch. Supporting Children with Visual Impairment and Additional Difficulties*. London: David Fulton.

Mangold, S. (1978) The importance of precision teaching in the education of visually impaired students being mainstreamed into public schools. Part I, *Education of the Visually Handicapped*, 10(1): 1–9.

Mason, H., McCall, S., Arter, C., McLinden, M. and Stone, J. (eds) (1997) *Visual Impairment Access to Education for Children and Young People*. London: David Fulton

Millar, S. (1997) *Reading by Touch*. London: Routledge.

Miller, O. (1996) *Supporting Children with Visual Impairment in Mainstream Schools*. London: Franklin Watts.

Olson, M. R. and Mangold, S. S. (1981) *Guidelines and games for Teaching Efficient Braille Reading*. New York: American Foundation for the Blind.

Pavey, S., Douglas, G., McCall, S., McLinden, M. and Arter, C. (2002) *Steps to Independence: The Mobility and Independence Needs of Children with a Visual Impairment. Recommendations and Summary Report*. London: RNIB.

Rex E. J., Koenig A. J., Wormsely, D. P. and Baker, R. L. (1996) *Foundations of Braille Literacy*. New York: American Foundation for the Blind.

Spragg, D. and Stone, J. (1997) The peripatetic/advisory teacher, in H. Mason, S. McCall, A. Arter, M. McLinden, and J. Stone (eds) *Visual Impairment Access to Education for Children and Young People*. London: David Fulton.

Tobin, M. J. (1993) The educational implications of visual impairment, in A. R. Fielder, A. B. Best, and M. C. O. Bax (eds.) *The Management of Visual Impairment in Childhood*. London: MacKeith Press.

Tobin, M.J. (n.d.) Bibliography of learning and teaching Braille. (http://www.education.bham.ac.uk/research/victar/).

Walker, E., Tobin, M. and McKennell, A. (1992) *Blind and Partially Sighted Children in Britain: The RNIB Survey, Volume 2*. London: HMSO.

Webster, A. and Roe J. (1998) *Children with Visual Impairments. Social Interaction, Language and Learning*. London: Routledge.

Wormsley, D. P. (1981) Hand movement training in Braille reading, *Journal of Visual Impairment and Blindness*, 75: 327–31.

Wormsley, D. P. and D'Andrea, F. M. (eds) (1997) *Instructional Strategies for Braille Literacy*. New York: AFB Press.

CHAPTER FOUR

Deafblindness
Olga Miller and Liz Hodges

Introduction

Over the past hundred years or so, writers, philosophers and more recently psychologists and neuroscientists have become increasingly fascinated by the role of the senses in the evolution of brain function and the emergence of thought. Much of this work has developed as scientists and others continue to seek to understand the nature of consciousness (Ramachandran 2003). As part of this search psychologists and neuroscientists have studied the effects of sensory loss or impairment on the individual in the hope that, in explaining what is atypical in human development, they will gain a better understanding of what constitutes the typical, or, more emotively, 'the norm'. The subject of deafblindness therefore holds particular fascination. As Alexi Leontiev (1948: 108) wrote:

> Deaf-blindness is the most extreme experiment on man, an experiment devised by Nature herself, and one of the most complex and awe-inspiring phenomena – the inner mechanism of the emergent human consciousness in the objective relationships which mould that consciousness.

Deafblindness is rare and congenital deafblindness rarer still. There is an estimated incidence rate (QCA 1999) in the UK of around 1.8 per 10,000 of the total population. Rubella has traditionally been the major cause of deafblindness but, as populations of children emerge with more complex needs, deafblindness is associated with a range of syndromes such as Goldenhaar syndrome or CHARGE, and other neo-natal factors such as low weight premature births. As with sensory loss in general, children who are deafblind from birth are the minority within a minority. For the majority of those affected, sensory loss is acquired in later life following a lifetime's experience of vision or hearing or both. This makes the needs of children who are congenitally deafblind especially distinct. The effects of congenital deafblindness are likely to include difficulty in communicating, problems in environmental navigation and difficulty in gaining understanding and feedback from actions. However, there are several other factors to consider (based on Warren 1994):

- degree of loss or impairment;
- presence of any other disability;
- personality of the child.

Aitken *et al.* (2000: 8) expand Warren's list in relation to deafblindness:

- congenital or early onset hearing and visual impairment;
- congenital or early onset hearing impairment with acquired visual impairment;
- congenital or early onset visual impairment with acquired hearing impairment;
- later onset hearing and visual impairment.

Definitions

Definitions of deafblindness stress the effects of the combined loss or impairment of both hearing and vision. McInnes and Treffry (1982: 1) describe the deafblind child as having one of the least understood of all disabilities because of the unique impact of the loss of the effective use of both distance senses. They therefore consider the needs of such children as arising from *multisensory deprivation*. More recently, writers such as Aitken *et al.* (2000: 3) point to the number of different terms used. They note the loss of the hyphen in deafblindness in 1993 as a means of highlighting the combined effect of deafblindness. Deafblind thus became the preferred term in the UK (and is the term used throughout this chapter), while the USA retains the hyphen, as in deaf-blindness.

However, there is a still greater debate around definition and the approaches used in education. The debate hinges on the specificity of the definition of deafblindness. Much of the work concerned with the development of what are considered to be 'distinct' approaches in the education of children who are deafblind addresses the population of children who are congenitally deafblind with no other disabilities. This is an important distinction for the purposes of this chapter as even the term 'multisensory deprivation' has come to embrace a range of needs, including children considered to have profound and multiple learning difficulties.

We believe there are a number of problems associated with a broader concept of deafblindness:

- research is difficult, and often inconclusive, without an agreed definition of deafblindness and the population;
- claims for a distinct pedagogy become confused when the population is too diverse;

- provision may not be appropriate because it does not address the unique needs of the population;
- the knowledge base of educators is weakened by lack of contact with children affected by congenital deafblindness;

Historical factors

The history of pedagogy and deafblindness can be traced back as far as the eighteenth century but it is the experience of Helen Keller (1889–1969), who became deafblind from an early age, that has come to symbolize the adaptability of the human brain when faced with massive sensory deprivation. Helen Keller and Laura Bridgman before her became famous for what were seen as their amazing abilities, despite their deafblindness, in learning to communicate with others and to understand what was happening around them. This was at a time when the general orthodoxy suggested that there was limited, if any, potential for those considered to be deafblind.

Pockets of educational provision for children who were deafblind were developed from the nineteenth century onwards. However, it is the pioneering work in what was then the Soviet Union, at a school in Zagorsk (now renamed Sergiev Posad), that has had a major influence on the education of children who are deafblind. The work at Sergiev Posad is part of a long tradition in what is described as 'defectology'. Defectology grew out of the work of psychologists such as Vygotsky. Defectology is defined by Knox and Stevens (1993: v) as concerned with abnormal psychology learning disabilities and special education.

Theoretical perspectives

Alexander Meshcheryakov (1974: 31) notes in his seminal study of the education of deafblind children, *Awakening to Life*, that one of the key figures in defectology who 'paved the way for a new approach to the study of the mind' was Lev Vygotsky. Meshcheryakov goes on to note:

> Vygotsky's research paved the way for a new approach to the study of the mind not only viewed from the historical angle, but also in the context of man's development as an individual. Research in the sphere of genetic psychologists carried forward the ideas formulated by Vygotsky, who sought to reveal the significance of objects and norms of human culture, and also of interaction between adult and child for the development of the latter's mind.

Vygotsky's work influenced Meshcheryakov, who emphasises the importance of 'action' (*ibid.*: 295) and the use of 'tools' by the deafblind child. Tools are broadly defined as objects (spoons, clothes, house etc.) and also as norms of social/cultural behaviour (timetables, rules, customs etc.). This emphasis on the 'socio-cultural' and 'activity' within the context of pedagogy is reflected in the work of Jan van Dijk.

In the West probably the most influential figure in the field of deafblindness over the past 30 years is Professor Jan van Dijk. Van Dijk (2001) traces his own approach back to the rubella epidemics in Europe and America in the early 1960s, when a 'new' population of deafblind children emerged. The outcome of these epidemics saw a sharp rise in the number of deafblind, rubella-damaged children (Robbins and Stenquist 1967). Many of these children had more complex needs than earlier populations and the large number of children affected challenged existing provision (Robbins and Stenquist 1967).

The work of van Dijk, while reflecting an interest in Vygotsky's theories around the socio-cultural influences on development, also utilizes the work of psychologists such as Piaget and Bowlby in combination with that of modern neuroscientists. Unlike the work of the early educators in the nineteenth century (such as Howe in America), who worked in the context of provision for children who were blind, van Dijk's work stems from his association with Sint-Michielsgestel, an 'Institute for the Deaf' based in the Netherlands. Much of van Dijk's work builds on his links with the provision for deafblind pupils within Sint-Michielsgestel.

The conceptual framework that underpins the work of van Dijk is drawn from a number of sources. Broadly speaking, he brings together concepts of deprivation, attachment and socialization in order to evolve an approach to pedagogy (Nelson *et al.* 2002).

Deprivation theory

Sensory and experience deprivation

Van Dijk and Nelson (1998) argue that the congenitally deafblind child is potentially deprived in a number of ways. These can be summarized as sensory, experiential and social. In terms of the effect on the developing child this deprivation can be catastrophic. Van Dijk and Nelson suggest that a dual sensory loss or impairment limits not only the child's understanding of what is around them but also their opportunity to gain meaningful experience. In particular, van Dijk and Nelson stress the fragmentation of the sensory input the child receives and the consequent unpredictability of events. As a result of this unpredictability it is difficult for the child to understand the implications of their actions. The child is therefore unable to modify their behaviour or understanding as a result of these actions, and thus their opportunities for learning are limited. Consequently, the child is not motivated to explore and to seek further interactions.

Social deprivation

In his description of social deprivation van Dijk (1991) characterizes the deafblind child as suffering the effects of sensory and social deprivation, often in combination with neurological impairments such as cerebral palsy. The child consequently *lives in an environment with extremely limited stimuli*. At both physiological and emotional levels the child seeks compensation in self-stimulation. There are a number of such behaviours, such as rocking, 'eye-pressing' and light gazing. When engaged in these behaviours the child does not respond to other attempts to help him or her to become aware of a world outside his or her own body.

Van Dijk goes on to examine the impact of deafblindness on the early mother–child relationship and learning. He suggests that the child may not only withdraw from contact with the carer into his or her own patterns of self-stimulation and stereotypical behaviours but may also develop idiosyncratic modes of communication that carers fail to understand. This seeming lack of response may also be coupled with the impact on the child and family of unusual sleep patterns, hospital visits and medical interventions, as well as the involvement of many professionals. The end results are often confusion and misunderstanding between carers and child. This is combined with fear and uncertainty on the part of the child and feelings of disempowerment on the part of the carer.

The possible effects of this are also described by Anne Nafstad (1991: 19), who suggests that the congenitally deafblind child may not be able to learn to organize his interaction into a meaningful entirety. Much like van Dijk, she sees the results for the child as a tendency to remain passive or to be locked into self-stimulatory behaviours that further restrict the child's opportunities for social interaction. Nafstad also emphasizes the subsequent lack of spontaneous or exploratory behaviours.

Teaching and learning

The work of van Dijk has led to the development of a variety of pedagogic strategies. The most comprehensive attempt to evaluate and exemplify the main tenets of his 'approach' has been undertaken by Stephanie MacFarland. MacFarland (1995) sets out an overview of what she describes as the 'van Dijk curricular approach'. She divides this into four components:

1 Learner outcome: development of initial attachment and security.
2 Learner outcome: development of near and distance senses in relation to the world.
3 Learner outcome: development of the ability to structure his or her world.
4 Learner outcome: development of natural communication systems.

These components are underpinned by a series of theoretical principles drawn from studies of typical child development. The principles can be summarized as:

- The importance of the integration of sensory pathways (hearing, vision, touch, taste and proprioception) in the development of perception.
- The role of motor patterns that are 'involved in the handling of things-of-action' and the significance of these patterns in the development of concept formation.

- Attachment and security as an outcome of close human contact between teacher and child. The role of 'imitative (co-active) movements between the child and a consistent partner (response-contingent interaction)'.
- What van Dijk describes as distancing: the gradual transition from concrete and iconic representations towards 'conceptual and schematized representations of the world'.
- The growth of a sense of agency in the child and an awareness of the 'ordering of time and space' facilitating the child's ability to anticipate events.
- The child structuring his or her world around situations that are anticipated and learning to deal with the unexpected.
- How in response to everyday events and interactions the child develops a 'repertoire of natural symbols', which include signs, gestures and referential objects.
- The child's use of this 'repertoire of natural symbols' within the form of pragmatic communication.

Theory into practice

Van Dijk, writing in 1986, outlined what he considered to be the key aspects of an education programme building on his theoretical principles and leading the child from the precursors of 'attachment' to the development of communication. One key element is the use of 'resonance': this is a strategy that capitalizes on the developing child's reflex response to external stimuli (e.g. movement, vibration, vocal). In the case of the deafblind child the aim is to 'shift self-stimulatory behaviours to behaviours that involve other persons and objects' (MacFarland 1995).

This is followed by the introduction of co-active movement. Co-active movement is where the educator follows and then joins in the movement of the child in order to encourage later turn-taking. Van Dijk and Nelson (1998) highlight the importance of this approach in helping the child to develop what they describe as a 'feeling of competence'. By competence they mean that the aim is to promote a 'locus of control' within the child. Co-active movement is unlike earlier techniques that were based on behaviourism, which tried to force the child away from his or her stereotypical behaviours by preventing his or her hand movements or rocking. In co-active movement the educator takes his or her lead from the child. The educator then seeks to sense the child's intentions through his or her movement and to begin a movement-based 'conversation' with the child.

Co-action becomes a basis for bringing movements or actions together in a chain or circuit and structuring the child's daily routine through the establishment of a 'chain of expectancies' (van Dijk acknowledges the particular influence of Vygotsky in this strategy). A chain or routine is established (usually in relation to daily living activities). When the child has become used to the routine a component is omitted. The critical factor is how the child responds to this sudden change. The aim is that the change in routine will encourage the child to react in a way that facilitates the involvement of the teacher. For instance, the child (if physically able) may search for the missing bread during a mealtime routine. The teacher is then able to use the opportunity to respond to the child's interest in locating the missing bread and a form of dialogue takes place.

Tangible symbol systems

Of all van Dijk's work the use of tangible symbol systems such as object referents has been the most influential. At the same time it is also the most widely misunderstood. Van Dijk traces his approach back to the work of Werner and Kaplan (1963), who identify in typical language development the stage at which the child discovers the similarity between object and referent. Van Dijk stresses that these are 'natural' symbols discovered by the child. Writers such as Russell (1996) have explored in some depth the complexity behind the use of objects in what Russell describes as symbol processing and 'the language of thought'.

Although there is not space here to rehearse the numerous theories around language acquisition, it is important to stress that agency and its role in cognition are at the heart of tangible symbol systems. Unfortunately, this is most often what is lost in the use of what have come to be called 'objects of reference'. Often objects of reference are seen as a teaching activity rather than part of a holistic approach to communication (Porter *et al.* 1997). If part of a coherent approach, the use of object referents can enable the child to exert control and to make real choices. However, in many cases the focus of the approach becomes one of giving an object to the child for the teacher to use as a referent in order to direct and thus control the child.

The use of signifiers

'Characterization' strategies are used to help the child to develop a form of vocabulary of referents. A 'characteristic' of an individual or an event, which is significant to the deafblind child, is used as a means of helping the child to locate the individual or event within a context he or she can anticipate and thus remember. It may be a bracelet or ring that an individual always wears when greeting or working with the child or a particular smell or texture linked to an activity. In the case of a child with some vision this could also be a photograph or later a drawing. For the child this referent comes to 'signify' one person rather than another or a particular day of the week when an event may occur. Van Dijk extended this work through the use of what came to be known as 'calendar' or 'memory' boxes. These boxes contain the signifier or referent for the individuals or activities the child will encounter during a particular day. Calendar boxes can reduce anxiety and help the child to anticipate change (for example, if his or her key worker is away). However, van Dijk is keen to point out that this strategy will not work unless the child has reached an awareness of object permanence.

Evidence from research

Although pedagogy and deafblindness have a long history, there is relatively little empirical evidence as to the efficacy of particular approaches or strategies. There is, however, a gloriously rich source of anecdotal information from parents, teachers and deafblind individuals supported by some studies such as the work undertaken in Russia.

In 1991 the All Russia Association of the Blind held a symposium that sought to examine some of the methodological issues underpinning research into pedagogy and deafblindness. The results of the symposium illustrate what remains a major barrier to researching the outcome of teaching, learning and deafblindness. Participants of the symposium were critical of much of the research carried out by key Soviet figures working in the field of deafblindness. This was on the basis of the lack of clarity in relation to the characteristics of the population being researched. This, it was argued, led to assumptions and claims based on inaccurate or misleading data. In particular, research undertaken by Sokoliansky and Meshcheryakov (and subsequently used to support claims of successful interventions) was described by the researchers as derived from data drawn from children who were congenitally deafblind or those who were totally deafblind from early childhood. However, the research was criticized by members of the symposium on the basis that it was said to have involved children who had lost vision and hearing in later life. Some of these children, it was claimed by critics, had been verbal and so had established patterns of language and communication before becoming deafblind.

The very diversity of the population is one of the enduring dilemmas for research in the field of deafblindness. Added to the problem of diversity are the methodological and ethical issues of researching low incidence and vulnerable populations. Where research has been more prolific (though in some ways controversial) is in the field of neuro-science. Although this research focuses on more general populations, there are many similarities between the findings from these studies and those of van Dijk. In 1999 van Dijk returned to his research on the importance of co-active movement and contingency. This was in the wake of a number of studies of brain formation and the ability of the child to cope with stress (Boyce *et al.* 1992; Nelson and Carver 1998; Perry and Pollard 1998). Van Dijk suggests that from these studies it becomes clear that imposing activities on 'a young child in such a way that he is unable to escape, undermines the development of the neurological system and even destroys existing neuronal pathways' (van Dijk 1999). This brought into question the wholesale use of pedagogic strategies such as co-active movement with populations of children with multiple and often profound needs when teachers did not have a full understanding of the theoretical and philosophical roots of such approaches. In some cases, far from helping the child to develop a sense of competence, van Dijk points out that such ill conceived attempts promoted only learned helplessness and greater passivity.

In 1997 one of the authors of this chapter worked on a research project with Jill Porter and Laura Pease. The research had a series of objectives. These included gathering information on the range of pedagogic strategies employed by teachers, how teachers made decisions about what type of strategy to use and the effectiveness of the range of different strategies.

At the time of the research the majority (53 per cent) of pupils were following what was described as a developmental curriculum. Teachers drew their strategies from a variety of sources but the predominant theorist remained van Dijk, whose ideas were enormously influential. One of the difficulties identified was that of translating his ideas into a British curricular context. Teachers sometimes used van Dijk's terminology without a clear understanding of its range of theoretical underpinning (as with van Dijk's observations on the problems associated with co-active movement). Much depended on teachers' knowledge of child development and their initial training. Teachers from secondary (subject-based) backgrounds were therefore at a particular disadvantage.

Conclusions

Much of the emphasis in this chapter has been on presenting the needs of children who are congenitally deafblind as distinct from those of other learners. However, we have also suggested that the population of children now described as deafblind or multisensorily deprived is no longer easily defined and encompasses a multiplicity of combinations of sensory impairment, together with other forms of disability. The real question focuses on whether there is a pedagogy that is specifically related to a group of learners described as deafblind or whether the change in the population of learners has diluted the notion of distinctiveness. While recognizing the complexity of the current population we would still argue that any child who has a significant hearing and visual loss or impairment, whether in combination with other disabilities or not, should be considered to be deafblind. Further, we argue that without an understanding on the part of educators of sensory function and the impact of its loss, access to an appropriate curriculum and pedagogy is unlikely to be achieved. Pedagogy therefore has to be seen to underpin entitlement.

The notion of entitlement and disability is reiterated in terms of the curriculum through numerous discourses around access and inclusion. The introduction of a National Curriculum within the UK in 1988 gave rise to a mountain of material and guidance endorsed by statutory requirements. Teachers were required to follow the content and structure of this curriculum. Teacher training was reconfigured in such a way that the emphasis became one of delivering a prescribed curriculum rather than following the outcome of detailed study of child development and learning. In combination with this mechanistic approach, the area of sensory function has always been a neglected aspect of teacher education. Usually seen within the context of medical study rather than pedagogy, sensory function is perceived as being on the periphery of teaching and learning. Consequently, very few teachers feel competent to assess the educational needs of children who have sensory impairments.

Because of the impact on communication of deafness, and particularly deafblindness, there is additional uncertainty on the part of the majority of teachers. This uncertainty was compounded with the introduction of a curriculum with a linear structure and a starting point of a chronological equivalence of five years. The learning needs of many pupils fell outside this newly created 'norm'-focused curriculum. Given the rarity of deafblindness (in all its forms) the needs of these pupils seemed all the more extreme.

It would be wrong to suggest that before the advent of the National Curriculum all pupils who were deafblind in the UK received appropriate provision. Indeed, apart from one or two notable examples, the needs of such pupils were often misunderstood and their potential untapped. In our experience some of the casualties of this lack of understanding ended up being consigned to long-term care in the sub-normality wards of mental hospitals. Fortunately, more recently there has been some recognition of the need for a more flexible approach to the curriculum.

The devolved nations within the UK now have their own documentation, so more than one model of the curriculum now exists and attempts have been made to unravel the rather simplistic notion of linear progression to allow for greater access to an appropriate curriculum. The publication of curriculum guidance in the UK (QCA 1999) specifically for those professionals working with deafblind pupils has helped to raise awareness of the importance of monitoring the curriculum to ensure that the needs of pupils who are deaf-blind are addressed.

There is also a growing emphasis on early intervention. This concern for the early years has to some extent reawakened interest by the UK government in funding studies and research into child development. There is also increased interest in training those professionals working in the early years who are likely to play a critical role in supporting families of deafblind children. At present these seem positive trends that will, we hope, contribute to a wider understanding of deafblindness and its impact on the developing child.

Summary

Nature of the group

- Defining this population is problematic – there is no agreed definition.
- There is a strong likelihood of co-occurence in a significant subset of the deaf-blind population.
- In the literature, there is a confounding of evidence concerning children who are deafblind from birth and children who develop deafblindness during childhood.

Pedagogy

- Vygotskian influences (co-action) can be seen.
- The influence/relevance of mainstream theorizing – attachment behaviour, deprivation, socialization, language acquisition, recent work in neuro science – can also be seen.

- There is a strong dependence on work derived from van Dijk (informed by the development of 'typical' children).
- Evidence about effectiveness draws heavily on Russian research plus, from there and elsewhere, anecdotal evidence.

Curriculum

- There is little evidence about this; what little there is draws heavily on van Dijk.
- The use of object referents is seen as important.

Knowledge

- This is not covered explicitly in the chapter.

Unique versus general differences position as pedagogic base

- The position taken by contributors is of 'individual', not general or group differences.
- In line with this, there is a reiteration in various contexts of 'normal' child development as a helpful reference point.

Notable aspects introduced

- Repercussions of difficulties concerning group definition, i.e. consequent problems in hypothesizing pedagogic principles.
- Neglect of sensory aspects of learning/development. This is disadvantageous for deafblind children but also for other groups, in that the direction of influence regarding a common pedagogy goes from special to mainstream as well as the reverse.

References

Aitken, S., Buultjens, M., Clark, C., Eyre, J., and Pease, L. (eds) (2000) *Teaching Children who Are Deafblind: Contact Communication and Learning*. London: David Fulton.

All Russia Association of the Blind (1991) *Deaf-Blindness: Historical and Methodological Aspects. Myths and Reality*. Moscow: VOS.

Black, J. E. (1998) How a child builds its brain: some lessons from animal studies of neural plasticity, *Preventive Medicine*, 27(2): 168–171.

Boyce, Barr and Zeltzer (1992) Temperament and the psychobiology of childhood stress, *Pediatrics*, 90(3): 483–6.

Bridgett, G. (1995) Curiosity in deaf-blind children: a starting point for teaching, *JVIB News Service*, 89(3): 8–9.

Janssen, M., Riksen-Walraven, J., Marianne, J. and van Dijk, J. (2002) Enhancing the quality of intervention between children and their educators, *Journal of Developmental and Physical Disabilities*, 14(1), 87–109.

Knox, J. and Stevens, C. B. (1993) English translation and introduction, in R. W. Rieber and A. S. Carton (eds) *The Collected Works of L. S. Vygotsky, Volume 2: The Fundamentals of Defectology*. New York: Plenum Press.

Landesman, C. (1997) *An Introduction to Epistemology*. Oxford: Blackwell.

Leontiev, A. H. (1948) *How I Form a Picture Around Me*. Moscow: Progress Press.

MacFarland, S. Z. C. (1995) Teaching strategies of the van Dijk curricular approach, *Journal of Visual Impairment and Blindness*, May/June: 222–8.

McInnes, J. M. and Treffry, J. A. (1982) *Deaf-blind Infants and Children: A Developmental Guide*. Toronto: University of Toronto Press.

Meshcheryakov, A. (1974) *Awakening to Life*. Moscow: Progress Press.

Nafstad, A. (1991) *Space of Interaction*, Oslo: NUD.

Nelson, C. A. and Carver, J. (1998) The effects of stress and trauma on brain and memory: a view from developmental cognitive neuroscience, *Development and Psychopathology*, 10: 793–809.

Nelson, C., van Dijk, J., McDonnell, A. P. and Thompsom, K. (2002) A framework for understanding young children with multiple disabilities: the van Dijk approach to Assessment, *Research and Practice for Persons with Severe Disabilities*, 27(2): 97–111.

Perry, B. and Pollard, D. (1998) Homeostasis, stress, trauma, and adaptation. A neuro-developmental view of childhood trauma, *Child and Adolescent Psychiatry Clinics of North America*, 7: 33–51.

Porter, J., Miller, O. and Pease, L. (1997) *Curriculum Access for Deafblind Children*. London: Department for Education and Employment and Sense: the National Deafblind and Rubella Association.

QCA (1999) *Shared World – Different Experiences*. London: Qualifications and Curriculum Agency.

Ramachandran, V. S. (2003) The emerging brain, the Reith Lectures. (www.bbc.co.uk/radio4/reith2003/).

Rieber, W. and Carton, A. S. (eds) (1993) *The Collected Works of L. S. Vygotsky, Volume 2: The Fundamentals of Defectology*. New York: Plenum Press.

Robbins, N. and Stenquist, G. (1967) *The Deaf-Blind 'Rubella' Child*. Watertown, MA: Perkins School for the Blind.

Rowland, C. and Schweigert, P. H. (1988) *Tangible Symbol Systems*. Eugene: Oregon Research Institute.

Russell. J. (1996) *Agency – Its Role in Mental Development*. London: Taylor and Francis.

Schellingerhout, R., Smitsman., G. and van Galen, P. (1997) Exploration of surface textures in congenitally blind infants, *Child Care, Health Development*, 23(3): 247.

van Dijk, J. (1986) An educational curriculum for deaf-blind multi-handicapped persons, in D. Ellis (ed.) *Sensory Impairments in Mentally Handicapped People*. London: Croom Helm.

van Dijk, J. (1991) *Persons Handicapped by Rubella. Victors and Victims*. Amsterdam and Lisse: Swets and Zeitlinger.

van Dijk, J. (1999) *Development through relationships – entering the social world*, Paper presented at the Twelfth DB World Conference on Deafblindness.

van Dijk, J. (2001) Congenital rubella: victims and victors, Paper presented at the American Symposium on Deafblindness: Communities and Connections.

van Dijk, J., Carlin, R. and Janssen, M. (1989) Stereotyped behaviour in rubella-deaf and deaf-blind people, *Deaf-blind Education* 3: 8–10.

van Dijk, J. and Nelson, C. (1998) History and change in the education of children who are deaf-blind since the rubella epidemic of the 1960s: the influence of methods developed in the Netherlands, *Deaf-Blind Perspectives*, 5(2): 1–5.

Vygotsky, L. (1934) *Thought and Language*, 1996 edn revised by Alex Kozuin, London: MIT Press.

Warren, D. H. (1994) *Blindness and Early Childhood Development*. New York: American Foundation for the Blind

Werner, H. and Kaplan, B. (1963) *Symbol Formation*. New York: John Wiley.

CHAPTER FIVE

Severe learning difficulties

Jill Porter

Two different starting points can be taken to analysing the evidence for specialized teaching methods for children with severe learning difficulties. On the one hand, one can start with the practices and look at the evidence for their effectiveness and explanations that account for this. This approach places the prime focus on educational practices and an analysis of pedagogy as it relates to education. Thus one might search the literature for pedagogy in relation to the curriculum. An initial trawl through the British Education Index indicates that if one starts with the key words of severe learning difficulties and disabilities with a focus on literature from 1996 to the current time, a generous analysis suggests that some 30 articles have been published. However, few of these can be described as robustly evaluative. It would be difficult on this slender research base to provide an answer to the question 'Are we using a distinctive pedagogy for teaching pupils with severe learning difficulties?' that is grounded in clear evidence for its effectiveness. This is unsurprising, as it largely looks to educators to carry out and publish this research. A review of trends in research in learning difficulties suggests that international research in the field of education is small and diminishing (Porter and Lacey 2004) compared, for example, to that relevant to social service provision. Others commenting on the state of international research have also indicated concerns about the paucity of empirical research in special education (Gersten *et al.* 2000).

The alternative approach starts from an examination of the evidence to suggest that pupils with severe learning difficulties have particular needs or characteristics that make learning different for them. We might then make a tentative assumption that they therefore require some approaches to teaching that are distinctly different and look for evidence that supports this contention. Here the literature is more extensive, although much of it might now be considered historical. This research reflected the early interests of different groups of psychologists in investigating learning and developmental processes in atypical populations. One group espoused a defect theory of learning difficulties, suggesting that this population demonstrated differences in the learning process. For example, Ellis and colleagues (Ellis 1969; Ellis and Cavalier 1982) strove to investigate how people of different IQs performed on particular learning tasks, with the result that many different deficits were proposed in, for example, attention and discrimination (Zeamon and House 1979), memory (Ellis 1963; Ellis and Woodridge 1985; Marcell and Weeks 1988) and generalization (Zeamon and House 1984). On this basis one might look for approaches to teaching that specifically took account of these difficulties in attention, discrimination, memory and generalization.

The contrasting position, the developmental position, expressed by Zigler (1969, 1982), held that the mentally retarded passed through the same stages of development as non-retarded children, but with a slower rate of progression and a lower ceiling, a proposition that is not inconsistent with a continuum view of need. This approach was originally limited to studying those individuals without organic damage and utilized an experimental design that matched children according to mental age in order to reveal that they performed equally on developmental tasks. The developmentalists have become increasingly differentiated as a group and the theories have widened along with the individuals investigated. Some researchers have adopted a 'similar structure' approach, arguing that not only do individuals pass through the same sequence but they reveal similar reasoning at each stage (Weisz *et al.* 1982), and encompass individuals who have organic damage through study of the patterns of development of particular aetiological groups, notably children with Down's syndrome (see Chapter 7 for a review), as they constitute a relatively large and identifiable group. In contrast, this approach suggests that if children simply lag behind there may be no special approach needed other than those adopted for younger children.

An analysis of published research in the field suggests that aetiology-specific research continues to form an important segment of publications but with a growth in studies of children with autism (Porter and Lacey 2004). In contrast, there is less research that is generic to learning difficulties and seeks to answer questions about how children with SLD learn. In part this probably reflects the domination of the literature by relatively few researchers (Logan and Lott 2000) and the commitment to research around behaviour phenotypes that is a strong movement in the United States. While in time one might look to neuroscience to provide us with more tangible evidence (Blakemore and Frith 2001), it is the research on learning processes that this chapter reflects on before looking more specifically at the implications for teaching particular curriculum areas. As we shall see, more recent studies question whether the identified needs are distinct or whether they reflect the decontextualized methods that are used to study learning. They also raise issues about the methodological difficulty of separating out aspects of the learning process to suggest specific deficits.

How can one conceptualize severe learning difficulties?

First, it is necessary to try to delineate the group of pupils referred to here as having severe learning difficulties. Characteristically in the UK definitions have been indicative of provision, and severe learning difficulties were generally seen as those children who required a different curriculum – a developmental curriculum (DES 1985). This is not unlike definitions that were used in the United States that referred to the sorts of self-help skills that children would need help in learning (Seltzer 1983). There is an expectation, one that is reflected in the early American literature (Yesseldyke 1978), that these children are unlikely to progress to a level beyond that of an average seven- or eight-year-old by the end of their school career.

These kinds of definition create a number of difficulties for the researcher in drawing together the evidence. For example, the basis for distinguishing between groups of children with different needs is imprecise and lends itself to subjective judgements, especially for those individuals who fall on the margins. The lack of precision creates difficulties communicating with personnel outside education in the UK, as the terms and methods for distinguishing between groups may well have little meaning for them. Internationally, researchers are more likely to adopt a classification based on either severity or aetiology (Hodapp and Dykens 1994) and one way of indicating the level of severity is to use a normative measure such as IQ or mental age (MA). Convention rather than legislation suggests that pupils with SLD fall between IQs of 20 and 50/55 in the UK (British Psychological Society 1963; Kushlick and Blunden 1974). The most recent WHO (2001) definitions have moved away from IQ to a complex system based on activity, participation and function. It will be interesting to examine the extent to which this approach is utilized in the research literature. Historically international definitions have made reference to IQ (WHO 1968, 1980, 1992; APA 2000) and it is important to recognize how the cut-off points and the descriptors used vary between countries. Notably, the American literature will use the term 'severe' for individuals with an IQ of 20/25 to 35/40 and 'moderate' for those described as having an IQ in the range 35/40 to 50/55. Many other countries have adopted similar cut-off points, so in the UK when we refer to children with severe learning difficulties we are including children who, elsewhere, might be described as having moderate learning difficulties or mental retardation.

Given definitional differences, prevalence rates are notoriously difficult to determine (Larson *et al.* 2001), not least because of regional variations in the way learning difficulties are recognized and resourced. OECD (2000) figures highlight this: Italy has the highest figure of 0.88 per cent of the school population registered as having severe learning difficulties, New Zealand has 0.45 per cent and the Netherlands 0.44 per cent. These issues are well discussed in relation to mental retardation, where an estimate of prevalence in the States is 0.78 per cent of the population. This would of course include all those with intellectual disability and significant limitations in everyday functioning that occur early in life and before the age of 18 years (APA 2000).

At this point it is also important to recognize that children with severe learning difficulties often do not simply experience a cognitive impairment. Research has consistently pointed to the higher incidence of sensory, motor and health difficulties in this group and also to limitations in speech and language, with many pupils having multiple communication forms (Male 1996; Smith and Phillips 1992; Mar and Sall 1999).

Research identifying particular cognitive difficulties in learning

Early research, as we have seen, adopted an information processing approach to learning and sought to identify deficits particularly in the areas of attention, discrimination and memory. Clements, writing in 1987, reviewed this literature with a schematic model of cognitive functioning that considered (a) the structures (e.g. memory and attention), (b) the processes or strategies a person has for learning (e.g. how people remember material) and (c) the higher order structures (the knowledge the person has about the learning process, what strategies to use when). This model leads him to believe not in a single dysfunction, but in a diversity of difficulties. It is worth taking a moment to consider what this means in practice by looking at one aspect, working memory, that underpins key aspects of school learning (Gathercole and Pickering 2001).

Working memory is important because it enables us to keep in mind information while we perform some mental operation, such as holding in mind the beginning of a sentence until the speaker reaches the end or making comparisons between things we can see or hear. Limitations in working memory (and consequent difficulties in such areas as literacy and numeracy) can be attributed to deficits in any one of a number of areas. The fluency with which one speaks, the speed with which one is able to process information and one's ability to use a strategy all influence how well we hold information in mind. Evidence suggests that children with SLD may experience difficulty in taking in information and be poor at noting visual changes of colour, form or presence. These difficulties are possibly due to different search strategies (Bruscia 1981; Whitley et al. 1987; Yando et al. 1989; Burack et al. 2001; Carlin et al. 2003). The quality of information to be remembered may therefore be poor. If it is auditory information, children may have difficulties 'keeping it alive' in working memory as they process words slowly and often show poor articulation and dysfluencies in speech (Dodd 1976, Willcox 1988) both of which limit how much can be retained. Additionally, research suggests that they are poor at using strategies for remembering and monitoring their performance (Henry and Maclean 2002). Consistently in the literature there is more efficient processing of spatial and visual, compared to verbal and auditory, material. In considering the implications of this research one needs to take into account familiarity of material and individual differences but we can hypothesize that individuals will respond better to visual material and small chunks of information especially when this is presented in auditory form and that they need to be helped to use strategies such as rehearsal. While memory studies almost uniformly point to a deficit, more naturalistic studies suggest that we should interpret these with caution and recognize that children's difficulties may not be apparent in all situations.

So far, therefore, while we have noted research that identifies particular difficulties that pupils with SLD experience, we have also drawn attention to the fact that we need to take into account the differential impact of children's response to laboratory tasks, which is not necessarily replicated in naturalistic settings.

Particular difficulties and instructional literature

Looking at the empirical literature on pedagogy, it is possible to identify some studies that link instructional design to the specific difficulties children have been found to experience. Wolery and Schuster (1997: 68) review instructional strategies for pupils with significant disabilities and, as others have done, propose a continuum based on structure or 'the extent to which they influence control over students' interactions with the environment'. Here we will use the distinctions made by them to illustrate research on the effectiveness of different aspects of pedagogy. However, as others have argued, while the research points to effectiveness, on the occasions where there have been comparisons between methods, the differences have usually been small, and there are individual differences in the way learners have responded (Browder 1997).

Specific methods

Traditional behavioural approaches to teaching faced a number of criticisms, not least their failure to produce learning that was maintained over time and generalized to new situations (Porter 1986). In consequence there has been a shift towards more naturalistic methods of teaching so that aspects that naturally occur in the environment help to shape and control behaviour. While early approaches espoused the use of errorless learning, with prompting being faded from greatest assistance to least, more recent research implicitly questions the use of these methods. The use of delayed prompting is now a feature of many successful interventions. Further, there is some research to suggest that time delay is a better system of prompting than increasing assistance over trials (Wolery and Schuster 1997).

Visual cues

There has also been a growing literature on using visual cues to prompt responses in order to reduce the dependency on the presence of adults to elicit a correct response. Here we see recognition of the greater efficiency in visual processing with the use of photographs and symbols serving as prompts. For example, Copeland and Hughes (2000) report on the touching of pictures as a prompt to initiate a task and turning the picture over as a sign of completion; in this way pupils were learning to monitor their own behaviour and become independent learners.

Enhancing cues

In recognition of pupils' difficulty with discrimination, errorless learning methods have been used to produce a technology for enhancing the cues to which pupils are expected to attend in discrimination tasks. MacKay *et al.* (2002) provide a recent example using an approach that produced successful matching to sample in nine of their 12 learners. They based their study around the idea that it is easier to find a target when it is surrounded by identical distracters: the red football shirt among a group of blue phenomenon. Training therefore starts with the odd one out of eight identical distracters and proceeds with the gradual withdrawal of distracters until there are only two, the correct match and one distracter.

This type of methodology has proved a powerful influence on the teaching of both numeracy and literacy where children were taught to respond to presentations rather than given an underlying understanding of the task. The correct stimulus might be produced larger than the incorrect or be presented nearer to the subject than the incorrect, or the essential features may be exaggerated. An alternative approach described by Carlin *et al.* (2001) is to use the 'aha' factor where clues are gradually introduced that promote understanding and solutions to a problem and that actively engage the student cognitively in a discrimination task.

Embedding learning in routines and natural contexts

One of the ways in which these specific approaches have developed is to teach in more naturalistic contexts so that new learning is embedded within existing routines. A well researched example is that of the Behaviour Chain Interruption Strategy (BICS), where a purposeful flow of well established behaviour is interrupted in a way that demands new types of communication. There is a growing body of evidence for its effectiveness as a method of teaching communication (Carter and Grunsell 2001). Interestingly, this technique is not unlike the sabotage strategies described by Goldbart (1986).

Self-management

All pupils will be more effective learners if they are able to evaluate their own progress and set their own targets. Copeland and Hughes (2002) review the effects of encouraging goal or target setting and its impact on the performance of pupils with SLD across 17 studies. In some of these studies participants were taught to monitor their own performance but in all studies learners were guided in their selection of goals. One of the most frequent strategies was the use of visual cues, either as reminders of their target or to provide a tangible measure of progress. Unsurprisingly, more training led to stronger effects, but providing feedback specifically on the accuracy of their performance was identified by the reviewers as critical to success. Notably, most of the studies reviewed were carried out prior to 1990.

More recent research (Porter *et al.* 2000) has explored the range of methods that teachers are using in the classroom to promote pupils in target setting. This highlighted the load on memory of self-monitoring and recording and the importance of being able to draw on concrete materials as well as visual images as a way of assessing one's progression towards a goal. It also, however, emphasized the careful use of adult questioning and discussion to help pupils to remember and elaborate on these responses. Teachers use a whole range of strategies, which are not well represented in the research literature, to promote shared attention and communication through creating scenarios that nurture curiosity and interest and increase learners' ability to reflect on the learning process.

Literature on teaching literacy

The UK government review of the Literacy Strategy (DfES 2000) indicated how few published studies mirror current practice and highlighted the fact that, typically in the past, a functional approach has been adopted to the teaching of reading. They chart the emphasis in the past on developing readiness for reading, which children typically did not progress beyond, and the teaching of functional social sight words. These limitations are not restricted to practice in the UK. Katims (2000) takes a historical look at teaching literacy and reviews the guidance given in contemporary American texts for teachers across the range of learning difficulties and disabilities. He finds only one textbook that could be described as providing useful information; that is, containing information relevant to assessment and procedures for teaching. He contrasts these with the socially constructed approaches that are available for people with specific learning disabilities.

One response to developing individualized instruction has been the use of technology. Basil and Reynes (2003) describe the evaluation outcomes of using computer-assisted learning to support the teaching of reading and writing to children with severe learning difficulties who had made little progress using conventional methods (matching words to pictures, writing words to pictures). They describe a programme using a whole word selection strategy to make sentences, which led to significant gains in learning in a three-month period. The authors do not simply account for this in relation to the massed practice, but argue that the self-produced and directed methods prompted more problem-solving approaches to understanding, as well as enabling learners to work at their own pace and speed. They also provide evidence for implicit learning as the post-test situation revealed gains in children's linguistic knowledge that had not been a specific part of the programme. Motivation is likely also to have played a role as the programme introduced unusual characters and strange situations.

Increasingly, however, it has been recognized that we need to view literacy in a wider context than simply reading. Kliewer and Bikklen (2001) decry both a connectionist approach and a developmental approach, which presupposes that cognitive mastery is required in early stages before literacy can be understood. Powerfully they argue for greater recognition of the symbolism involved in literacy and literature. There are diverse ways in which this can be seen to translate into practice. There has been the development and use of symbolic systems acting as a 'bridge to traditional literacy' (Detheridge and Detheridge 1997) that has its sources outside the research literature.

A second approach lies in the introduction of pupils to the experience of literature, not simply as a vehicle for teaching communication but to provide access to a 'cultural heritage' (Grove and Park 1996; Grove 1998; Park 1998). The creativity and interactive characteristics of an approach rooted in drama contrast strongly with the more easily evaluated but narrowly defined approaches to reading that are more widely represented in the research literature.

Maths and severe learning difficulties

If there is little empirical research on teaching literacy to pupils with SLD there is even less on aspects of numeracy. A review of research with pupils with mild to moderate mental retardation highlights a similar picture to that of literacy (Butler *et al.* 2001). Approaches typically involved the use of highly structured direct instruction methods and techniques such as constant time delay. Butler *et al.* do note a shift towards problem-solving instruction but these approaches were fewer in number and largely involved pupils with mild learning difficulties.

The limitations of the instruction literature should not be taken as evidence that children with severe learning difficulties are unable to learn about number. As with other aspects of learning there are large individual differences, with some pupils providing little formal evidence of learning to count, through to those who are proficient in counting and demonstrate an underlying understanding of what it means to count (Porter 1998, 1999). Some pupils are not only able to show proficient skills but able to apply them to problem-solving. One area in which the profile of pupils with SLD has been found to be different generally from that of pre-schoolers is their acquisition of the counting string (Porter 1998). Learning the sequence of number words is an auditory sequential memory task and therefore these findings should not surprise us.

Conclusion

In this chapter we have explored some of the more recent literature that attempts to determine the specific difficulties experienced by this population in learning. It has highlighted the difficulty of attempting to separate particular aspects of learning and the importance of context in providing multiple cues that support the acquisition process. The studies typically involve participants who are on the margins of severe and moderate learning difficulties, and where they use matched samples, are methodologically problematic. For any teacher it is perhaps unsurprising that research has focused on those most amenable to assessment and intervention. This literature is dominated by psychologists working within particular paradigms that, many would argue, provide a very narrow view of learning. It has, however, provided some empirical evidence for a link between specific deficits and strategies in teaching that meet these needs. While its application to curriculum practices has been criticized, the work does draw attention to the importance of learning to learn skills, those of self-management, self-assessment and target setting.

However, as the reader will note, there are a number of tensions in accounts of this kind. In our search for a specialist pedagogy we have inevitably ended up with a catalogue of deficits rather than a celebration of achievements. The focus on limitations can lead, and has led until recently, to limited expectations in a number of key areas, notably core skills of numeracy and literacy, and to research focusing almost exclusively on a narrow range of learning paradigms. While the field is indebted to psychologists who have systematically proved learning ability in youngsters who were thought ineducable at one time, they have also constrained what has been taught as well as the approaches to teaching. The notion of pedagogy can be difficult to separate from that of content. The use of adapted materials and structured support systems can fundamentally change the nature and context of learning. Therefore, there comes a point on the continuum where the combined methodologies are so fundamentally different, and applied in a different context, that one can only refer to them as distinct.

Perhaps more fundamentally, research evidence is not sufficient to inspire teachers to adopt particular approaches. Arguably, we need to examine more closely teachers' beliefs about the nature of learning and also what evidence they look for in evaluating their impact (Jordan and Stanovich 2003). Stephenson's (2002) research suggests that teachers look for intervention strategies that promote interactions with pupils. We might therefore look to paradigms of learning that are consistent with this emphasis in developing and evaluating pedagogies. Daniels (2003), drawing on Vygotskian accounts of learning, argues that teachers of children with SLD should be placing more emphasis on social and participatory learning, thus fundamentally changing the contexts of learning and ultimately our view of the communities in which learning takes place.

In summary, the somewhat tentative conclusions that we draw from examining the empirical evidence are:

* there is evidence of particular difficulties in learning;
* it is not altogether meaningful to attempt to try to pin these to particular parts of an information processing system without recognizing their interactive component;
* research has typically not taken into account the meaningfulness of the task and its potential differential impact on learners;

- empirical evidence is also constrained by the weakness of research designs that seek to compare groups of children;
- specific instructional methods that take into account these difficulties in learning have been evaluated as effective, although we need to recognize the evidence of individual differences and idiosyncratic responses;
- while these may be conceived as lying along a continuum, traditional structured responses now use methodologies that mirror more closely naturally occurring learning contexts but are applied in a systematic way;
- the use of these methods can be seen to constrain what is taught, and therefore it becomes difficult to separate discussion of pedagogy from curriculum content;
- alternative accounts of learning are likely to prove more inspirational to teachers, and could lead to greater creativity and problem-solving about how to teach pupils with SLD effectively.

And the continuum debate? We are left with the view that there is a point along the continuum where the presenting features are such that the approach is likely to appear to be different. The point at which this occurs is, we would argue, dependent on the perception of the viewer, and more specifically the paradigm of learning that they adopt.

Summary

Nature of the group

- Historically, definition of the group in the UK was by provision attended; this is associated with lack of precision and subjectivity.
- Internationally, reference is made to definitions by IQ and/or aetiology (and this is subject to criticism).
- There is a higher incidence of health, motor and sensory difficulties with this group.

Pedagogy

- Errorless learning is now being questioned.
- There is increasing use of visual cues (e.g. photographs, symbols) to prompt response.
- Self-monitoring and self-management are increasingly seen as important (also reflecting motivation and linked with some ICT-based approaches).
- Enhancement of key cues is used as a teaching strategy.
- Modelling of responses followed by prompting is a useful strategy.

Curriculum

- Behavioural approaches are criticized in relation to the maintenance and generalization of learning.

- There is a resultant shift to more naturalistic methods.
- There is a preponderance of reductionist research designs in relation to curriculum evaluation in this field.
- There has been a shift to a 'cultural heritage' perspective regarding literacy.

Knowledge

- There is a bias towards aetiology-specific studies (US influence).
- Historically, there has been an association with deficits in working memory, but this has been contested in more recent work characterized by higher ecological validity.

Unique versus general differences position as pedagogic base

- The nature of the research evades this point (can only be inferred).
- Presenting features of teaching strategies may appear different (but, by implication, be similar).
- Perceptions of difference in relation to teaching strategy will reflect the viewer's stance about learning (and pupils?).

Notable aspects introduced

- A key question is posed: at what point does 'difference' along a continuum (or several continua?) of teaching strategy become distinctive?
- A research design issue is whether robust designs are associated with reductionist methods, while more creative methods are less amenable to (conventionally defined) rigorous evaluation.

References

American Psychiatric Association (2000) *Diagnostic and Statistical Manual of Mental Disorders*. DSM-IVR-TR, 4th edn. Washington, DC: APA.

Basil, C. and Reynes, S. (2003) Acquisition of literacy skills by children with severe disability, *Child Language Teaching and Therapy*, 19(1): 27–48.

Blakemore, S. and Frith, U. (2001) The implications of recent developments in neuroscience research on teaching and learning. A consultation paper prepared for the ESRC Teaching and Learning Research Programme.

British Psychological Society (1963) Report of the working party on subnormality, *Bulletin of the British Psychological Society*, 16(53): 37–50.

Browder, D. M. (1997) Educating students with severe disabilities: enhancing the conversation between research and practice, *Journal of Special Education*, 31(1): 137–44.

Bruscia, K. E. (1981) Auditory short-term memory and attentional control of mentally retarded persons, *American Journal of Mental Deficiency*, 85(4): 435–7.

Burack, J. A., Evans, D. W., Klaiman, C. and Iarocci, G. (2001) The mysterious myth of attention deficits and other defect stories: contemporary issues in the developmental approach to mental retardation, *International Review of Research in Mental Retardation*, 24: 299–320.

Butler, F. M., Miller, S. P., Lee, K. and Pierce, T. (2001) Teaching mathematics to students with mild-to-moderate mental retardation: a review of the literature, *Mental Retardation*, 39(1): 20–31.

Carlin, M. T., Soraci, S. A., Dennis, N., Nicholas, A., Chechile, A. and Loiselle, R. (2001) Enhancing free-recall rates of individuals with mental retardation, *American Journal on Mental Retardation*, 106(4): 314–26.

Carlin, M. T., Soraci, S. A., Strawbridge, P., Dennis, N., Loiselle, R. and Chechile, A. (2003) Detection of changes in naturalistic scenes: comparisons of individuals with and without mental retardation, *American Journal on Mental Retardation*, 108(3): 181–93.

Carter, M. and Grunsell, J. (2001) The behavior chain interruption strategy: a review of research and discussion of future directions, *Journal for the Association of the Severely Handicapped*, 26(1): 37–49.

Clements, J. (1987) *Severe Learning Disability and Psychological Handicap*. Chichester: Wiley.

Copeland, S. R. and Hughes, C. (2000) Acquisition of a picture prompt strategy to increase independent performance, *Education and Training in Mental Retardation and Developmental Disabilities*, 35(3): 294–305.

Copeland, S. R. and Hughes, C. (2002) Effects of task performance of persons with mental retardation, *Education and Training in Mental Retardation and Developmental Disabilities*, 37(1): 40–54.

Daniels, H. R. J. (2003) *Vygotsky and the Education of Children with Severe Learning Difficulties*. London: SLD Experience.

Department of Education and Science (1985) *Better Schools*, Cmnd 9469. London: HMSO.

Detheridge, T. and Detheridge, M. (1997) *Literacy through Symbols: Improving Access for Children and Adults*. London: David Fulton.

Dodd, B. (1976) A comparison of the phonological system of mental age matched, normal, severely subnormal and Down's syndrome children, *British Journal of Disorders of Communication*, 11(1): 27–42.

Ellis, N. R. (1963) The stimulus trace and behavioural inadequacy, in N. R. Ellis (ed.) *Handbook of Mental Deficiency*. New York: McGraw-Hill.

Ellis, N. R. (1969) A behavioral research strategy in mental retardation: defense and critique, *American Journal of Mental Deficiency*, 73: 557–66.

Ellis, N. R. (1970) Memory processes in retardates and normals, in N. R. Ellis (ed.), *International Review of Research in Mental Retardation, 14*. London: Academic Press.

Ellis, N. R. and Cavalier, A. R. (1982) Research perspectives in mental retardation, in E. Zigler and D. Balla (eds) *Mental Retardation. The Developmental-difference Controversy*. Hillsdale, NJ: Lawrence Erlbaum.

Ellis, N. R. and Woodridge, P. W. (1985) Short-term memory for pictures and words by mentally retarded and nonretarded persons, *American Journal of Mental Deficiency*, 89(6): 622–6.

Gathercole, S. and Pickering, S. (2001) Working memory deficits in children with special educational needs, *British Journal of Special Education*, 28(2): 89–97.

Goldbart, J. (1986) The development of language and communication, in J. Coupe and J. Porter (eds) *The Education of Children with Severe Learning Difficulties*. London: Croom Helm.

Grove, N. and Park, K. (1996) *Odyssey Now*. London: Jessica Kingsley.

Henry, L. C. and MacLean, M. (2002) Working memory performance in children with and without intellectual disabilities, *American Journal on Mental Retardation*, 107(6): 421–32.

Hodapp, R. M. and Dykens, E. M. (1994) Mental retardation's two cultures of behavioral research, *American Journal on Mental Retardation*, 98(6): 675–87.

Jordan, A. and Stanovich, P. (2003) Teachers' personal epistemological beliefs about students with disabilities as indicators of effective teaching practices, *Journal of Research in Special Educational Needs*, 3(1) (on line journal).

Katims, D. S. (2000) Literacy instruction for people with mental retardation: historical highlights and contemporary analysis, *Education and Training in Mental Retardation and Developmental Disabilities*, 35(1): 3–15.

Kliewer, C. and Bikklen, D. (2001) 'School's not really a place for reading': a research synthesis of the literate lives of students with severe disabilities, *Journal for the Association of the Severely Handicapped*, 26(1): 1–12.

Kushlick, A. and Blunden, R. (1974) The epidemiology of mental subnormality, in A. M. Clarke and A. D. B. Clarke (eds), *Mental Deficiency*, 3rd edn. London: Methuen.

Larson, S. A., Lakin, K. C., Anderson, L., Kwak, N., Lee, J. H. and Anderson, D. (2001) Prevalence of mental retardation and developmental disabilities: estimates from the 1994/5 National Health Interview Survey Disability Supplements, *American Journal on Mental Retardation*, 106(3): 231–52.

Logan, J. R. and Lott, J. D. (2000) Top researchers and institutions in mental retardation 1979–1999, *Research in Developmental Disabilities*, 21(4): 257–61.

McDade, H. L. and Adler, S. (1980) Down syndrome and short-term memory impairment: a storage or retrieval deficit?, *American Journal of Mental Deficiency*, 84(6): 561–7.

MacKay, H. A., Soraci, S., Carlin, M., Dennis, N. and Strawbridge, C. P. (2002) Guiding visual attention during acquisition of matching-to-sample, *American Journal on Mental Retardation*, 107(6): 445–54.

Male, D. B. (1996) Who goes to SLD schools?, *Journal of Applied Research in Intellectual Disabilities*, 9(4): 307–23.

Mar, H. M. and Sall, N. (1999) Profiles of the expressive communication skills of children and adolescents with severe cognitive disabilities, *Education and Training in Mental Retardation and Developmental Disabilities*, 34(1): 77–89.

Marcell, M. M. and Weeks, S. L. (1988) Short-term memory difficulties and Down's syndrome, *Journal of Mental Deficiency Research*, 32: 153–62.

Norwich, B. (1990) *Reappraising Special Needs Education*. London: Cassell.

OECD (2000) *Special Needs Education. Statistics and Indicators*. Paris: OECD.

Park, K. (1998) Dickens for all: inclusive approaches to literature and communication with people with severe and profound learning difficulties, *British Journal of Special Education*, 25(3): 114–18.

Porter, J. (1998) Understanding of counting in children with severe learning difficulties and nursery children, *British Journal of Educational Psychology*, 68: 331–45.

Porter, J. (1999) The attainments of pupils with severe learning difficulties on a simple counting and error detection task, *Journal of Applied Research in Intellectual Disabilities*, 12(2): 87–99.

Porter, J. and Lacey, P. (in preparation) *Research and Learning Difficulties*. London: Sage.

Porter, J., Robertson, C. and Hayhoe, H. (2001) *Self-assessment and Learning Difficulties*. London: QCA.

Seltzer, G. B. (1983) Systems of classification, in J. L. Matson and J. A. Mulick (eds) *Handbook of Mental Retardation*. New York: Pergamon.

Smith, B. and Phillips, C. J. (1992) Attainment of severely mentally retarded adolescents by aetiology, *Journal of Child Psychology and Psychiatry*, 33(6): 1039–58.

Stephenson, J. (2002) Characterization of multisensory environments: why do teachers use them?, *Journal of Applied Research in Intellectual Disability*, 15(1): 73–90.

Weisz, J. R., Yates, K. O. and Zigler, E. (1982) Piagetian evidence and the developmental-difference controversy, in E. Zigler and D. Balla (eds), *Mental Retardation. The Developmental-difference Controversy*. Hillsdale, NJ: Lawrence Erlbaum.

Whitley, J. H., Zaparniuk, J. and Asmundson, G. J. G. (1987) Mentally retarded adolescents' breadth of attention and short-term memory processes during matching-to-sample discrimination, *American Journal of Mental Deficiency*, 92(2): 207–12.

Willcox, A. (1988) An investigation into non-fluency in Down syndrome, *British Journal of Disorders of Communication*, 23(2): 153–70.

Wolery, M. and Schuster, J. W. (1997) Instructional methods with students who have significant disabilities, *Journal of Special Education*, 31(1): 61–79.

World Health Organization (1968) *Organization of Services for the Mentally Retarded, Fifteenth Report of the WHO Expert Committee on Mental Health*. Geneva: WHO.

World Health Organization (1980) *International Classification of Impairments, Disabilities and Handicaps*. Geneva: WHO.

World Health Organization (1992) *The ICD-10 Classification of Mental and Behavioural Disorders: Clinical Descriptions and Diagnostic Guidelines*. Geneva: WHO.

World Health Organization (2001) *The ICDH-2 International Classification of Functioning, Disability and Health*. Geneva: WHO.

Yando, R., Seitz, V. and Zigler, E. (1989) Imitation, recall, and imitativeness in children with low intelligence of organic and familial etiology, *Research in Developmental Disabilities*, 10(4): 383–97.

Ysseldyke, J. E. (1987) Classification of handicapped students, in M. C. Wang, M. C. Reynolds, and H. J. Walberg (eds) *Handbook of Special Education: Research and Practice. Volume 1, Learner Characteristics and Adaptive Education*. Oxford: Pergamon Press.

Zeamon, D. and House, B. J. (1973) The role of attention in retardate discrimination learning, in N. R. Ellis (ed.) *Handbook of Mental Deficiency*. New York: McGraw-Hill.

Zeamon, D. and House, B. J. (1979) The review of attention theory, in N. R. Ellis (ed.), *Handbook of Mental Deficiency, Psychological Theory and Research*, 2nd edn. Hillsdale, NJ: Lawrence Erlbaum.

Zeamon, D. and House, B. (1984) Intelligence and the process of generalization, in P. H. Brookes, R. Sperber and C. McCauley (eds) *Learning and Cognition in the Mentally Retarded*. Hillsdale, NJ: Lawrence Erlbaum.

Zigler, E. (1969) Developmental versus difference theories of mental retardation and the problem of motivation, *American Journal of Mental Deficiency*, 73: 536–56.

Zigler, E. (1982) MA, IQ, and the developmental difference controversy, in E. Zigler and D. Balla (eds) *Mental Retardation. The Developmental-difference Controversy*. Hillsdale, NJ: Lawrence Erlbaum.

CHAPTER SIX

Profound and multiple learning difficulties

Jean Ware

Definition

When we originally introduced the term 'profound and multiple learning difficulties' (PMLD; Evans and Ware 1987) it was in an attempt to overcome the problems caused by the lack of a clear definition for that group of children who had both a profound level of learning difficulty and other severe impairments, and who, in England and Wales at that time, were normally educated in the 'special care' classes of SLD schools. Since we originally coined the term there has been much debate about its utility and appropriateness, and a number of alternatives have been suggested (e.g. complex needs, SCAA 1996; profound intellectual and multiple disability (PIMD), Hogg 1991).

Hogg (1991), in expressing his preference for PIMD, argues that to refer to the problems experienced by this group as 'learning difficulties' fails to recognize the full impact of profound intellectual impairment on all aspects of information processing, ignores the extensive organic brain damage that many of them have and inaccurately suggests that sensory and physical disabilities are essentially difficulties in learning. There is little space within this chapter for a debate about terminology, but, despite the force of these objections, I have chosen to stay with PMLD because it is widely accepted within education in Britain and I believe reflects the conceptualization of special needs underlying current legislation and guidance (Education Act 1996; DfES 2001). That is, in an educational context what is important about disabilities and difficulties, however caused, is their impact on learning. This is not to deny that PMLD has profound consequences for all areas of life; instead it is to reiterate that at the heart of the educational enterprise for all children is enabling learning. It follows from this that a wide variety of approaches to overcoming or circumventing pupils' learning difficulties may be appropriate, not all of which would traditionally be considered as educational (see Chapter 1).

In 1987 I defined PMLD with reference to a definition of multiple handicap given by De Jong:

> De Jong ... has suggested that the term 'multiply-handicapped' should only be used to describe those persons who have two or more severe impairments. By severe impairment he means one which *by itself* would constitute a hindrance to learning such as to lead to the necessity for special methods to ensure development.
>
> (Ware 1987: 21)

According to this definition, someone with PMLD has at least two severe impairments, one of which is profound learning difficulties. Profound learning difficulties are, in turn, defined according to the international classification of diseases (ICD) manual published by the World Health Organization, according to which people with profound learning difficulties (mental retardation in ICD terminology) have an IQ score of below 20.

In the context of this book, it is interesting to note that this definition with its reference to the need for 'special methods to ensure development' implicitly adopts a group (general) differences position. Since 1987 there have been a number of attempts to refine the definition of PMLD. Most recently ACCAC (2003) has proposed the following:

> Pupils with PMLD have a profound cognitive impairment/learning difficulty, leading to significant delay in reaching developmental milestones. Such pupils will be operating overall at a very early developmental level and are likely to display at least one or more of the following:
>
> * Significant motor impairments
> * Significant sensory impairments
> * Complex health care needs/dependence on technology
>
> Pupils with PMLD will have a statement of Special Educational Needs and are likely to be working at p levels 1–3 for the majority/all of their school life. Staff will almost certainly experience great difficulty in establishing reliable and consistent methods of communicating with them and due to high levels of dependency for basic self care such as dressing, toileting and feeding they are also likely to require extra resources in school such as:
>
> * Specialist staffing and substantial support
> * Adapted curriculum and Individual Educational Plans
> * Mobility aids and therapy programmes
> * Frequent assistance and medical support
>
> N.B. This definition does not include those whose difficulties are believed to result from ASD unless this is also combined with a profound level of general learning difficulties.

This definition (which draws on earlier work by Byers (2000) and Julian

(2002) and will be used for the remainder of this chapter) attempts to define PMLD in terms of its educational implications. It reflects what seems to be a general agreement among classroom teachers about the existence of a group of children who present special pedagogical challenges due both to the overall complexity and severity of their disabilities and to the profundity of their intellectual impairment. As McInnes and Treffry (1993) state in relation to deafblindness, it is not possible to separate out the different aspects of their disability because the problem lies in the combination. This definition excludes from the PMLD group two groups of children who have often been included among those with complex needs: (a) children with both severe physical difficulties and severe learning difficulties; and (b) children with autistic spectrum disorders. The rationale for these exclusions is that pupils with PMLD have educational needs that are sufficiently different from these other groups to justify separate consideration. Thus it is arguable that this definition, compiled by a group of experienced teachers in the field, also implies a group differences approach. This contrasts with the philosophy that underlies the Code of Practice, which tends to emphasize unique individual differences, and is likewise reflected in the way in which different groups of pupils with special educational needs are defined and described. Even at the level of definition, then, it is difficult to avoid leaning towards one or the other position.

Two characteristics of people with PMLD that are not mentioned in the definition above, but that are of considerable importance with regard to pedagogy, are behavioural state and behavioural rate. Studies of behaviour states in normal young infants suggest that they are only 'ready to learn' when awake and alert, which may be as little as 20 per cent of the time. A significant issue with regard to behavioural state – which causes considerable problems for teachers – is the amount of time some children with PMLD spend either actually asleep or drowsy. For example, Guess *et al.* (1990) found that in the group they studied, students spent less than half their time awake and alert. These students therefore spent half their school time in states that were not conducive to learning.

The term 'behavioural rate' is used to refer to the average number of voluntary behaviours or actions that an individual produces per minute. Individuals with PMLD often have very low behavioural rates. For example, in my own observations of children in four special care classes I found that the average behavioural rate in each class was around five behaviours per minute (Ware 1987), considerably lower than that of a normal young infant.

Another crucial issue for pedagogy is whether there is evidence of differences in information processing between people with PMLD and those with different special educational needs or without any such needs. Unfortunately, there is little research on information processing in people with PMLD, but what there is suggests that, in general, development parallels that of young infants operating at a similar developmental level (Kahn 1976; Remington 1996). However, the combination of an extremely low behavioural rate with a short-term memory span, which would normally be found in a young infant with a much higher behavioural rate, has profound implications for learning and thus potentially for teaching strategies. Furthermore, there is some tentative evidence that short-term memory span may be less good than that of normal young infants (Kail 1990).

Prevalence

There are few studies of the prevalence of PMLD, and this probably reflects a generally high level of agreement about prevalence, at least amongst school-age children in developed societies. Studies from France (Rumeau-Rouquette *et al.* 1998), Norway (Stromme and Valvatne 1998) and Western Australia (Wellesley *et al.* 1992) all indicate a prevalence rate of between 0.6 and 0.8 per thousand. Studies also agree that there are few people with a profound level of intellectual impairment who are not multiply disabled (Kelleher and Mulcahy 1985; Arvio and Sillanpaa 2003) and that life expectancy among this group is considerably shorter than average. Arvio and Sillanpaa also suggest that (in contrast to some other groups) prevalence rates have changed little in the past few decades. Although almost all have organic brain damage, children with PMLD form a very diverse group, with a large number of rare syndromes each being responsible for a small percentage of the overall total. The one exception is cerebral palsy, which accounts for between 20 and 30 per cent of the group (Evans and Ware 1987; Wellesley *et al.* 1992).

Despite their low numbers, children with PMLD represent a particular challenge for education. As the definition above suggests, from a developmental perspective they are likely to spend their entire school career at a developmental level that other children, including the majority of those with severe learning difficulties, have passed before school entry. Furthermore, there are considerable limitations to a developmental perspective for this group, all of whom have several severe impairments.

Teaching strategies for children with PMLD

Despite the group differences perspective implied in some definitions, few teaching strategies are promoted exclusively or specifically for use with children with PMLD. Indeed, Ault *et al.* (1995) claim that developments in education for people with PMLD have not kept pace with innovations in other areas of SEN. Those teaching strategies that have been devised specifically for this group are mainly to be found in the area of communication. This is agreed as a major focus in the education of pupils with PMLD, although the debate continues about the relevance of English as an academic subject. Two main types of specialised approach can be identified: those based on caregiver–infant interactions (Nind and Hewett 1994; Ware 1994, 1996), and those that capitalize on the ability of ICT to provide an alternative means of communication for children with severe physical disabilities as well as a severe or profound level of learning difficulty. These approaches are discussed in some detail here; other approaches sometimes used with this group, but not specific to them (such as PECs), are not discussed here.

Approaches based on caregiver–infant interaction

Responsive environments
Responsive environments, according to Ware (1996, 2003), are interactive environments in which people get responses to their actions, get the opportunity to respond to the actions of others and have an opportunity to take the lead in interaction. These three principles are used to summarize the characteristics of positive caregiver–infant interactions, on which the responsive environments approach is based. As would be predicted from the caregiver interaction research, when staff modified their interactions to fit more closely with these principles the children made progress in the areas of communication and socialization. The research project used a multiple baseline design to demonstrate that when staff changed their interactive style to one that was more responsive, pupil behaviour also changed and more sophisticated communication behaviours began to develop (Ware 1994).

Intensive interaction
Intensive interaction is the name given by Nind and Hewett to the teaching approach they devised for 'students who experienced severe difficulties in learning and relating to others' (Nind 1996: 48). It was specifically designed to address the needs of students who, in addition to severe or profound learning difficulties appear remote or withdrawn. Like my own responsive environments approach, Intensive Interaction is based on research into the interactions between infants and caregivers. It similarly seeks to replicate central features of 'good' care-giver infant interaction but in 1:1 sessions. (Nind and Hewett 1994)

The main differences in approach between Ware and Nind and Hewett lie in the explicit use of targets, which is advocated by Ware and rejected by Nind and Hewett, and the use of timetabled, structured 1:1 interaction sessions by Nind and Hewett, while Ware advocates deliberate use of the basic principles in all activities.

Evaluating intensive interaction is problematic because its proponents repeatedly claim that it is about process rather than product and that it is therefore inappropriate to set learning targets (Nind and Hewett 1994; Nind 1996). In practice, however, claims *are* made for intensive interaction in terms of developmental gains – for example, the development of anticipation and ways of asking for 'more' (Nind and Hewett 1994: 196) – which are part of the recognized sequence of communication development. Furthermore, the theoretical underpinnings of intensive interaction are essentially developmental, with the use of techniques that are taken from 'normal' caregiver–infant interaction being based in research that demonstrates the crucial role of interaction in the development of cognition, communication and socialization. Thus it seems reasonable to attempt to evaluate intensive interaction both in its own terms (the extent to which mutually enjoyable interactions are established where they were previously absent) and in terms of its efficacy in promoting communication development, since this is increasingly seen as central to the education of pupils with PMLD.

Although intensive interaction has never been compared directly with any alternative approach there have been a number of attempts to evaluate its effectiveness using either case studies or single subject research designs. In general the case study reports (Watson 1994; Hewett 1998) give too little detail for the effectiveness of the approach in terms of its impact on the development of communication and socialization to be properly assessed. However, Watson and Fisher (1997) report on a group of five children with PMLD from whom data were collected over a school year during intensive interaction and teacher-directed 'group time'. They state that by the end of the study all the children showed more advanced and consistent behaviour during the intensive interaction sessions, but the study can be criticized for the choice of comparison activity (a group activity not specifically aimed at the development of communication). However, studies using a single-subject approach (Nind 1996; Kellett 2000; Nind and Kellett 2002) provide good experimental evidence for the efficacy of daily intensive interaction sessions in developing communication, and increased involvement in positive social interaction. There is also some evidence that intensive interaction sometimes leads to the reduction of stereotyped behaviour (Nind and Kellett 2002), but none that it is more effective in this regard than other strategies (such as behaviour modification). However, Goldbart (2002) points out that this paper highlights the tension between the developmental basis of intensive interaction and the espousal of a non-directive approach in which particular behaviours are not targeted, but, for example, the reduction of stereotyped behaviour is welcomed when it occurs. However, it is clear that intensive interaction, used regularly, can increase mutual participation and enjoyment and contribute to the development of communication.

In summary, while further research is needed, the evidence so far available from both the responsive environments approach and intensive interaction supports the use of teaching strategies based on caregiver–infant interaction with children with PMLD.

Using ICT

The use of ICT, especially switches (see below), with pupils with PMLD has grown considerably over the past decade, and a number of authors describe the use of ICT to facilitate communication and social interaction with these pupils. The extent to which the use of a switch to enable an individual to communicate more effectively can be regarded as a *teaching strategy* is questionable. However, the use of switches as part of a strategy for teaching communication skills is described by Schweigert and Rowland (Schweigert 1989; Schweigert and Rowland 1992) and a number of authors also describe the use of switches or switch-based communication aids to teach choice-making.

Schweigert and Rowland have devised an instructional sequence designed to teach children with severe multiple disabilities the early steps in intentional communication using microtechnology, going from what they describe as social contingency awareness (the knowledge that one's own behaviour can reliably affect the behaviour of another person) to making choices using symbols.

Choice-making

Schweigert and Rowland see choice-making as part of an overall early communication sequence, but teaching choice-making as a discrete skill has attracted a good deal of attention from researchers working with people with PMLD. Choice-making is seen as important, not only because it is a step in the development of communication, but because the ability to make choices is seen as an important component of both autonomy and quality of life. Two main strategies are used to teach choice-making: the provision of switch-activated reinforcers, and prompting. In practice these two strategies are often combined, with prompting being used to teach switch activation and/or discrimination between the different choices available. In general, published studies report that choice-making was successfully acquired by the participants (Kearney and McKnight 1997), with some participants successfully choosing items via symbolic means (e.g. Parsons *et al.* 1997).

Teaching communication skills through the medium of academic subjects

Subsequent to the introduction of the National Curriculum in England and Wales and the 1999 revision of the Primary Curriculum in Ireland there has been much discussion of using academic subjects as a context or vehicle for teaching. An example of this approach is the work of Grove and Park (1996, 2001; Park 1998), which uses 'classic literature' (*The Odyssey, Macbeth, A Christmas Carol*) as a way of teaching communication skills to groups of children with severe and profound learning difficulties. There are no formal evaluations of this work, although there is anecdotal evidence of positive responses from individual pupils with PMLD (e.g. Park 2002).

Contingency awareness

The acquisition of contingency awareness – 'a generalised cognitive awareness of the relationship between behaviours and their consequences' (Hanson and Hanline 1985) – is a crucial step in early development, which for normal infants takes place between three and six months. Scattered through the psychological literature is evidence that some, but not all, people with PMLD acquire contingency awareness. Research into strategies by which it may be taught is therefore of great importance.

Two main approaches can be identified, both involving the use of switch-operated reinforcers. The first of these strategies involves applying directly to children with PMLD the paradigm used to demonstrate contingency awareness in young infants. In this paradigm the child is carefully positioned so that some voluntary movement that they make on a relatively frequent basis operates a switch connected to a reinforcer. Operation of the switch delivers a predetermined amount of reinforcer. Learning is judged according to two main criteria: a significant increase in the movement that operates the switch and (sometimes) affective responses (smiling, vocalizing etc.). By no means all the studies employing this approach are using it as a *teaching* strategy. Instead, most have as their aim the demonstration of the existence of contingency awareness, with intervention sessions often being continued over a week or less (e.g. Watson *et al.* 1982; O'Brien *et al.* 1994).

The second approach entails prompting the child to operate the switch in an attempt to facilitate learning. This approach is based on the hypothesis that in order to learn contingency awareness, the child needs to experience the link between their action and the consequence frequently to overcome the possible brevity of short-term memory, and that prompting can help to establish this link.

We (Ware *et al.* 2003) have recently compared these two strategies as part of a larger study in which we are attempting to teach children with PMLD contingency awareness using frequent physical prompts. Our strategy uses a microcomputer to assist the teacher to prompt frequently and consistently, and to record data. The prompting regime has its basis in what is known about the short-term memory span at very early developmental levels, which is estimated by Watson, among others, to be around 5–7 seconds (Watson 1967). Using a multiple baseline design we have compared the learning of identical twin girls using the unprompted and prompted paradigms. Since the child who was not initially prompted showed no evidence of learning while her prompted twin began to learn, and the initially unprompted twin also began to learn once prompted, we tentatively conclude that frequent prompting is the more successful teaching strategy at these very early developmental levels.

Teaching knowledge

A number of common factors can be identified in the different successful teaching strategies for pupils with PMLD:

1 They have strong theoretical underpinnings, usually in cognitive or developmental psychology.
2 All involve frequent (daily where possible) intervention sessions carried out over an extended period.
3 All involve highly structured interventions, which normally require a degree of staff training for their successful implementation.
4 Systematic and detailed data-gathering is used to inform assessment and teaching decisions.

This clearly places these approaches at the high intensity end of continua of pedagogic strategies (see Chapter 1). What initially appear to be highly specialized methods can be conceptualized as at one end of a continuum of strategies that are applicable to *all* children. The use of switch-operated reinforcers, for example, is designed to provide clear consistent and immediate feedback;

systematic data-gathering enables the teacher to monitor learning effectively; frequent sessions ensure sufficient practice for learning and mastery.

It is clear from the foregoing discussion of effective strategies for teaching pupils with PMLD that they are often operating at very early developmental levels. The *content* of teaching is frequently derived from the study of normal development in infancy. Targets include things such as developing contingency awareness, or making a choice between two events. Teachers working with this group therefore need in-depth knowledge of infant development. Additionally, since pupils with PMLD also have severe motor and/or sensory impairments, teachers require knowledge of how these impact on development. Interestingly, even those authors who see developmental goals as of questionable relevance for pupils with PMLD regard in-depth knowledge of early development as crucial for teachers (e.g. Ferguson and Baumgart 1991). While some of this knowledge may also be required by teachers working with multisensory-impaired pupils or profoundly autistic pupils, it is not required by teachers working with other groups. It is, in essence, specialized knowledge. Furthermore, there is some evidence to suggest that such specialized knowledge has a positive impact on teaching effectiveness.

For example, Nind (1996) argues that in order to use intensive interaction, teachers will need to draw on their knowledge of 'good' caregiver–infant interactions, and that in-depth knowledge is essential in order for teachers to make appropriate teaching decisions in the course of interactions with pupils. Furthermore, there is some evidence that teachers who have some degree of specialised knowledge deploy teaching strategies more effectively. Ware et al. (1996) found that teachers who had completed a specific Induction Course for working with this group interacted more effectively with their pupils. The responsive environments project included a staff training component, which was most effective for those staff who had previously lacked specialist knowledge relating to teaching this group. Each of these studies examines the impact of short, highly focused training on particular aspects of teaching pupils with PMLD. This evidence is not extensive, but it is sufficient to suggest that further research into the impact of specialized knowledge on teaching effectiveness is needed.

Curriculum adaptations

If the requirement for specialized knowledge derives in part from the nature of the goals for children with PMLD, this implies a question about the level at which a common curriculum may be said to apply to this group. In England, there has been fierce debate about the relevance of traditional curriculum subjects, or even areas of learning for this group. If learning becomes more differentiated as it progresses then there is a corollary that at very early levels it is relatively undifferentiated (i.e. there are fewer discrete areas). This provides a possible resolution of the problem: if academic subjects can be seen to emerge from areas of learning, then what may be different for pupils with PMLD is the earliness of the stage at which they enter the curriculum; thus areas of

learning, broadly interpreted, could be regarded as common rather than simply aims and principles. This does not, however, entirely resolve the difficulty.
As Ferguson and Baumgart (1991) have highlighted, the issue of what to teach
and with what aim has continued to be a major challenge. Thus programme
objectives remain a problem, with the underlying issue being not whether
they are the same or different from those for other pupils, but whether we are
able to conceptualize them in such a way as to make a real difference to
children's lives.

The international context

Children with PMLD are still only fully within the education system in relatively few countries. The research on teaching strategies referred to in this
chapter comes almost exclusively from these countries, and particularly from
Britain and North America, where there is now 30 years' experience of educating this group. There is also interesting work being carried out in Japan and the
Netherlands, where the reportedly excellent provision for children with PMLD
within the health service raises interesting issues about the context for
education.

Implications for future research

As will be clear from the preceding discussion, little research has been carried
out with children with profound and multiple learning difficulties, and even
less that takes a specifically educational perspective. There are a number of
reasons for this: examination of the research that does exist shows that there
are huge problems of attrition, partly due to the high health needs of many
participants. Additionally, the length of time that it takes for people with
PMLD to learn means that research is necessarily long-term and expensive.
None the less, it is possible to identify three critical areas where research could
currently make a real impact on the development of effective teaching strategies for this group. Information processing, and the neurobiological basis for
this, is perhaps the most critical area. Little is currently known about the
extent to which findings about the development of memory in normal infants
can be applied to this group. The effective utilization of ICT is also an important area. A final, crucial, issue is the evaluation of the impact of specialist
knowledge and training on the extent to which teachers employ effective
teaching strategies.

Conclusions

There is still comparatively little research evidence about education for pupils
with PMLD in general and the efficacy of specialized pedagogy in particular.
The difficulties of doing research with this group, particularly the time needed
to demonstrate progress, remain a major obstacle. However, even where

techniques appear highly specialized, they share common characteristics with 'good' teaching in general, and it is possible to conceptualize them as lying at the high intensity extreme continua of strategies (see Chapter 1). The evidence also suggests that educational progress depends heavily on skilled and knowledgeable teaching that takes account of the pupils' developmental level, both in setting goals and in teaching methodology.

A more pressing issue for teachers working with this group is the extent to which even skilled and successful teaching makes a real difference to children's lives. There is conclusive evidence that pupils with PMLD can learn (e.g. Remington 1996). What is in doubt for some is whether, for pupils with the most profound disabilities, this learning constitutes significant progress towards the common aims. To some extent conclusions on this point inevitably reflect individual value positions. The real difficulties faced by teachers in the classroom should not be underestimated. None the less, for me, the evidence that children with PMLD enjoy learning is compelling evidence that the enterprise is worthwhile.

Summary

Nature of the group

- There is debate about terminology and defining criteria.
- Profound cognitive impairment and learning difficulties are agreed as the basis.
- Children operate at very early developmental level, and are likely to display significant motor impairments, to have significant sensory impairments and to have complex care needs.
- Children with autistic spectrum disorders are not included.

Pedagogy

- This is largely subsumed in discussion of curriculum.
- Contingency awareness is seen as underpinning learning.

Curriculum

- A 'responsive environments' approach is used (includes use of targets).
- An intensive interaction approach is used (excludes use of targets).
- Communication is a major focus.
- ICT is used as a facilitator for communication.
- The teaching of choice-making is seen as a discrete skill.
- There are fewer discrete areas of learning ('subjects') than at later developmental levels.

Knowledge

- Behavioural state is important; possibly awake and alert less than 20 per cent of the time.

- Behavioural rate is important; possibly only five behaviours per minute.
- In general, development parallels that of very young infants at similar developmental levels but there may be differences due to the interaction of impairment, so normal infant development can only be a rough guide.
- But short term memory span may be less good that that for otherwise developmentally similar young infants.

Unique versus general differences position as pedagogic base

- The definition implies a group/general differences position.
- Teaching content is often derived from study of normal infant development.
- Specialized knowledge is very important with this group.
- Children are distinctive in the level at which they enter the curriculum.
- Highly specialized techniques share common characteristics with 'good' teaching in general.
- The 'high intensity' end of continua of pedagogic strategies is illustrated.

Notable aspects introduced

- The 'developmentally normal' is a strong reference point.
- There are difficulties in researching claims about distinctive pedagogies for this group, especially the time needed to show change.
- Distinctiveness lies in the interaction of specialized knowledge with the high intensity end of the pedagogic strategies continuum.

References

ACCAC (2004) Personal, health and social education for pupils with PMLD (http://www.accac.org.uk).

Arvio, M. and Sillanpaa, M. (2003) Prevalence, aetiology and comorbidity of severe and profound intellectual disability in Finland, *Journal of Intellectual Disability Research*, 47(2): 108–12.

Ault, M., Guy, B., Guess, D., Bashinski, S. and Roberts, S. (1995) Analyzing behavior state and learning environments: application in instructional settings, *Mental Retardation*, 33(5): 304–16.

Byers (2000) *Enhancing Quality of Life Project: Newsletter 1*. Cambridge: Cambridge University.

Committee of Enquiry into the Education of Handicapped Children and Young People (1978) *Special Educational Needs: Report of the Committee of Enquiry into the Education of Handicapped Children and Young People (The Warnock Report)*. London: HMSO.

Department for Education and Skills (2000) *Curriculum Guidance for the Foundation Stage*. London: DfES.

Department for Education and Skills (2001) *Special Educational Needs Code of Practice*. London: DfES.

Evans, P. and Ware, J. (1987) *Special Care Provision*. Windsor: NFER-Nelson.

Ferguson, D. and Baumgart, D. (1991) Partial participation revisited, *Journal of the Association for Persons with Severe Handicaps*, 16(4): 218–27.

Goldbart, J. (2002) Commentary on Melanie Nind and Mary Kellett (2002) Responding to individuals with severe learning difficulties and stereotyped behaviour: challenges for an inclusive era, *European Journal of Special Needs Education*, 17(3): 283–7.

Grove, N. and Park, K. (1996) *Odyssey Now*. London: Jessica Kingsley.

Grove, N. and Park, K. (2001) *Social Cognition through Drama and Literature for People with Learning Disabilities: Macbeth in Mind*. London: Jessica Kingsley.

Guess, D., Siegel-Causey, E., Roberts, S., Rues, J., Thompson, B. and Seigel-Causey, D. (1990) Assessment and analysis of behavior state and related variables among students with profoundly handicapping conditions, *Journal of the Association for Persons with Severe Handicaps*, 15: 211–30.

Hanson, M. and Hanline, M. (1985) An analysis of response-contingent learning experiences for young children, *Journal of the Association for Persons with Severe Handicaps*, 10: 31–40.

Hewett, D. (ed) (1998) *Interaction in Action: Reflections on the Use of Intensive Interaction*. London: David Fulton.

Hogg, J. (1991) Developments in further education for adults with profound intellectual and multiple disabilities, in J. Watson (ed.) *Innovatory Practice and Severe Learning Difficulties*. Edinburgh: Moray House Publications.

Julian, G. (2002) Curriculum and provision for pupils with profound and multiple learning difficulties in England, Wales and Ireland: a comparative study. Unpublished PhD thesis, School of the Social Sciences, Cardiff University.

Kahn, J. V. (1976) Utility of the Uzgiris and Hunt Scales with severely and profoundly retarded children, *American Journal of Mental Deficiency*, 80: 663–5.

Kail, R. (1990) *The Development of Memory in Children*, 3rd edn. New York: W. H. Freeman and Company.

Kearney, C. A. and McKnight, T. J. (1997) Preference, choice, and persons with disabilities: A synopsis of assessments, interventions and future directions, *Clinical Psychology Review*, 17(2): 217–38.

Kelleher, A. and Mulcahy, M. (1985) Patterns of disability in the mentally handicapped, in J. M. Berg and J. M. DeJong (eds) *Science and Service in Mental Retardation*. London: Methuen.

Kellett, M. (2000) Sam's story:evaluating Intensive Interaction in terms of its effect on the social and communicative ability of a young child with severe learning difficulties, *Support for Learning*, 15(4): 165–71.

McInnes, J. M. and Treffry, J. (1993) *Deaf-blind Infants and Children: A Developmental Guide*. Toronto: University of Toronto Press.

Nind, M. (1996) Efficacy of intensive interaction: developing sociability and communication in people with severe and complex learning difficulties using an approach based on caregiver–infant interaction, *European Journal of Special Needs Education*, 11(1): 48–66.

Nind, M. and Hewett, D. (1994) *Access to Communication*. London: Fulton.

Nind, M. and Kellett, M (2002) Responding to individuals with severe learning difficulties and stereotyped behaviour: challenges for an inclusive era, *European Journal of Special Needs Education*, 17(3): 265–82.

Nind, M., Kellett, M. and Hopkins, V. (2001) Teachers' talk styles: communicating with learners with severe and complex learning difficulties, *Child Language Teaching and Therapy*, 17(2): 143–59.

O'Brien, Y., Glenn, S. and Cunningham, C. (1994) Contingency awareness in infants and children with severe and profound learning disabilities, *International Journal of Disability, Development and Education*, 41(3): 231–43.

Qualifications and Curriculum Authority (2001) *Planning, Teaching and Assessing the Curriculum for Pupils with Learning Difficulties*. London: QCA.

Park, K. (1998) Dickens for all: inclusive approaches to literature and communication with people with severe and profound learning disabilities, *British Journal of Special Education*, 25(3): 114–18.

Park, K. (2002) Macbeth: a poetry workshop on stage at Shakespeare's Globe Theatre, *British Journal of Special Education*, 29(1): 14–19.

Parsons, M., Harper, V., Jensen, J. and Reid, D. (1997) Assisting older adults with severe disabilities in expressing leisure preferences: a protocol for determining choice-making skills, *Research in Developmental Disabilities*, 18(2): 113–26.

Remington, B. (1996) Assessing the occurrence of learning in children with profound intellectual disability: a conditioning approach, *International Journal of Disability, Development and Education*, 43: 101–18.

Rumeau-Rouquette, C., du Mazaubrun, C., Cans, C. and Grandjean, H. (1998) Definition and Prevalence of School-age Multi-handicaps, *Archives of Pediatric and Adolescent Medicine* 5(7) 739–744.

School Curriculum and Assessment Authority (1996) *Planning the Curriculum: For Pupils with Profound and Multiple Learning Difficulties*. London: SCAA.

Schweigert, P. (1989) Use of microswitch technology to facilitate social contingency awareness as a basis for early communication skills, *Augmentative and Alternative Communication*, 5: 192–8.

Schweigert, P. and Rowland, C. (1992) Early communication and microtechnology: Instructional sequence and case studies of children with severe multiple disabilities, *Augmentative and Alternative Communication* 8 273–284.

Stromme, P. and Valvatne, K. (1998) Mental retardation in Norway: prevalence and sub-classification in a cohort of 30,037 children born between 1980 and 1985, *Acta Paediatrica*, 87(3): 291–6.

Ware, J. (1987) Providing education for children with profound and multiple learning difficulties: a survey of resources and an analysis of staff:pupil interactions in special care units. Unpublished PhD thesis, University of London Institute of Education.

Ware, J. (1994) Using interaction in the education of pupils with PMLDs. (i) Creating contingency-sensitive environments, in J. Ware (ed.) *Educating Children with Profound and Multiple Learning Difficulties*. London: Fulton.

Ware, J. (1996) *Creating a Responsive Environment for People with Profound and Multiple Learning Difficulties*. London: David Fulton.

Ware, J. (2003) *Creating a Responsive Environment for People with Profound and Multiple Learning Difficulties*, 2nd edn. London: David Fulton.

Ware, J., Thorpe, P. and Mehigan, P. (2003) Teaching contingency awareness in the classroom to pupils with profound and multiple learning difficulties. Paper presented at the Annual Conference of BERA Edinburgh, 11–13 September.

Watson, J. S. (1967) Memory and contingency analysis in infant learning, *Merrill Palmer Quarterly*, 11: 55–76.

Watson, J. (1994) Using interaction in the education of pupils with PMLDs. (ii) Intensive interaction: two case studies, in J. Ware (ed.) *Educating Children with Profound and Multiple Learning Difficulties*. London: David Fulton.

Watson, J. and Fisher, A. (1997) Evaluating the effectiveness of Intensive Interactive teaching with pupils with profound and complex learning difficulties, *British Journal of Special Education*, 24(2): 80–7.

Wellesley, D., Hockey, K., Montgomery, P. and Stanley, F. (1992) Prevalence of intellectual handicap in Western Australia: a community study, *Medical Journal of Australia*, 156(2): 94–6, 100, 102.

Children with Down's syndrome

Jennifer Wishart

The task of this book is to evaluate whether meeting the special educational needs (SEN) of pupils with learning difficulties requires a different set of pedagogical skills and a new knowledge base or whether the portfolio of skills normally held by any good teacher, appropriately differentiated, is sufficient. The rapid move towards mainstreaming necessitates an urgent answer to this question. Teachers today are increasingly expected to be able fully to meet the requirements of pupils with SEN from within resources currently available to them. Classroom assistants and learning support teachers are often on hand, but the responsibility for providing appropriate educational support ultimately resides with the classroom teacher. Some will not have expected to meet this challenge within their teaching career and some may be unwilling to try to meet it if they do not feel they have ready access to the pedagogic strategies best suited to this group of children.

This chapter looks at what is known about teaching children with Down's syndrome. As we shall see, the evidence base for assessing the efficacy of contrasting pedagogies with children with Down's syndrome is very thin indeed. At the very fundamental level of information processing and motivational processes, there is evidence that children with Down's syndrome may show some syndrome-specific difficulties in learning. However, many of the problems the children face are undoubtedly shared by other children with similar levels of learning difficulties arising from other causes. To ensure a broader picture of the issues, this chapter should therefore be read in conjunction with the chapters covering mild, moderate, severe and profound difficulties, as all these levels of learning difficulty can be found in children with Down's syndrome (see Chapters 15, 14, 5 and 6 respectively).

Down's syndrome

Down's syndrome is a genetic disorder that accounts for the largest single sub-grouping of pupils with severe learning disabilities.[1] In the 1920s, it was unusual for someone with Down's syndrome to survive into their teens and, even in the 1960s, most children and adults with Down's syndrome were still being cared for in residential institutions, with no access to formal education. Today, in most developed countries, children with Down's syndrome now have essentially the same rights to education as other children and many receive their education, or at least part of it, in mainstream schools. Many adults now live semi-independently in the community and are in some form of supported part-time employment. Most enjoy relatively good health and average life expectancy is now around 50 (Yang *et al.* 1997).

As well as these changes in health, social and educational circumstances, there have been very significant advances in our understanding of the genetic and neurological mechanisms that underlie the cognitive impairments typically seen in Down's syndrome. These advances have provided helpful insights into the origin of the learning difficulties experienced but as yet have not led to any treatment that might prevent or reduce these. Some children do comparatively well in school but average academic achievement levels remain low and investment in early intervention programmes and in special education has so far failed to produce substantive or lasting benefits for the majority of children (for an overview see Spiker and Hopmann 1997). Few children reach developmental ages of more than six to eight years, with language development often even further delayed in terms of age equivalence. This clearly poses some very real challenges to educational inclusion, especially at secondary level, where the developmental gap between pupils with Down's syndrome and their age peers can be very wide indeed.

Down's syndrome is the most easily recognizable of the many childhood disorders leading to special educational needs. Members of the general public will readily offer views on likely personality characteristics (Wishart and Johnston 1990), developmental, social and educational potential (Wishart and Manning 1996; Gilmore *et al.* 2003), lifespan and health needs (NOP/Down Syndrome Association 2003) – despite having had little, if any, contact with anyone with Down's syndrome. Most also have low expectations of academic potential, often unnecessarily low (Wishart and Manning 1996). What runs common to these views is a tendency to consider all people with Down's syndrome as being alike. In reality, children with Down's syndrome can vary in their ability, progress and personalities as much as ordinary children. It is not surprising, though, that only a minority of the public – 20 per cent in a recent Australian study – believe that a regular classroom is the best educational setting for such children. More surprising perhaps is the fact that many teachers share these views (Gilmore *et al.* 2003). Public and professional acceptance of those with Down's syndrome may have changed to some extent but there is limited evidence that underlying beliefs or knowledge have changed to the same extent.

What is Down's syndrome?

Down's syndrome is the result of a random accident at the very earliest stage in development, at the point before sperm and egg first come together. Down's syndrome can occur in any pregnancy at any maternal age. Although for reasons not yet understood older mothers are more at risk, higher fertility rates in younger women result in the majority of Down's syndrome babies being born to mothers in the normal child-bearing age range. Down's syndrome results from the presence of an extra copy, in whole or part, of chromosome 21; in many publications, especially medical ones, the term 'trisomy 21' is also used. Chromosome 21 is one of the smallest human chromosomes. This was previously believed to have around 1500 genes but was estimated in the Human Genome Project to have 225 genes, now revised to 329 (Roizen & Patterson, 2003). Whatever their number, the resulting extra copies of these genes – in themselves all perfectly normal – lead to harmful 'gene dosage' effects from conception onwards. The extra copy disrupts physical and mental development throughout childhood and into adult life. Inherited genetic characteristics, environmental factors, upbringing and educational opportunities also play an important role in determining developmental outcomes, however, just as they do for other children (Buckley and Bird 2001; DSA 2003).

Space limits the amount of information on Down's syndrome that can be provided here. A number of readily available, up-to-date sources provide useful introductions for both parents and professionals, however (e.g. Stratford and Gunn 1996; Selikowitz 1997; Lewis 2003; see also the websites listed at the end of this chapter). It is important to note that, contrary to common belief, Down's syndrome is not a disability that will soon no longer be with us. Approximately 1 in every 1000 babies is born with Down's syndrome. Two babies are born every day in the UK, around 5000 each year in the USA and around 100,000 per year worldwide. Incidence rates are broadly similar across countries and have shown no marked decline in recent years. Religious views on abortion influence birth rates in some countries, as does the availability of pre-natal screening, but the latter has failed to have as great an impact on incidence as initially predicted. Life expectancy has increased greatly in all but the most disadvantaged of countries and so prevalence rates are rising rather than falling.

As most people with Down's syndrome can expect to lead a relatively healthy and long life these days, providing more effective education is crucial. Some children benefit more than others from schooling, some may need more help than others, but all can be expected to make measurable progress during these important years. However, it is important to be realistic about what may be achieved and to recognize how hard a child with Down's syndrome will have to work to reach the same educational milestones as other children.

Health

Children with Down's syndrome used to have a very short lifespan, often succumbing to infections or heart disease in early childhood. Advances in antibiotics and in surgical techniques – along with changes in attitudes to medical interventions for children with SLD – now mean that most can look forward to a comparatively healthy childhood. A life expectancy of 50–60 years is now average and in some countries people with Down's syndrome are living into their eighties and nineties. At the cellular level, there is evidence of an accelerated ageing process but this is not always accompanied by evidence of mental deterioration or Alzheimer-like dementia in later adulthood (Holland 2000). Many adults benefit from access to further educational opportunities and continue to add to their skills in useful ways throughout life.

Around 40 per cent of children are born with heart defects of varying degrees of severity but in most cases these can be surgically corrected or managed through carefully monitored medication. Susceptibility to leukaemia and some other childhood diseases is also raised but is still more uncommon than common. Over 50 per cent of children with Down's syndrome have to cope with a hearing and/or visual impairment. Again, this can be of varying severity. Visual impairments are not always properly diagnosed and hearing impairment is often missed, especially if intermittent, with classroom difficulties often wrongly attributed solely to the child's learning disability. Clearly sensory impairments need to be considered carefully in planning lessons, as often the child may be having unnecessary additional difficulty in accessing subject materials or teacher instructions. This is often mistaken as being solely due to their learning disability.

Levels of learning disability

Learning difficulties can vary from mild to severe but can also be profound if other disabling conditions are present. Most children fall into the moderate-to-severe range. Reaching even early academic milestones often proves to be an uphill task and many children reach adulthood without developing the basic literacy and numeracy skills taken for granted in much younger children; a minority, however, do make significant academic progress. IQ scores in child and adult samples can range over 50–60 IQ points (Carr 1995), a similar spread to that found in the general population, albeit displaced to the lower end of the normal distribution. Given its genetic basis, this wide variation is surprising and is as yet unexplained. It is clear that Down's syndrome in itself does not necessarily put a very low ceiling on what can be learned, although adverse learning styles may impede developmental progress (see below).

Language development

Children with Down's syndrome are typically very slow to develop language and in the early years many parents encourage the use of a sign language such as Makaton to help to bridge the gap between comprehension and production that is characteristic of the condition (Miller 1999; Chapman and Hesketh 2001). Low muscle tone in the tongue and lips often makes even simple speech difficult for others to understand. An American survey indicated that as many as 95 per cent of children have difficulty in being understood (Kumin 1994) and even family members often depend heavily on contextual clues to decipher speech intent.

Language is often more delayed than would be predicted from other areas of cognitive functioning. Recent work suggests that language profiles are similar to those seen in non-disabled children who have a specific language impairment: both groups have more severe deficits in phonological development and in grammar acquisition than in vocabulary acquisition (Laws and Bishop 2003). Continuing growth in vocabulary often disguises how poor syntax is, as does a tendency to speak very little spontaneously or in only short sentences. Fowler (1990) found few children and young adults with grammatical abilities beyond the three-year-old level in her studies, although once again the picture was of considerable individual variation.

Some children have much better language than others but we do not yet know why this is so. Variation is not accounted for by differences in cognitive ability, early intervention, hearing status, mothers' education or socio-economic status, parental language input, general health status or structural differences in the speech production mechanism (see Laws and Bishop 2003 for an overview). Variation may be related to auditory short term memory (the store used to hold and process spoken language) or to phonological memory deficits (Laws & Gunn, 2004). Genetic allelic variation may also play a role but whatever its basis, the wide variation in language outcomes once again demonstrates that Down's syndrome in itself does not inevitably constrain language development to very low levels. With increasing understanding of factors influencing outcomes, greater progress may be possible for more children.

The DownsEd team in the UK have long advocated the use of reading as an effective way of developing speech and language skills on the grounds that vision is an easier route into language for children with Down's syndrome than auditory processing. Some remarkable successes with individual children have been reported and many schools follow this team's recommendations, using the comprehensive set of resources they have recently made available (Buckley 1985; Buckley and Bird 2001). More research studies are needed, however, to establish exactly which approaches provide maximum benefits and whether these are Down's syndrome-specific or could be equally beneficial to children with similar levels of learning difficulties.

Memory

As we have seen, working memory is not a strength in children with Down's syndrome (Jarrold & Baddeley, 1997). Working memory problems lead to difficulties in processing and retaining new words, understanding and responding to spoken language, following verbal instructions, learning rules and routines, developing organizational skills and remembering sequences and lists (DSA 2003).

Children can quickly switch out of teaching that places too many demands on auditory memory. Teachers who work regularly with children with Down's syndrome have all sorts of strategies to try to circumvent these inherent difficulties, such as supporting verbal input in visual forms (using symbols or drawings), simplifying and shortening instructions, checking that the child has understood instructions by asking them to repeat them back and so forth. Many of these techniques are also recommended for children with non-specific learning difficulties of similar severity, however, so their pedagogical utility is unlikely to be restricted to children with Down's syndrome. This notwithstanding, the memory limitations inherent to Down's syndrome do make the teaching of basic academic skills such as literacy and numeracy challenging, especially when taken in combination with the children's associated language difficulties.

Learning

There are many misconceptions about the nature and extent of the difficulties associated with Down's syndrome but the one thing that all children with Down's syndrome *do* have in common is a significant degree of learning disability. A number of excellent books have reviewed the research literature on this and readers are encouraged to consult these for more in-depth information (e.g. Cicchetti and Beeghly 1990; Carr 1995; Stratford and Gunn 1996; Lewis 2003).

Early developmental progress is often highly encouraging but all too often this promise fails to be realized in later years. Generalization and consolidation of new skills seem to pose particular problems (Morss 1985; Duffy and Wishart 1994; Wishart 1996) and it is essential to find out why this is the case in order to identify ways of helping the children to maintain early rates of progress. To date, little has been possible to prevent the gap between the children and their peers widening with increasing age. This poses social and academic challenges for educational inclusion, particularly at secondary levels.

As we have seen, the stereotype of children with Down's syndrome often translates into very low expectations of academic potential. Low expectations in learning partners may be compounded by the emergence of an adverse learning style in the children themselves. Even as infants, they can show an unwillingness to take the initiative in their learning and, as personal learning histories lengthen, they sometimes develop highly successful strategies, often socially based, for avoiding new learning (Wishart 1991, 1993). At times, social skills are used to divert learning partners into doing the work for them – a short-term 'fix' that is unlikely to be helpful in the longer term (Pitcairn and Wishart 1994; Wishart 1996). Responses to successes and failures also seem to differ qualitatively (Wishart and Duffy 1990; Pitcairn and Wishart 1994) with self-regulation and mastery motivation behaviours showing subtle differences in comparison to similarly disabled or typically developing peers (Cuskelly *et al.* 1998; Dayus 1999; Niccols *et al.* 2003).

A number of studies have recently examined the assumption that social understanding is somehow protected in Down's syndrome in comparison to more general learning ability. Findings suggest that this assumption may be wrong. In comparison to both ordinary children matched on mental age and other learning disabled groups, children with Down's syndrome show difficulties from a very early age with some very specific aspects of social interaction, including theory of mind, empathizing, requesting behaviours and social referencing (Franco and Wishart 1995; Wishart and Pitcairn 2000; Kasari *et al.* 2001; Binnie and Williams 2002; Williams *et al.* 2004). There is also evidence that imitation, often thought to be the foundation stone of social learning, is not used to support learning in the same way as in typical development (Wright 1997). As we have seen, social behaviours produced in a variety of learning contexts indicate that the children may intentionally misuse their social skills to avoid engaging in difficult tasks. These behaviours often prove not to be truly 'social' in that the children show little accommodation to their partner and indeed often break some of the most basic ground rules of interpersonal interaction. This may explain why the children show few benefits from collaborative learning opportunities unless skilfully scaffolded by an adult partner (Goodall 2002; Willis *et al.* 2003).

Different or similar pedagogical needs?

This chapter has so far sidestepped the focus of this book: whether differing teaching approaches are necessary when working with children who have Down's syndrome. There are two reasons for this. The most obvious – and disappointing – is the paucity of relevant research findings from which to draw robust conclusions. In the case of psychological research, developmental researchers largely ignore Down's syndrome in favour of more recently identified and 'interesting' conditions such as autism and Williams syndrome; there is currently very little research being conducted with the children beyond pre-school years. Despite learning and teaching being inextricably intertwined, the educational literature on children with Down's syndrome is even thinner. Educational research seldom focuses specifically on children with Down's syndrome and, where it does, comparison of outcomes to other groups of children, either typically developing or with similar levels of learning difficulties, is rarely included in the design. This leaves interpretation of findings hugely problematic, especially when ability at entry to the study is poorly defined, details of pedagogical approaches are slight and progress is rather loosely measured. Recent advances in neuropsychology and the completion of the Human Genome Project may have brought us much closer to understanding at the biological and physical level exactly how Down's syndrome affects learning and development, but in terms of identifying effective educational interventions we are very much still struggling in the dark. We have very little knowledge of how the children learn – or fail to learn – in formal classroom contexts.

Psychological and educational research has tended to focus on identifying relative strengths and weaknesses in cognitive profiles (for overviews see Cicchetti and Beeghly 1990; Carr 1995; Stratford and Gunn 1996; Lewis 2003). The following are usually said to be characteristic of Down's syndrome learners: strong visual learning skills, poor auditory learning skills, delayed speech and language development, good ability to learn from peers (particularly through imitation and cue-taking), immature social skills, delayed fine and gross motor skills (leading to clumsiness and manipulation difficulties) and a short concentration span. While this general profile is supported by a range of studies in the research literature, cited studies have not always included comparison with other groups of learners. Recommendations made in relation to specific areas of the curriculum, such as literacy and maths, are likewise seldom grounded in findings from controlled comparative studies, drawing instead on what is currently judged as best practice. In the UK, the USA and other countries, a number of resource packs and texts specifically for teachers who work with children with Down's syndrome are now widely available (see e.g. Oelwein 1995; Lorenz 1998; Buckley and Bird 2001). However, authors are generally careful to point out that the advice given is often based on hands-on experience of what 'works' with children with Down's syndrome rather than on findings from educational research. Although there is frequent reference to the specific learning profiles of children with Down's syndrome, the number of studies that can legitimately claim to have produced evidence to back up this claim is very small indeed.

Many experienced teachers of pupils with special educational needs often find much commonality in the kinds of learning 'styles' described as Down's syndrome-specific and those seen in other children with learning disabilities of a similar degree of severity. Recommended pedagogies show much overlap with more general MLD/SLD pedagogic strategies, but with a particular emphasis on trying to circumvent the language and auditory memory problems associated with Down's syndrome by capitalizing on relative strengths in visual processing ability. Readers are therefore advised to cross-refer Down's syndrome texts with the broader PMLD, MLD, SLD and special needs literature. Ware (2003), Lewis (1995), Carpenter, Ashdown and Bovair (1996), Watson (1996), Farrell (1997) and Dyson and Millward (2000), for example, all offer insightful analyses and balanced evaluations of educational theory and current practice, often placing these usefully in the wider context of recent and far-reaching changes in educational provision for children with learning difficulties.

This brings us to the second reason for this chapter sidestepping the central question of this book. Children with Down's syndrome have traditionally been educated in special schools and consequently what little research there has been of direct relevance to pedagogy has mostly been carried out in these settings. Most research has been carried out in small classrooms, with staff with extensive experience of working with children having special educational needs but over a fairly restricted curriculum. This makes it almost impossible to generalize findings to mainstream classrooms and the wider curriculum. We have to recognize that meeting the additional needs of a child with Down's syndrome in a large mainstream classroom while continuing to meet the diverse needs of all of the other children is a challenge that many teachers may not relish. A recent Scottish report (Audit Scotland 2003) was highly critical of the 'patchy preparation', 'minimal planning' and 'inadequate resourcing' of this major educational shift and in the case of children with Down's syndrome it is already apparent that additional adult classroom support is often being used inappropriately and ineffectively (Lorenz 1999). Many teachers, while publicly endorsing the principles of inclusion and the values that drive it, may not be sufficiently convinced of its educational value to be willing to carry it forward into their own professional practice. In the absence of any solid evidence base from which to endorse the efficacy of either innovative or traditional pedagogical methods, this is understandable.

For real inroads to be made into helping children with Down's syndrome to achieve to their full potential, a more focused and unified research effort will be needed. Mainstreaming now makes research into Down's syndrome far less attractive to many researchers. Achieving large samples is much more time consuming and access has to be negotiated through many more channels, not all of them welcoming of researchers. We are, however, at a very exciting time in research into learning difficulties, a time when educationalists, psychologists, sociologists, biomedical scientists and geneticists can pool their respective expertises to reach a much fuller understanding of the nature and impact of genetically based syndromes such as Down's syndrome on development and learning – respecting individual differences while also explaining them. There will, though, need to be a greater willingness for psychological and educational researchers to cross the interdisciplinary divide and dig deeper into what can at first seem like a totally alien literature, based on very different methodologies and in very different value systems.

Many educationalists reject any focus specifically on children with Down's syndrome as it smacks of a return to labelling and a 'within-child' blame culture. For many psychologists, this is the only way forward, seen as neither disrespectful to the individual child, denying of commonalities across special needs groups nor reflecting a belief that environmental factors are unimportant in determining outcomes. Special educators, surprisingly perhaps, are sometimes the most resistant to any aetiology-specific approach to teaching, fearing a return to the discredited 'medical model' of learning disabilities (Hodapp and Dykens 1994). Medical and genetic research can tell us a great deal about conditions like Down's syndrome. Neither has yet identified any way of alleviating the associated learning difficulties, however, and it is here that psychological and educational research can contribute most. The current disciplinary stand-off means that very little research is being carried out on children with Down's syndrome by either psychologists or educationalists, however. There are a few studies that have directly investigated classroom learning in children with Down's syndrome but few report on large numbers of children (essential given the wide range in developmental outcomes seen in this group) and many are single case studies. Some have been designed specifically to identify differences in development in children with Down's syndrome, but most have not. Very few have compared the outcomes of specific pedagogic strategies for children with Down's syndrome to outcomes either for typically developing children of the same chronological or developmental age or for children with learning difficulties of the same severity but differing (or unknown) aetiology and even these few studies are often misreported in the practitioner literature (e.g. Duffy and Wishart 1994).

Conclusion

This chapter has tried to establish whether meeting the educational needs of pupils with Down's syndrome requires a different set of pedagogical skills and a new knowledge base or whether the portfolio of skills normally held by any good teacher, appropriately differentiated, can be equally effective. It unfortunately has to be concluded that there is as yet no substantive evidence base from which to answer this question at this time. What *is* clear is that children with Down's syndrome face very significant obstacles to their learning and experience difficulties at the most fundamental of levels. A large number of studies have compared basic psychological functioning in Down's syndrome to developmental pathways shown by children who are either typically developing, have some other form of genetic learning disability (such as Fragile X, autism or Williams syndrome) or have learning difficulties of a similar severity but unknown aetiology (see Chapman and Hesketh 2001; Chertkoff Walz and Benson 2002). Although many of the impairments evident in the areas of language, memory and the like are shared with other MLD and SLD children, profiles of strengths and weaknesses do show qualitative and quantitative differences, although these are sometimes very subtle. Given the effects that Down's syndrome has on brain development and functioning – from conception onwards – such differences are hardly surprising (Karrer *et al.* 1998). It is also important to remember that Down's syndrome is one of the few learning disabilities that can be diagnosed at birth and can be easily identified by others. At an experiential level, the learning environments of children with Down's syndrome, both in and out of school, are also therefore likely to differ from those experienced by children with later emerging and less readily identifiable learning disabilities.

So far little has been said in relation to the unique versus general differences framework introduced in Chapter 1 and interwoven into other chapters in this book. Again, one of the difficulties in writing from a psychology viewpoint is that these conceptualizations – and the terminology in which they are expressed – are difficult to reconcile with the treatment of similar issues in child psychology and in the wider learning disability field. Research on children with Down's syndrome has had a particularly chequered past few decades. Difficulties in communicating across disciplinary divides have been exacerbated by the 'two cultures' that until recently have divided research on learning disabilities (Hodapp and Dykens 1994): research based on aetiologically distinct groups (usually in the 'harder' empirical sciences) and research focusing on level of impairment (special education research and educational psychology). Child development straddles these two cultures, at times uncomfortably. However, increasing realization that syndrome-specific research can advance knowledge of both typical and atypical development has led to a recent upsurge in aetiology-led research and increased interdisciplinary collaboration among geneticists, psychologists and educators (see Hodapp *et al.* 2003). One of the longest-standing debates in psychological research – now thankfully put to one side – has been between supporters of difference versus delay theories of learning disability, with further debate centring on whether differences, if they exist, lie in the structure of cognition across domains and/or the sequence in which development unfolds (see Hodapp 1998 for an overview). In terms of the commonality/differentiation model laid out in Chapter 1, the 'difference' theory equates at some level more to the 'general differences' position (where commonality within group needs are acknowledged, but the pedagogical relevance of current groupings queried) than to the 'unique differences' model (where approaches to pedagogy are informed only by common and individual needs). For some commentators, however, the case will always depend on the level of analysis: the more detailed the analysis, the more likely fine grained differences are to show up, at both group and individual levels. The same seems true for pedagogies: when does a continuum become a series of related but distinctive pedagogic strategies and when do these individually become so differentiated as to become specific to the group of learners with whom they are used? The current absence of evidence of the need for separate pedagogical strategies for children with Down's syndrome should be taken as just that. We are still a long way away from being able to conclude that such strategies do not exist in current practice or are not needed.

Summary

Nature of the group

- Down's syndrome arises from a genetic 'random accident' associated with a range of learning difficulties from mild to severe and (if occurring with other disabling conditions) profound.
- There are overlaps with other groups experiencing learning difficulties.
- There is a wide range in IQ (over 50 60 IQ points) across children with Down's syndrome.
- Down's syndrome is associated with sensory impairments for the majority of children.
- There is an association with heart disease for a large minority of children with Down's syndrome.
- There have been shifts in the developed world towards more rights, longer life expectancy and more independent living for people with Down's syndrome.
- Generalization and consolidation of new skills are particular problems.
- Often children have an adverse learning style (avoiding new learning, unwilling to take initiative).
- The assumption that social understanding is protected is not supported by the research evidence.
- Early diagnosis means that early environments may be atypical compared with the experiences of children without Down's syndrome.

Pedagogy

- There is a paucity of robust research evidence.

- There is a dearth of systematic studies involving children with Down's syndrome after pre-school.
- Claims have been made (in the literature) for the specificity of approaches but the research base required to support such claims is weak.

Curriculum

- There is some evidence that vision is an easier route into language and learning than is auditory processing (reflected in some approaches to the teaching of literacy with this group).

Knowledge

- See above regarding the nature of children with Down's syndrome.
- Children often have an adverse learning style (avoiding new learning, unwilling to take initiative).
- Generalization and consolidation of new skills are a particular problem.

Unique versus general differences position as pedagogic base

- Recommended (in literature) pedagogic strategies have much in common with those recommended for other groups of learners with similar levels of difficulties.
- It is not possible to take a clear cut position as research designs have lacked external and internal validity, thus failing to provide answers to question posed here about individual versus general differences as the pedagogic base.

Notable aspects introduced

- Given the genetic distinctiveness of this group, the absence of research-based evidence about pedagogy is disappointing.
- Mainstreaming is an obstacle to unambiguous (quasi-experimental) research designs required to address causal outcome questions.
- There are potential strengths in synthesizing psychological, educational and medical perspectives and research evidence on learning in children with Down's syndrome, but potential conflicts in relation to acceptable research paradigms and methodologies.

Note

1 The term 'learning disability' is used here in its UK sense and interchangeably with 'learning difficulties', the preferred term among educationalists. Internationally, 'intellectual disability' is increasingly used to describe those with significantly impaired cognitive and adaptive abilities. In the USA, the term 'mental retardation' is still favoured, with 'learning disability' used to describe children who have normal intelligence but show a significant discrepancy between this intellectual potential and their academic achievement. Great care is therefore necessary when accessing the international literature on children with a 'learning disability' or with 'learning

difficulties'. US studies reporting on the effective application of specific pedagogies with children with 'learning disabilities' are often cited inappropriately in the special needs literature. This is not only misleading but also makes it less likely that the necessary studies relating specifically to special educational needs will be carried out.

References

Audit Scotland/Her Majesty's Inspectorate (2003) *Moving to Mainstream: The Inclusion of Pupils with Special Educational Needs in Mainstream Schools*. Edinburgh: Audit Scotland/ Her Majesty's Inspectorate.

Binnie, L. M. and Williams, J. M. (2002) Intuitive psychological, physical and biological knowledge in typically developing preschoolers, children with autism and children with Down's syndrome, *British Journal of Developmental Psychology*, 20: 343–59.

Buckley, S. (1985) Attaining basic educational skills: reading, writing and number, in D. Lane and B. Stratford (eds) *Current Approaches to Down's Syndrome*. London: Holt, Rinehart and Winston.

Buckley, S. and Bird, G. (eds) (2001–3) *Issues and Information* (series of linked publications with resources for teachers). Portsmouth: Down Syndrome Educational Trust.

Carpenter, B., Ashdown, R. and Bovair, K. (eds) (1996) *Enabling Access: Effective Teaching and Learning for Pupils with Learning Difficulties*. London: David Fulton.

Carr, J. (1995) *Down's Syndrome: Children Growing up*. Cambridge: Cambridge University Press.

Chapman, R. S. and Hesketh, L. J. (2001) Behavioral phenotype of individuals with Down syndrome, *Mental Retardation and Developmental Disabilities Research Reviews*, 6: 84–95.

Chertkoff Walz, N. and Benson, B. A. (2002) Behavioral phenotypes in children with Down syndrome, Prader-Willi syndrome, or Angelman syndrome, *Journal of Developmental and Physical Disabilities*, 14: 307–21.

Cicchetti, D. and Beeghly, M. (eds) (1990) *Children with Down Syndrome: A Developmental Perspective*. Cambridge: Cambridge University Press.

Cuskelly, M., Zhang, A. and Gilmore, L. (1998) The importance of self-regulation in young children with Down syndrome, *International Journal of Disability, Development and Education*, 45: 331–41.

Dayus, B. (1999) The development of mastery motivation in infants with Down syndrome. Unpublished PhD dissertation, Liverpool John Moores University.

Down's Syndrome Association. (2003) *Education Support Pack for Schools. Mainstream: Primary and Secondary*. London: Down's Syndrome Association.

Duffy, L. and Wishart, J. G. (1994) The stability and transferability of errorless learning in children with Down's syndrome, *Down's Syndrome Research and Practice*, 2: 51–8.

Dykens, E. M. and Hodapp, R. M. (2001) Research in mental retardation: toward an etiologic approach, *Journal of Child Psychology and Psychiatry*, 42: 49–71.

Dyson, A. and Millward, A. (2000) *Schools and Special Needs: Issues of Innovation and Inclusion*. London: Paul Chapman Publishing.

Farrell, P. (1997) *Teaching Pupils with Learning Difficulties*. London: Cassell.

Fowler, A. E. (1990) Language abilities in children with Down syndrome: evidence for a specific syntactic delay, in D. Cicchetti and M. Beeghly (eds) *Children with Down Syndrome: A Developmental Perspective*. Cambridge: Cambridge University Press.

Franco, F. and Wishart, J. G. (1995) The use of pointing and other gestures by young children with Down's syndrome, *American Journal on Mental Retardation*, 100: 160–82.

Gilmore, L., Campbell, J. and Cuskelly, M. (2003) Developmental expectations, personality stereotypes and attitudes towards inclusive education: community and teacher views of Down syndrome, *International Journal of Disability, Development and Education*, 50: 63–78.

Goodall, K. (2002) The effect of collaborative learning on the problem-solving skills of children with Down syndrome. Unpublished PhD dissertation, University of Edinburgh.

Hodapp, R. M. (1998) *Development and Disabilities: Intellectual, Sensory and Motor Impairments*. Cambridge: Cambridge University Press.

Hodapp, R. M., DesJardin, J. L. and Ricci, L. A. (2003) Genetic syndromes of mental retardation: should they matter for the early interventionist?, *Infants and Young Children*, 16: 152–60.

Hodapp, R. M. and Dykens, E. M. (1994) Mental retardation: two cultures of behavioral research, *American Journal on Mental Retardation*, 98: 675–87.

Holland, A. (2000) Ageing and learning disability, *British Journal of Psychiatry*, 176: 26–31.

Jarrold, C. and Baddeley, A. D. (1997) Short-term memory for verbal and visuospatial information in Down's syndrome, *Cognitive Neuropsychiatry*, 2: 101–22.

Karrer, J. H., Karrer, R., Bloom, D., Chaney, L. and Davis, R. (1998) Event-related brain potentials during an extended visual recognition memory task depict delayed development of cereberal inhibitory processes among six-month-old infants with Down syndrome, *International Journal of Psychophysiology*, 29: 167–200.

Kasari, C., Freeman, S. F. N. and Hughes, M. A. (2001) Emotion recognition by children with Down syndrome, *American Journal on Mental Retardation*, 106: 59–72.

Kumin, L. (1994) Intelligibility of speech in children with Down syndrome in natural settings: parents' perspective, *Perceptual and Motor Skills*, 78: 307–13.

Laws, G. and Bishop, D. V. M. (2003) A comparison of language abilities in adolescents with Down syndrome and children with specific language impairment, *Journal of Language, Speech and Hearing Research.* 46: 1324–1339.

Laws, G. & Gunn, D. (2004). Phonological memory as a predictor of language comprehension in Down syndrome: a five year follow up study, *Journal of Child Psychology and Psychiatry*, 45: 326–337).

Lewis, A. (1995) *Primary Special Needs and the National Curriculum*, 2nd edn. London: Routledge.

Lewis, V. (2003) *Development and Disability*, 2nd edn. Oxford: Blackwell.

Lorenz, S. (1995) The placement of pupils with Down's syndrome: a survey of one Northern LEA, *British Journal of Special Education*, 22: 16–19.

Lorenz, S. (1998) *Children with Down's Syndrome: A Guide for Teachers and Learning Support Assistants in Mainstream Primary and Secondary Schools*. London: David Fulton.

Lorenz, S. (1999) *Experiences of Inclusion for Children with Down's Syndrome in the UK*. London: Down's Syndrome Association.

Miller, J. F. (1999) Profiles of language development in children with Down syndrome, in J. F. Miller, M. Leddy and L. A. Leavitt (eds) *Improving the Communication of People with Down Syndrome*. Baltimore: Paul H. Brooke.

Morss, J. R. (1985) Early cognitive development: difference or delay?, in D. Lane and B. Stratford (eds) *Current Approaches to Down's Syndrome*. London: Holt, Rinehard and Winston.

National Opinion Poll Research Group/Down Syndrome Association. (2003) *Barriers to Inclusion for Persons with Down's Syndrome: A Survey*. London: NOP/DSA.

Niccols, A., Atkinson, L. and Pepler, D. (2003) Mastery motivation in young children with Down's syndrome: relations with cognitive and adaptive competence, *Journal of Intellectual Disability Research*, 47: 121–33.

Oelwein, P. L. (1995) *Teaching Reading to Children with Down Syndrome: A Guide for Parents and Teachers*. Bethesda, MD: Woodbine House.

Pitcairn, T. K. and Wishart, J. G. (1994) Reactions of young children with Down's syndrome to an impossible task, *British Journal of Developmental Psychology*, 12: 485–90.

Roizen, N. J. and Patterson, D. (2003) Down's syndrome, *Lancet*, 361: 1287–9.

Selikowitz, M. (1997) *Down Syndrome: The Facts*, 2nd edn. Oxford: Oxford University Press.

Spiker, D. and Hopmann, M. R. (1997) The effectiveness of early intervention for children with Down syndrome, in M. J. Guralnick (ed.) *The Effectiveness of Early Intervention: Directions for Second Generation Research*. Baltimore: Paul H Brooke.

Stratford, B. and Gunn, P. (eds) (1996) *New Approaches to Down Syndrome*. London: Cassell.

Ware, J. (2003) *Creating a Responsive Environment for People with Profound and Multiple Learning Difficulties*, 2nd edn. London: David Fulton.

Watson, J. (1996) *Reflection through Interaction: The Classroom Experience of Pupils with Learning Difficulties*. London: Falmer Press.

Williams, K. R., Pitcairn, T. K., Wishart, J. G. and Willis, D. S. (2004) Emotion recognition in children with Down's syndrome: investigation of a specific impairment, in revision for *American Journal of Mental Retardation*.

Willis, D. S., Wishart, J. G., Williams, K. R. and Pitcairn, T. K. (2003) Peer collaboration and problem solving in children with Down's syndrome. Paper presented at Eleventh European Conference on Developmental Psychology, Milan, August.

Wishart, J. G. (1991) Taking the initiative in learning: a developmental investigation of infants with Down's syndrome, *International Journal of Disability, Development and Education*, 38: 27–44.

Wishart, J. G. (1993) The development of learning difficulties in children with Down's syndrome, *Journal of Intellectual Disability Research*, 37: 389–403.

Wishart, J. G. (1996) Avoidant learning styles and cognitive development in young children with Down syndrome, in B. Stratford and P. Gunn (eds) *New Approaches to Down Syndrome*. London: Cassell.

Wishart, J. G. and Duffy, L. (1990) Instability of performance on cognitive tests in infants and young children with Down's syndrome, *British Journal of Educational Psychology*, 59: 10–22.

Wishart, J. G. and Johnston, F. (1990) The effects of experience on attribution of a stereotyped personality to children with Down's syndrome, *Journal of Mental Deficiency Research*, 34: 409–20.

Wishart, J. and Manning, G. (1996) Trainee teachers' attitudes to inclusive education for children with Down's syndrome, *Journal of Intellectual Disability Research*, 40: 56–65.

Wishart, J. G. and Pitcairn, T. K. (2000) The recognition of identity and expression in faces by children with Down syndrome, *American Journal on Mental Retardation*, 105: 466–479.

Wright, I. (1997) The development of representation in children with Down's syndrome. Unpublished PhD dissertation, University of Warwick, Coventry.

Yang, Q., Rasmussen, S. A. and Friedman, J. M. (1997) Mortality associated with Down's syndrome in the USA from 1983 to 1997: a population-based study, *Lancet*, 359: 1019–25.

Useful internet sites (with good links to other international sources of info):

Down Syndrome Educational Trust (UK): http://www.downsed.org
Down's Syndrome Association (UK): http://www.dsa-uk.com
National Down Syndrome Society (USA): http://www.ndss.org
Down Syndrome Research Foundation (Canada): http://www.dsrf.org

English as an additional language and children with speech, language and communication needs

Deirdre Martin

Introduction

The imperative driving an examination of specialist teaching approaches is the inclusion agenda. For learners with educational language needs this means developing language within the context of academic learning, and for teachers and speech and language therapists it entails collaborative work to integrate language and academic learning. This chapter examines teaching approaches and strategies for language learning needs of two groups of learners who, traditionally, have been carefully distinguished: bilingual learners of English as an additional language (EAL) and learners with speech, language and communication needs (SLCN). I argue that although the underlying causes are different for their educational language learning needs, these learners share educational needs for a pedagogic approach to academic learning that integrates language learning with academic (subject domain) learning. A theoretical framework is presented that supports the integration of language knowledge and academic knowledge in teaching and learning in a mainstream inclusive curriculum.

The premise for a 'common' pedagogic approach in inclusive education is that one teaching approach will enable all learners with diverse educational needs to access the curriculum and subject knowledge, and afford opportunities and possibilities for teachers to differentiate this access through strategies and techniques sensitive to individual learners' needs. I argue for a common pedagogic approach through integrating language and subject knowledge, focusing on an inclusive pedagogic approach developed for EAL learners and applied to learners with SLCN in the mainstream. This common pedagogic approach could be applicable to all learners, since it challenges the assumption that all 'typical' children enter the education system with language abilities capable of academic learning.

There are learners who challenge the assumption often made about 'typical' language ability: children of poverty. Research has shown (e.g. Locke *et al.* 2002) that children of poverty have significantly less vocabulary and other language resources than children from more socio-economic advantaged groups. Other research (e.g. Heath 1983) indicates that some social groups may not use language as a tool for learning in the same way as school does. The 'mismatch' between school expectations and children's communicative practices and resources has implications for academic and curriculum learning, and teaching approaches that integrate language and learning.

The first part of the chapter describes the language needs of EAL learners and learners with SLCN. The second part critically examines selected studies of pedagogic strategies for the two groups of learners and evaluates the evidence for claims about specialist knowledge informing teaching for language learning and academic learning. The chapter concludes that pedagogic strategies integrating language development and domain knowledge offer a common approach for diverse learners with or without educational language needs. Moreover, they allow for differentiation so that individual learners' needs can be met, including those with more complex language needs. However, an integrated approach to language and learning is not typical of mainstream pedagogic strategies, and consequently could be regarded as 'special'. Nevertheless, there is evidence that policy-driven collaborative work practices across professional groups are bringing about shared pedagogic strategies and consequently a 'common' approach for integrating language and learning.

Definition and description of focal pupil groups: EAL and SLCN

A critical comment: it is easy to slip into descriptions of groups of learners that assume homogeneity across individual members and make generalizations about normative language and learning development that are contraindicated by studies of communicative practices, which reveal the importance of interaction and context. The aim of this section is to explore, in the context of school learning, the language learning needs of the two focal groups, EAL learners and pupils with SLCN. The areas of language learning need shared by the two groups are discussed and differences that might affect teaching and learning strategies are considered. The extent to which their individual differences and language learning needs do not have the same causes means that there might be reasons to require different, or 'special', pedagogic approaches is considered.

Theoretical background

It is generally accepted that we have a biological and cultural predisposition to learn language. Our brains are predisposed to recognize and process linguistic information, whether this is for one or several languages. It is also widely accepted that language develops through interaction with the social world, so that children build a communication system that relates the content and structure of language to its social meanings.

Current psychological theories about language development propose that children apply powerful cognitive strategies to make sense of their complex language environments (Bates and McWhinney 1987; Tomasello and Brookes 1999). The relationship between cognitive strategies and language development is currently regarded as central to understanding children's difficulties developing language as a first or additional language (Dockrell and McShane 1993). Cognitive strategies and children's implicit and explicit awareness of them are currently understood to be important in formal language teaching, literacy teaching and intervention. Other learning theories, such as Skinner's behaviourist approach, that emphasize the roles of imitation, repetition, reward and reinforcement are less favoured now, although still drawn on in formal language teaching situations.

Within the psycholinguistic theoretical approach, the aetiology of delay experienced by some children developing their first language is attributed to intrinsic difficulties in applying cognitive strategies to process and interpret their complex linguistic environment. The framework developed by Stackhouse and Wells (1997, 2001) draws on this approach to interpret speech and language difficulties. Difficulties may be with short- or long-term memory abilities, perceptual and discrimination segmentation abilities or programming and coordinating motor sequences. Substantial social trauma and deprivation can inhibit the development of these abilities in children (Bishop and Mogford 1993).

Learners with SLCN (also known as speech and language impairment, SLI, or specific speech and language difficulties, SSLD; Dockrell and Lindsay 1998) have a specific difficulty in developing language as their primary educational need when 'language acquisition is abnormal or delayed [despite] sufficient exposure to language input, normal capacity to perceive language, a brain which is adequate for learning in the non-verbal domain and intact articulatory structures' (Bishop 1992: 2). The specific difficulty is not due to hearing difficulties or loss, general learning difficulties, emotional problems and environmental factors (Adams *et al.* 1997). Surface behaviours and test scores may appear to be similar but underlying processing difficulties and compensatory behaviours can be different (Constable 1993).

Learners who have SLCN have their difficulties described in cognitive (psychological) terms as difficulties in processing, storing, retrieving and manipulating language, and linguistically when difficulties affect different aspects of language. Difficulties in phonological development (speech sounds) may involve difficulties in perceiving and discriminating between speech sounds, and between real and nonsense words, as well as motor difficulties in learning speech sound sequences in new words.

Some children have difficulties in making sense of patterns of word sequences (sentence grammar) or learning word endings. One interpretation is that children with this difficulty cannot recognize the grammatical role that words play in utterances, an ability known as 'syntactic bootstrapping'. Another interpretation is that grammatical difficulties are due to short-term memory and organizational problems.

Many children with speech and language needs have difficulties developing vocabulary and relating it to underlying concepts (semantic difficulties). Common difficulties are learning new words, 'word-finding', using words appropriately and learning multiple meanings of words. There may be several reasons for these difficulties. Phonological difficulties may impede the learning of new words. Processing difficulties in accessing and retrieving words may result in word-finding difficulties. Conceptual inflexibility may inhibit attributing several meanings to one word form (e.g. dog is an animal and a pet; table meaning 'furniture' and 'grid'). There are implications of vocabulary difficulties for conceptual development and academic learning.

Children who have difficulties in the appropriate use of language in social situations (pragmatic difficulties) usually have the correct forms of language but what they say may not match the meaning expected for the situation. The social context in which speaking occurs allows speakers and listeners to construct inferences and implications that are drawn from knowledge of social interactions and knowledge of the world. Consequently, difficulties in using language appropriately are due as much to children's difficulties in understanding language meaning as to cognitive and emotional understanding of social contexts.

Almost all children with expressive language difficulties have varying difficulties in understanding language. Furthermore, they usually have difficulties in developing literacy skills and practices, which has implications for teaching and learning. Children with language difficulties related to conceptual and cognitive development, such as difficulties with meaning, appropriateness and understanding, are likely to need assistance with academic learning, with implications for pedagogic strategies.

Bilingual learners are a heterogeneous group, differing across first languages, ethnicities, cultural heritages and beliefs, as well as having individual differences; for example, in their learning potential, proficiency in their first language, ability to learn additional languages, educational history and gender. Bilingual learners who are developing EAL have usually developed one language successfully, their home language, in which they may have extensive communicative, social and literacy practices. They need to develop English in order to function successfully in school, and later to get employment and to participate in wider society.

Bilingualism is not a cause of educational difficulties and most EAL learners do not have intrinsic learning difficulties in the way described for SLCN.

However, statistics show that in many countries, including England, the USA and Australia, bilingual pupils constitute the lowest bands of educational achievement and continue to be over-represented in special educational needs provision (Gillborn and Youdell 2000). This may be attributable to several factors: such as poverty of many linguistic minority pupil populations, pupils' constructs of their academic identity and teachers' perceptions of difference and disability. It is likely that teaching practices for academic curriculum learning through learners' additional language also contribute to low achievement.

The distinction between pupils with EAL needs and those with educational needs is summed up by Mattes and Omark (1984):

> Second language learners who perform poorly in the school setting because of limited familiarity with English and/or cultural differences need to be distinguished from children who demonstrate communicative disorders and/or abnormalities that require special education intervention.

This distinction is recognized in education legislation in many countries but not all. The UK 1981 Education Act distinguished between the educational needs and subsequent provision for EAL learners and learners with SLCN. EAL learners were offered increasingly inclusive provision with additional specialist teacher support, while specialist support for learners with SLCN has mainly been offered outside the education system, by health services, and until recently had limited inclusion in mainstream.

The brief summary of characteristics of EAL learners and learners with SLCN suggests that their learning needs through language have similarities that teaching approaches could make the most of. Many learners in both groups potentially have cognitive capabilities to achieve similarly to their peers. Low academic achievement must pose questions about the role and effect of teaching approaches and strategies on learning for these pupils.

Cummins (1984) offers a theoretical framework that explores the interface between conceptual, academic learning and learning through language. Cummins distinguishes between language learning for social and conversational purposes (basic interpersonal communication skills, BICS) and language for academic learning (cognitive academic language proficiency, CALP). Research shows that most bilingual children develop BICS within two years of being immersed in the additional language. Studies also show that bilingual learners can take between five and seven years to be able to use language for academic curriculum learning as their monolingual peers do (Collier 1989). Cummins argues that underpinning CALP is the relationship between language and higher order thinking skills, such as analysing, synthesizing and evaluating information, as well as inferring, predicting and understanding implications. The crucial aspect of language development for CALP is the development of vocabulary because of the connection between words and underlying concepts. Cummins, along with others, attributes language and learning difficulties and low achievement to pedagogic strategies rather than to aetiology factors within the EAL learner.

To summarize, I have shown that the aetiologies of language learning needs between EAL learners and learners with SLCN are very different. However, I argue that the aetiology of difficulty is less important for educational progress than learning needs. The learning needs of both groups require a teaching approach and strategies that focus on the relationship between language and learning, and language for academic learning. In the next section, I select studies to illustrate a continuum of pedagogic strategies that foreground language as a means of supporting language development as well as supporting academic learning. The continuum of pedagogic strategies allows for further differentiation for individual learners' needs.

Integrating language and learning

The challenge is to inform pedagogic practice with a theoretical base that affords curriculum learning for learners with SLCN while at the same time supporting their individual needs in language development and skills. We turn to an approach that informs pedagogic strategies with EAL learners. Drawing on Cummins's notion of embedding language development in curriculum learning, pedagogic strategies need to integrate subject knowledge of content and processes with language domain knowledge. This approach has immense implications for professionals involved in teaching learners with SLCN, which include issues of professional identity as well as professional development.

Continuum of integrating language and learning

A study by Stoddart *et al.* (2002) has looked at the challenge of developing subject domain teachers to be able to develop a pedagogic approach and pedagogic strategies that integrate language learning and subject content. They propose three approaches to integration of subject matter domains: thematic, interdisciplinary and integrated. Their framework, based on Dreyfus and Dreyfus (1986), proposes that these approaches form a continuum for integrating content and process across subject and language knowledge domains.

- Thematic: an overarching theme or topic creates the relationship across subject and language. For example, relating science and language may be developed around a topic, e.g. the sea.
- Interdisciplinary: the knowledge and processes of the secondary domain are used to support learning in the primary domain, e.g. language is used to help science learning, such as learning new scientific vocabulary.
- Integrated: both domains of knowledge (language and science) are equally balanced, learning in one domain complements and reinforces the other, learning is 'synergistic' and enhances learning in both areas.

Stoddart and colleagues, from evidence collected from teachers through observations of practice and interviews about their reflections of learning, develop concepts of practice about integrated pedagogic strategies. They propose five levels that identify teachers' conceptual pedagogic progression and indicators in teaching practices:

- Level 1: show no integration and conceptually consider language and subject learning as discrete and isolated domains; cannot be taught in the same lesson; knowledge is understood as rule-governed, with no consideration of context. There is little student input or initiation of inquiry.
- Level 2: understand that integration between language and subject areas is possible theoretically but have no understanding of relating theory to practice and no knowledge of appropriate pedagogic strategies. Thematic instruction, e.g. ocean, is used as an organizing topic. Integration of language and learning is described sequentially, e.g. talk about the topic then write about it.
- Level 3: emerging understanding of integration, and can clearly differentiate between domain knowledges, but with a limited understanding of common processes. For example, one domain is used to support the other – using skills, such as vocabulary building and writing tasks, to connect domains.
- Level 4: implicitly understand integration as a reciprocal relation between language and subject domain but the content in either domain may not be covered in depth. They can describe a plan for curriculum integration based on common processes between domains, while recognizing the challenges involved in integrated curriculum.
- Level 5: thorough explicit understanding of integration. They describe integration, and give examples of analysis and contextual considerations, and examples of transfer and application of understanding of integration to novel situations. They draw on a conceptual framework (e.g. inquiry) to implement an integrated curriculum across domains of knowledge, which emphasizes higher-order thinking skills that enhance learning; and talking and writing are to communicate ideas.

This continuum is a valuable metaphor to illustrate conceptual progression in teachers from understanding language proficiency as a set of skills in a discrete knowledge domain, towards integrating discursive practices with learning. Pedagogic strategies include language skills (such as knowledge of grammatical structures, vocabulary and meaning relations) but there is more emphasis on communicative and discursive practices for meaning-making in classroom interaction. Teachers draw on Palinscar's (1986) comprehension strategies, by discussing meanings of subject texts: identifying the main idea, guessing the teacher's questions, clarifying and repairing meaning, predicting and finding proof. Teaching and learning is embedded in hands-on, contextualized, collaborative work that affords cohesive learning between domains of language and subject knowledge.

Evaluating claims for special teaching and intervention

In this section I draw on Stoddart *et al.*'s model of conceptual progression by practitioners in understanding and implementing integrated pedagogic strategies to evaluate some of the models of pedagogic strategies for language and learning in clinical and educational settings. Two main aspects are considered in evaluating the evidence from studies that present the case for 'special' teaching and intervention for learners with SLCN. First, evaluating efficacy of an integrated approach is limited by few studies in this area and methodological difficulties. Second, there is evidence that strategies integrating language and learning are used successfully in pedagogic contexts with learners with SLCN, as they are with other language learners, such as EAL pupils.

Efficacy

Many research studies with learners with SLCN adopt a non-integrated approach, even though learners may be in educational settings. Intervention focuses on language proficiency being developed apart from curriculum learning. Tallal (2000) reviews studies on the impact of language training programmes with 'academically at risk' school-aged children with language difficulties. She concludes that, even though techniques and strategies for intensive practice done through withdrawal from class appear effective for language development, questions remain about how effectively pupils who have learnt comprehension strategies in isolation can 'transfer' and 'generalize' their new language skills to contexts of discussion about academic concepts. It remains to be seen in longitudinal study if the techniques can be applied to, or integrated into, curriculum learning. Moreover, Tallal (2000: 150) considers that future research should refocus 'away from their previous focus on aetiology [of SLCN], to a new focus on the development of practical and efficacious remediation techniques'.

Other reviews of the literature indicate that there are methodological difficulties in research evaluation of efficacy of intervention and teaching programmes (Conti-Ramsden and Botting 2000; Constable 2001; Popple and Wellington 2001). Criticisms focus on controlling the diversity of aetiology, shortcomings of the experimental paradigm and non-standard interventions. Where language skills are managed separately from learning skills studies look mainly at withdrawal interventions, where aims concern 'catching up'. Learners with SLCN may fall behind in their educational progress because of being excluded from learning in the mainstream class, and Conti-Ramsden and Botting's (2000: 221) non-integrated position is clear when they claim that 'If this is the case, it is even more imperative that the language skills of children with SLI are brought up to sufficient levels as efficiently as possible'.

Many language learning programmes that are used in schools and classrooms with children with SLCN (Rees 2002) (e.g. *Social Use of Language Programme*, Rinaldi 1995; *Teaching Talking*, Locke and Beech 1991) have not been researched for evaluation purposes. Although not evaluated, studies of metalinguistic pedagogic strategies integrating language and academic learning have demonstrated efficacy for learning academic language practices individually, in groups and whole classes, for both EAL learners (McWilliam 1998) and learners with SLCN (e.g. Hesketh *et al.* 2000; Goldfus 2001). Case studies of individual children with SLCN have shown that intervention is successful when some of the language demands of the curriculum are integrated into therapy plans.

Integrating language and learning for SLCN

Evidence for claims about pedagogic strategies based on developing explicit teaching of language and learning with learners with SLCN is, currently, very tentative. With reference to Stoddart *et al.*'s continuum, studies mainly reflect practice where teaching approaches are thematic with an emerging under-standing of integration (Level 3).

Evidence is found in studies of metalinguistic and metacognitive learning strategies, approaches used by EAL and SLCN, for monitoring language com-prehension and learning, and helping pupils to become independent learners. Metalinguistic awareness is used by learners when they are able to suspend their spontaneous use of language, which is concerned with communicating meaning, in order to reflect on some aspect of the language itself. A good example is the inclusion of metalinguistic strategies in developing phono-logical awareness in the literacy curriculum. This strategy was previously regarded as a 'special' pedagogic strategy for learners with speech and literacy difficulties. Now it is a mainstream literacy pedagogic strategy.

Phonological awareness as a pedagogic strategy affords opportunities for speech and language therapists to integrate interventionist approaches into curriculum learning. Studies have shown how it can be utilized by speech and language therapists and teachers for learners with speech difficulties (e.g. Hesketh *et al.* 2000). Case studies show that metalinguistic strategies in raising phonological awareness can be used beyond literacy learning for learning new curriculum vocabulary (Popple and Wellington 2001). Evidence from studies taking a metalinguistic approach to developing phon-ology (Howell and Dean 1994; Adams *et al.* 2000) suggests that learners use the new skills beyond the programme and across other areas of language learning.

There are many similarities between metalinguistic strategies used for EAL learners and those used for learners with SLCN. Constable (2001) notes that for learners with SLCN improving concepts and lexical representations through the accuracy of stored information relies on both strengthening semantic knowledge and raising phonological awareness. While methodological differ-ences in research studies offer conflicting results, certain features emerge as important:

- vocabulary selection – few, relevant to class learning, conceptually selected;
- plenty of repetitions in different contexts, and if possible with a baseline number of exposures;
- teaching vocabulary with explicit structured help to organize and store semantic information;
- memory difficulties mean vocabulary should be taught before, during and after learning experiences to help to store and integrate the information efficiently.

Teachers and therapists collaborated and specific technical knowledge was used about language when teaching vocabulary. Working through a structured teaching frame the child had a 'scaffold' for learning new vocabulary. Meta-linguistic strategies and communicative strategies are explicitly taught, and 'the aim is that strategies cease to be needed as a child's speech and language processing system becomes more efficient' (Constable 2001: 361). Similar constraints are recognized in EAL teaching.

Metalinguistic strategies are also used in 'rich scripting' (McWilliam 1998), a teaching approach for EAL learners to develop curriculum vocabulary. 'Target lexical items' are applied to a lexical framework that goes beyond giving definitions of words and requires learners to examine the meaning potential of words. This approach helps learners to plan processes of engagement with word meaning and to see how words change their meanings depending on their context and use. McWilliam notes that EAL learners need repetitive exposure to new words and opportunities to work with them. This pedagogic strategy would seem to complement the strategy taken by Constable and her colleagues, yet its application with learners with SLCN, and other mainstream learners, has not been reported yet.

Metacognition is a similar ability of pupils to suspend their spontaneous learning behaviour in order to reflect on aspects of their learning (O'Malley and Chamot 1990). Learners who are developing language in curriculum learning and through text, including learners with SLCN, bilingual learners of EAL and learners with dyslexia, have been shown to benefit in a whole-class teaching programme from being explicitly taught these comprehension strategies with text, with subsequent raised academic achievement over time (Goldfus 2001).

These studies illustrate some pedagogic strategies that are broadly similar and used for EAL learners and learners with SLCN. However, the researchers make no reference to this similarity and it seems unlikely that they are aware of shared practices because of discipline boundaries. These pedagogic strategies are moving along Stoddart et al.'s continuum towards a more integrated approach to language development and academic learning.

Further evidence is found in pedagogic strategies that seek to integrate language development and learning in early years. 'Special Times' is a programme originally envisaged as a non-directive approach to play that provides children with an arena for beginning to understand communication (Cockerill n.d.). It has been adapted, as 'Special Time', to support children with severe communication or social difficulties through routine and structure in reciprocal information exchanges. Special Time is examined by Cook (2003: 99–106) to see if anything was truly 'special' or 'different' from the everyday work and interaction of adults with children.

She concludes that the two important aspects of Special Time that make it 'special' relate to adult behaviours: adults' awareness of knowledge about language and learning and their application of that knowledge. She concludes that Special Time is an opportunity for adults to learn how to make their implicit knowledge of language into explicit knowledge. It affords possibilities for situated learning in the application of language knowledge for co-constructed communicative exchanges. Referring to Stoddart et al.'s continuum, Special Time reflects a Level 5 realization of integrating language and cognitive learning.

Conclusions

I have argued that there is evidence to support the case for a common pedagogic approach based on a continuum of integrating language and learning. The commonality of the approach implies that it is an effective teaching approach to all learners, not just those with educational difficulties, EAL needs or SLC needs. It challenges the assumption that most learners' language abilities can cope with academic curriculum language without an integrated pedagogy. In making this argument I have drawn on research from the fields of teaching in EAL and SLCN, which are traditionally distinct, to demonstrate that there are similarities in conceptualizing and implementing teaching language development integrated into subject knowledge, in the classroom.

A body of research and practice holds that particular language difficulties and needs of learners with SLCN determine the 'specialness' or discreteness of individualized interventionist programmes. This position is identified nearer one extreme on the language learning continuum where there is no or little integration of language learning with academic curriculum learning. The continuum passes through pedagogic strategies invoking metacognitive, metalinguistic and comprehension strategies towards conceptualization and implementation of pedagogic strategies for integration. Within these strategies there is space to develop differentiated techniques and practices, materials and outcomes to meet individual children's needs.

Finally, the 'specialness' of pedagogic strategies for language and curriculum learning lies more with raising teachers' awareness about their own language use in co-constructing learning with pupils. To realize these pedagogic strategies, professionals need to develop a language to talk about integrating language learning and academic learning. Therapists, subject teachers and specialist teachers need to acquire knowledge of language practices for academic learning as well as the application of this knowledge in integrating language and learning. Researching this professional development process is an important agenda.

Summary

Nature of the group

- This includes EAL and SLCN, but note the heterogeneity within and across these groups.
- SLCN are manifested by difficulties in cognitive skills such as processing, storing and retrieving language.
- SLCN encompasses expressive and receptive problems with phonology, syntax, semantics and/or pragmatics.

- SLCN difficulties are not due to hearing loss, general learning difficulties, emotional problems or environmental factors.
- Bilingual learners developing EAL have usually developed one language successfully.
- Both EAL and SLCN groups contain many children with cognitive capability potentially similar to that of their peers.

Pedagogy

- See below regarding curriculum.
- A range of methodological problems is noted (paralleling those noted in other chapters), making it difficult to establish clear research-based answers to questions about specificity of special needs pedagogy.

Curriculum

- There is a need to integrate subject knowledge and language domain knowledge.
- EAL work can be used to inform SLCN. Drawing on Stoddart *et al.*, three approaches are outlined for such integration: thematic, interdisciplinary and integrated.
- Following on from this, five levels of 'conceptual pedagogic progression and indicators in teaching practice' are identified.

Knowledge

- Subsumed under curriculum.

Unique versus general differences position as pedagogic base

- Aetiology is different but the learning needs are similar across the two groups, e.g. there is a need for repetition across different contexts.
- The relationship of EAL/SLCN and pedagogic practice with other special needs groups is not explored.
- The approaches outlined are useful for all learners, i.e. a unique differences (not general/group) differences position.
- In line with this, teachers and other professionals need to develop a language with which to discuss integrating language learning and subject learning.

Notable aspects introduced

- The position is strongly curriculum-based.
- Integration of subject knowledge and language domain knowledge (plus presumably knowledge of the individual learner) is highlighted.
- EAL and SLCN are used as exemplars of ways in which two distinct (pedagogically) fields can be brought together and commonalities highlighted.

References

Adams, C., Byers Brown, B. and Edwards, M. (1997) *Developmental Disorders of Language*, 2nd edn. London: Whurr.

Adams, C., Nightingale, C., Hesketh, A. and Hall, R. (2000) Targeting metaphonological ability in intervention for children with developmental phonological disorders, *Child Language Teaching and Therapy*, 16(3): 285–300.

Bates, E. and McWhinney, B. (1987) Competition, variation and language learning, in B. McWhinney (ed.) *Mechanisms of Language Acquisition*. Hillsdale, NJ: Erlbaum.

Bishop, D. V. (1992) The biological basis of specific language impairment, in P. Fletcher and D. Hall (eds) *Specific Speech and Language Disorders in Children*. London: Whurr.

Bishop, D. V. and Mogford, K. (eds) (1993) *Language Development in Exceptional Circumstances*. Hove: Erlbaum.

Cockerill, H. (n.d.) *Communication through Play: Non-directive Communication Therapy 'Special Times'*. London: Blackrose Press.

Collier, V. (1989) 'How long?' A synthesis of research in academic achievement in a second language, *TESOL Quarterly*, 23: 509–31.

Constable, A. (1993) Investigating word-finding difficulties in children, Unpublished MSc thesis, College of Speech Sciences, National Hospital, University College London.

Constable, A. (2001) A psycholinguistic approach to word-finding difficulties, in J. Stackhouse and B. Wells (eds) *Children's Speech and Literacy Difficulties 2*. London: Whurr.

Conti-Ramsden, G. and Botting, N. (2000) Educational placements for children with specific language impairments, in D. V. Bishop and L. Leonard (eds) *Speech and Language Impairments in Children: Causes, Characteristics, Intervention and Outcome*. Hove: Psychology Press.

Cook, T. (2003) Special Time: What's special about Special Time?, in F. Griffiths (eds) *Communication Counts: Speech and Language Difficulties in the Early Years*. London: David Fulton.

Cummins, J. (1984) *Bilingualism and Special Education: Issues in Assessment and Pedagogy*. Clevedon: Multilingual Matters.

Dockrell, J. and Lindsay, G. (1998) The ways in which speech and language difficulties impact on children's access to the curriculum, *Child Language Teaching and Therapy*, 14(2): 117–33.

Dockrell, J. and McShane, J. (1993) *Children's Learning Difficulties: A Cognitive Approach*. Oxford: Blackwell.

Dreyfus, H. L. and Dreyfus, S. E. (1986) *Mind over Machine: The Power of Human Intuition and Expertise in the Era of the Computer*. New York: Free Press.

Gillborn, D. and Youdell, D. (2000) *Rationing Education: Policy, Practice, Reform Equity*. Buckingham: Open University Press.

Goldfus, C. (2001) Reading comprehension and EFL adolescents with difficulties: a cognitive processing model. Unpublished doctoral thesis, University of Birmingham.

Heath, S. B. (1983) *Ways with Words*. Cambridge: Cambridge University Press.

Hesketh, A., Adams, C., Nightingale, C. and Hall, R. (2000) Phonological awareness therapy and articulatory training approaches for children with phonological disorders: a comparative study, *International Journal of Language and Communication Disorders*, 35(3): 337–54.

Howell, J. and Dean, E. (1994) *Treating Phonological Disorders in Children – Theory to Practice*. London: Whurr.

Locke, A. and Beech, M. (1991) *Teaching Talking*. Windsor: NFER-Nelson.

Locke, A., Ginsborg, J. and Peers, I. (2002) Development and disadvantage: implications for the early years and beyond, *International Journal of Language and Communication Disorders*, 37(1): 3–15.

McWilliam, N. (1998) *What's in a Word? Vocabulary Development in Multilingual Classrooms*. Stoke: Trentham Books.

Mattes, L. and Omark, D. (1984) *Speech and Language Assessment for the Bilingual Language Handicapped*. San Diego: College-Hill Press.

O'Malley, J. and Chamot, A. (1990) *Learning Strategies in Second Language Acquisition*. Cambridge: Cambridge University Press.

Palinscar, A. S. (1986) Metacognitive strategy instruction, *Exceptional Children*, 53(2): 118–24.

Popple, J. and Wellington, W. (2001) Working together: the psycholinguistic approach within a school setting, in J. Stackhouse and B. Wells (eds) *Children's Speech and Literacy Difficulties 2*. London: Whurr.

Rees, R. (2002) Language Programmes, in M. Kersner and J. Wright (eds) *How to Manage Communication Problems in Young Children*, 3rd edn. London: David Fulton.

Rinaldi, W. (1995) *Social Use of Language Programme for Primary and Infant School Children (SULP)*. Windsor: NFER-Nelson

Stackhouse, J. and Wells, B. (eds) (1997) *Children's Speech and Literacy Difficulties*. London: Whurr.

Stackhouse, J. and Wells, B. (eds) (2001) *Children's Speech and Literacy Difficulties 2*. London: Whurr.

Stoddart, T., Pinal, A., Latzke, M. and Canaday, D. (2002) Integrating inquiry science and language development for English language learners, *Journal of Research in Science Teaching*, 39(8): 664–87.

Tallal, P. (2000) Experimental studies of language learning impairments: from research to remediation, in D. V. Bishop and L. Leonard (eds) *Speech and Language Impairments in Children: Causes, Characteristics, Intervention and Outcome*. Hove: Psychology Press.

Tomasello, M. and Brookes, P. (1999) Early syntactic development: a construction grammar approach, in M. Barrett (ed.) *The Development of Language*. London: UCL Press.

CHAPTER NINE

Autistic spectrum disorders
Rita Jordan

The conceptualization and prevalence of Autistic Spectrum Disorders (ASDs)

Autistic spectrum disorders refer to a range of disorders related to the core disorder of autism and including Asperger's syndrome. What are common to the disorders within the spectrum are difficulties and differences within three areas of development, known as the 'triad of impairments' (Wing 1996). These are best characterized as difficulties in:

- social and emotional understanding;
- all aspects of communication;
- flexibility in thinking and behaviour (Jordan 2002).

The disorders are recognized as medical categories within both international systems for the classification of diseases (ICD-10, World Health Organization 1992; DSM-IV, American Psychiatric Association 1994), based on a set of features that represent broad descriptive areas rather than particular behaviours. The core disorder of autism has been recognized for 60 years (Kanner 1943) but the recognition of the broader spectrum is a more recent phenomenon, starting with Wing's 1981 description of what became known as Asperger's syndrome, after the psychiatrist who identified autism in a more cognitively and linguistically able group.

The strong genetic base to these disorders is well established (Bailey *et al.* 1995; Rutter 1999) and there is increasing evidence that the phenotype is an extreme form of normal variation in information processing style (Baron-Cohen 2003). Indeed, Baron-Cohen (2003) has supported the view of Asperger himself that autism represented the extreme form of 'maleness' and, while the evidence does not fully support this, there are strong gender biases in the spectrum (estimates ranging from 4:1 in favour of males to 14:1).

However, the characteristics only become pathological when they interfere with functioning and distort development. ASDs can be considered as representing a conjunction of extreme functioning on three dimensions of development but the categorical nature of the system of medical classification misleadingly suggests an absolute distinction between those with an ASD and those without (Jordan *et al.* 2001).

The argument against rigid categorization, however, is not the same as suggesting that ASDs are merely groupings of difficulties in three areas of development. The use of the diagnostic category is a kind of theory that the concurrence of these difficulties is not by chance. As with any developmental disorder, ASDs can be considered at the level of biology, psychology or behaviour. There is research (supporting the seminal work of Wing and Gould in 1979) to show the stability of the co-occurrence of the triad of impairments at the behavioural level and hence their use in diagnosis. Yet the behavioural symptoms vary considerably between individuals on the spectrum and within an individual over time. ASDs cannot be diagnosed simply by a behavioural 'count'; diagnosis is a clinical judgement based on a developmental history of the behavioural symptoms and other possible reasons for the behaviour (such as the follow-up study of 40 infants adopted from Romanian orphanages, who met criteria for autism on entry but all bar two of whom 'recovered' after a period of stability and care: Rutter *et al.* 1999). The undoubted biological bases are nevertheless diverse, with particular links to particular patterns of the ASD disorder not yet established. It is, therefore, at the level of psychology – how the individual is feeling, thinking, perceiving, attending, learning, memorizing and making sense of his or her environment – that the 'autism' is really located and this is the level of understanding that has to underlie the 'special' practice needed for work with those with ASDs (Powell and Jordan 1993, 1997; Jordan and Powell 1995; Jordan 1999a).

It is also important to recognize the totality of the triad in education and treatment. Conceptualizations of ASDs in terms of one of those areas (as in delineating national specialist standards: Teacher Training Agency 1999) encourage the idea that the difficulties faced by a child can be considered in isolation. Yet all development takes place in a context both intra and inter the individual level. Communication difficulties, for example, are different when the child has problems in understanding his or her own and others' emotions and social signals and when they have problems being spontaneous and monitoring feedback to their own actions. They also vary enormously according to the way the environment (people and physical) is geared to foster their understanding and so cannot be considered as 'attributes' of the child in isolation. ASDs are transactional disorders, appearing in their interactions with others and not to be understood without the contextualization from which special needs are determined.

Despite the clear biological base to ASDs (Bauman and Kemper 1994; Gillberg and Coleman 2001), there are as yet no reliable and valid biological markers. Thus it is difficult to obtain an accurate measure of the incidence (the number of new cases arising each year) and epidemiological data rely on prevalence figures (the number of new cases identified each year). Since prevalence reflects not only incidence, but also awareness and availability of knowledgeable diagnostic services, it is difficult to determine whether the incidence of ASDs is rising. It seems clear that prevalence is rising and that what was once regarded as a 'low incidence' disorder (at a rate of 4 per 10,000: Lotter 1966; Fombonne 1999) is now viewed as the most common of the developmental disorders (at a rate approximating to 1 per 160: Fombonne 2002). It does not follow that a diagnosis of an ASD will automatically imply special educational needs, but most research and reviews of provision suggest that the planning for meeting the special needs of such children in school is failing to make adequate provision even for the very conservative 'low incidence' figures, let alone for the later estimates of prevalence (Jordan and Jones 1996; NIASA 2003)

Educational needs in relation to ASDs

ASDs can and do occur across the spectrum of intellectual ability and may be accompanied by other disabilities and, especially in adolescence, by mental health problems (notably, depression and bipolar disorder). Some co-morbidities appear to have a genetic base, including dyslexia, dyspraxia and ADHD (Rutter 1999). Epilepsy (especially late-onset epilepsy) is common in core autism, as are general learning difficulties. It is clear (Wing 1996; Howlin 1998; Jordan 2001) that general learning difficulties can occur with autism, but there are problems because of the effects of autism in making cooperation with testing difficult. Some children with an ASD may have a specific problem in developing language, and sensory problems are also common.

Special needs in ASDs, as in other groups, are not a simple matter of translation from a medically designated disorder but need to be understood in terms of how that disorder is manifested in any particular individual at a particular time in a particular learning environment (Jordan 2001). Thus, there are few special educational needs that are uniform across the ASD group (and distinct from those without an ASD) and none that can be considered out of the context of the individual's pattern of strengths and weaknesses (including interests), learning style, personality, the learning environment and supports. Yet that is not to concede the distinct learning needs position. It is an argument for individual (unique) learning needs, but only as interpreted within the understanding of group attributes (Iovannone et al. 2003), as Norwich and Lewis (Chapter 1) suggest as a possible position.

Orkwis and McLane (1998) (cited Lewis and Norwich this volume) give a definition of the 'universal design' of curricula that is meant to make national curricula accessible to all (see also Lewis and Norwich 2001). This is taken as the starting point from which one might examine the 'nature, rationale and evidence base' (Norwich and Lewis, Chapter 1) of the necessary modifications to the curriculum, as applied to different disability areas. However, ASDs require two more fundamental issues to be considered. One is the transactional nature of ASDs, which means that 'solutions' cannot reside in mere curriculum adaptation, but must involve changes (based on a specific know-ledge base and an attitude of acceptance and openness) in those engaged in planning and teaching that curriculum (Peeters and Jordan 1999; Scheuermann *et al.* 2003). The knowledge, skills and attitude of teachers have been shown to be important variables in the success of all teaching (Medwell *et al.* 1998; Wragg *et al.* 1998; Crawford 2003) but it is even more important when natural intuitive and professional assumptions are challenged, as they are in ASDs.

The other challenge to the assumptions behind the notion of 'universal design' is that the values inherent in the 'curriculum for all' approach are problematic when it comes to ASDs, where it is important to consider separately education as the acquisition of culturally approved skills, knowledge and attitudes and a more therapeutic model of education as a form of 'treatment' for a disability. Oliver's (1992) rejection of the therapeutic role of education (or indeed of the need for 'therapy' at all) is a point of view that some with an ASD would endorse (Ward and Alar 2000) but by no means all (Blackburn 2000). Children with ASDs can be said to share common needs only to the extent that those needs are so broadly framed that they obscure real differences in how they can be addressed. Nevertheless, it is a useful reminder for teachers to recognize that principles of learning and teaching still apply in ASDs. For example, all children learn best when they are emotionally engaged in their learning. The difference in ASDs is that there are biological reasons why that is difficult. Teachers have to be aware of the problem, compensate for it in providing learning opportunities (by using other ways of making learning accessible) and at the same time develop therapeutic programmes (perhaps through drama: Sherratt and Peter 2002) to help to remediate the difficulty in becoming emotionally engaged. This example utilizes knowledge of distinct group differences but the unique differences will also need to be addressed at the level at which the particular way of making learning accessible is addressed and the particular therapeutic approach that is selected to engage the child.

In relation to the model proposed by Norwich (1996), then, I wish to argue that there are both group-specific pedagogic needs related to ASDs and individual unique needs, which, nevertheless are also related to ASDs. In addition, there are common needs, unrelated to ASDs but only in respect of broad pedagogical principles. The group needs primarily affect the changes (suggested above) in the individuals involved in planning and teaching (to understand the need for particular programmes), whereas the unique individual needs refer to the actual adaptations to curriculum goals, pedagogic approach and environment, inherent in the 'universal design' approach. The argument is that the unique individual needs of learners with ASDs can only be identified through the framework of the group needs arising from ASDs. Rather than seeing how the needs of children with particular disabilities (such as ASDs) can be incorporated into separately defined 'common needs', I would argue that the latter concept needs to be a true 'curriculum for all', informed by knowledge of the range and depth of the distinctiveness of individual needs (such as those arising from ASDs), phrased in terms of pedagogic principles and incorporating the required flexibility and adaptability. This is akin to the view voiced by Skrtic (1999). Norwich and Lewis (Chapter 1) also make the point that recognition of group differences in needs implies that common curricular needs/aims need to be formulated in general and very flexible terms.

The 'special' group needs of children with ASDs arise both directly from their developmental difficulties and also indirectly by preventing children with ASDs from participating in the socialization and enculturalization process through which development normally takes place. Difficulties in joint attention, imitation, social and emotional identification and sensitivity to social signals, for example, affect not just relationships with others but also how individuals come to understand themselves and the world around them (Hobson 1993, 2002; Rogers *et al.* 2003). The fact that social signals lack salience for them (Klin 1991) means they will need specific training, for example, to respond to their name as an attention-alerting signal and then teaching staff will need to use that signal appropriately. Missing out on early dyadic interaction (Trevarthen *et al.* 1996) means failures in learning about turn-taking, the timing of social interactions, the sharing of interests, the capacity to 'background' and 'foreground' information and the ability to modulate levels of arousal. Thus, many children with ASDs experience eye contact as intrusive and painful and, forcing them to make eye contact when being addressed, may make it impossible for them to attend to the auditory message. Teaching for meaning can help, because it is meaningless stimulation that is confusing and difficult to process (Williams 1996), but teachers will not be equipped to do this if they are responding at the level of behaviour alone and not benefiting from the transformation of meaning that a knowledge of ASDs can bring about (Cumine *et al.* 1997).

Learning needs arising from communication difficulties

ASDs are the only conditions where communication is separate from language in its development (Jordan 1996; Noens and van Berckelaer-Onnes, in press) and so learning needs in this area can illustrate the way in which group needs can be used to identify individual ones. Structural aspects of language are not always a problem for pupils with an ASD, although many have additional language problems. Where there are learning difficulties, there may be difficulties in acquiring speech because the normal foundation of communication is absent. Even those with good structural language skills may have difficulties with articulation and semantics – especially those aspects of meaning that shift according to context. Prosodic difficulties are also marked, speech often sounding flat and 'robot-like'. This makes it difficult for them to mark topic and comment structures in language and to understand how others use intonation to do that.

Communication remains a severe problem no matter how verbally skilled the pupil. The difficulties extend to all aspects, including gestures (e.g. indicative pointing), eye signalling, facial expression and body posture. The pupil will need to be taught what communication is for and how to go about it, regardless of apparent language skill. Language is often non-productive, failing to build on what others have said, not relating to the context, but reproducing familiar learned patterns of speech. Pupils with ASDs will not realize what knowledge and understanding can be assumed to be shared with their listeners and so will tend to be pedantic or ambiguous. They will try to understand what the words mean rather than what the speaker means, interpreting idioms or sarcasm literally, missing the point or even becoming distressed. Teachers will need to teach conversational skills (turn-taking, active listening, topic introduction, maintenance and change) and attempt to make pragmatic knowledge explicit; for example, looking for opportunities to point out when knowledge is shared or when someone knows something and others do not.

Some pupils with ASDs can read mechanically beyond their level of understanding and may find it easier to learn to read than to listen to stories or to tell them from picture books, so the normal stages in reading progression may not apply. Children with ASDs may have no idea about establishing mental models of the text, whether it is oral or written. In general, reading is likely to be a strength in ASDs and for some children reading may form a pathway into speech. On the other hand, dyslexia and ASDs may be linked genetically (Shea and Mesibov 1985), so there will be some pupils with ASDs who do struggle to learn to read and write. Clumsiness may also be a feature of the condition, leading to writing difficulties.

Literal understanding causes particular problems in schools. It may be difficult for pupils with ASDs to understand oral instructions, especially if expressed in indirect 'polite' forms; 'Can you draw another triangle like this one?' is meant to elicit more than a simple 'Yes'. Many questions asked in school are not 'genuine' in that they seek information that the questioner has not got; instead, they are asked to test the pupils' understanding, to encourage greater pupil participation or (as above) to issue instructions. Pupils with ASDs do not have a core of communicative competence on which to build and may mistake this educational use for the common use of questions and use it as a model for their own repetitive questioning on topics to which they already know the answer. They may also repeat questions because they want the reassurance of the same answer and the teacher will need to recognize the anxiety (or occasionally, the simple pleasure) behind such questioning rather than simply treating it as inappropriate behaviour. It is more appropriate to teach alternative ways of dealing with the anxiety or having fun with the sounds of words than to try to suppress expression.

A failure to appreciate the nature of conversations and the educational model of discourse may also lead to the pupil learning inappropriate ways of interacting with others. A straight modelling of a teacher's didactic style will lead to choosing the topic without regard to its appropriateness to the listener's focus of attention or the immediate context, and therefore producing bizarre irrelevant comments. It will also lead directly to pedantic, over-explicit styles, to ignoring signs of listener inattentiveness or boredom and contributions from others that do not fit the listener's predetermined goal for the 'conversation'. Teachers will need to be aware of this and make at least some attempt to provide a genuinely communicative environment for the pupil with an ASD for at least some of the time in school.

All these particular difficulties arise directly from ASDs, and so lend support to group differences in interpreting behaviour while supporting unique differences in the actual realization within each pupil.

ASD-specific approaches and curricula: origins and evaluation

The child with an ASD, like any other child, is entitled to a broad and relevant (not necessarily balanced) curriculum to meet his or her needs, with the issue being one of access. This common curricular goal, however, needs to be mediated through understanding of group and unique differences. At the same time, therapeutic approaches start with group rather than common needs, but also have to move to unique needs for implementation of programmes of action.

Ways of adapting mainstream curricula to meet the needs of pupils with ASDs have been developed (Cumine *et al.* 1997; Jordan and Jones 1999; Jones 2002; Seach *et al.* 2002; Mesibov and Howley 2003) and many educational authorities in the UK are developing outreach and support services for this group. Children with significant special needs as a result of their ASD are also likely to receive some individual support from a special assistant to enable further access. Here, too, training is essential since the mere addition of a support worker may do little to help the person with the ASD or his or her teachers. Nor may it effect true integration or inclusion (Jordan and Powell 1994). However, all these approaches concentrate on the compensatory, entitlement aspects of education for children with ASDs. The therapeutic aspects tend to centre on pre-school and special school curricula. This excludes the majority of children with ASDs from this therapeutic element of education.

Most of the evaluation studies of approaches to ASD have involved the use of education as therapy, rather than curricular adaptations or programmes to enable access. In a review of educational approaches in ASDs, Jordan *et al.* (1998) raise this issue as well as the inappropriateness of the clinical model of evaluation when applied to education. There are ethical and practical difficulties involved in establishing scientific models of research that would meet the clinical standard of a randomized control trial (MRC 2000). Jordan (1999b) deals with those issues in more depth and suggests some models for educational research that help to address these concerns.

A further evaluation problem lies in the eclectic nature of most educational settings in the UK. This means that it is hard to attribute success (or failure) to one aspect of the curriculum or situation rather than another, unless there are continual baselines taken and approaches are introduced systematically. Unfortunately, curriculum development and change, and the adoption of particular approaches, tend not to be systematic and the effects are poorly documented. In addition, the fact that most evaluation is by the practitioner increases the chance of bias and contamination. However, statistically based results are of limited value to the teacher trying to decide on the best approach for a particular child in a particular context (i.e. trying to meet unique needs). Most research designs focus on programmes developed to meet group needs, whereas it may be more important to know about the individual characteristics that led to success and/or failure. Action research models or single subject designs (Odom *et al.* 2003) may offer more ecologically valid ways of evaluating particular programmes with particular children in particular schools.

Conclusions

As indicated by Norwich and Lewis (Chapter 1), whatever position is adopted with respect to the common, different or unique needs of children with ASDs, it is neutral with respect to the existence and role of specialist provision in education. The degree to which individuals can and should be taught alongside typical peers depends on the severity of their unique needs, the expertise and attitude of the teaching staff (and their access to additional support) in mainstream settings and the adaptability and flexibility of the mainstream situation. The balance of advantage for one choice over another will always vary according to particular circumstances, although there can be value and policy guidelines to move provision in particular directions (e.g. towards inclusiveness); Lindsay (2003) has made the case for judgements of placement to be evidence- rather than dogma-based. The view is taken here that the balance of advantages is likely to change over time, in any particular case, so that placement always needs to be under continual review. There are not individuals who 'require' certain placements or even certain curricular adaptations, there are particular situations involving an individual that will determine those choices. However, within the context of planning and meeting needs, there will be a tension between the meeting of unique needs through very distinct curricula and pedagogy and the future effects on the individual's capacity to manage in less adapted environments. Whether the pedagogic differences required can be captured by the intensiveness and explicitness dimensions proposed by Norwich and Lewis (Chapter 1) is a separate issue. Children with ASDs often (but not always) require different approaches rather than just more (or more focused) of the same.

The issue of curriculum commonality versus difference, discussed by Lewis and Norwich (2001) and Norwich and Lewis (Chapter 1), can only be addressed in relation to ASDs by examining what is meant by 'commonality'. Reconceptualizing what is 'common' as setting principles in which group and individual needs can be met not only allows ASD approaches to be used but could see them (focused as they are on an individualised approach) as a model for others. Jordan *et al.* (1999) have given an example of how designing a pedagogical approach and physical environment adapted for those with ASDs can meet the needs of a far wider group in a special school. An inclusive curriculum is about its applicability to all from its inception and not about adaptations and extensions to make a non-inclusive curriculum more applicable to excluded groups. I reject the contention that there is a commonality (or typicality) beyond the broadest level, from which groups with special needs may or may not differ in their curriculum requirements. I suggest that 'commonality' is a pragmatic construct from the reality of individualization that is needed in any curriculum model. Naturally, the broader the curriculum principles, the more acceptable they are as common, and so the challenge here is to locate the areas of differentiation (Table 1.3) for ASDs.

The argument is that children with ASDs do have unique needs, which are recognized through, and derive from, group differences but are not fully determined by that group membership. Thus, a child with an ASD needs an individualized approach informed by understanding of ASDs. Can what is common encompass these needs? It cannot if 'common' is taken to mean 'the same' in terms of content and teaching but it could if what is common is a recognition of the uniqueness of needs in all, and the need to go beyond behaviour in understanding all children and providing the maximum learning opportunities for them. In adult care for the learning disabled, we are moving to a situation idealized as 'person-centred planning' (Department of Health 2001). This seems to me the best model for curriculum design, within curriculum principles and guidelines that reflect the values and educational goals of society. It is hard to fit such a model into a system based on centrally determined content and a didactic system of delivery, but increasing use of personal systems of instruction, as in IT, may make such an approach more accessible.

One of the arguments in this chapter is that the issues raised by inclusion are more fruitfully considered from a reverse perspective. In other words, rather than considering how what is available in curriculum and pedagogy for a presumed 'typical' group of learners might be adapted for individuals with ASDs, one could consider how far the curriculum and approach for all might be better based on recognizing the diversity of learner needs embodied in the group needs of children with special needs. Many aspects of 'best practice' for those with ASDs, for example, have a wider currency, even in the mainstream. The explicit teaching required, for example, will be of benefit to other children with different cultural backgrounds or missed experiences. The use of cueing will be good for any child who has ever daydreamed in class, as well as those with attention problems, and the learning style might be shared by many of the boys that our current educational system is failing (Frosh *et al.* 2003). That is not to say that all children will need, or benefit from, precisely the same curricular content and teaching as the child with an ASD, but all need the same recognition of their unique variability and the understanding of their behaviour as arising from a complex interplay of factors that determine its meaning. This involves a much more radical notion of the changes that need to be made to provide a genuinely inclusive environment, not just for those with special needs, but for all.

Summary

Nature of group

• There is a range of disorders related to the core disorder, including Aspergers's syndrome.

- These are not a mere grouping of difficulties; concurrence is not by chance.
- There is a strong genetic base but 'special practice' requires a psychological level of understanding.
- It has transactional origins; children should not be considered in isolation.
- It is accompanied by other disabilities and mental health problems.

Pedagogy

- Children with ASD have group-specific needs related to their individual needs as well as common needs.
- Unique needs can only be identified through a framework of group needs.
- Pedagogic approaches for ASD can benefit some wider groups, though not necessarily all other children.

Curriculum

- This rejects the universal curriculum design model where design leads to adaptations **relating to special educational needs**, and questions what is a common curriculum because: solutions require more than adaptations, links to teachers' characteristics; it marginalizes the therapeutic model of education.
- A common curriculum can only be formulated in broad terms that could obscure real differences.
- ASD children are entitled to a broad and relevant, not necessarily balanced, curriculum.
- The curriculum approach compensates for problems (access) while developing therapeutic approaches (remediate difficulties).

Knowledge

- Teachers' knowledge, skills and attitudes are important in appropriate ASD curricula.
- Teachers require knowledge of distinct ASD differences to address individual needs of children.

Individual versus general differences as pedagogic base

- A general differences position is adopted. Children often require different approaches, not just more of the same. ASD children have unique needs recognized through group differences, but not determined by them.

Notable aspects introduced

- An elaborate version of the general difference position is introduced.
- The person-centred planning model of common curriculum rejects central determination of content and teaching.

References

American Psychiatric Association (1994) *Diagnostic and Statistical Manual of Mental Disorders*, 4th edn. Washington, DC: American Psychiatric Association.

Bailey, A., Le Couteur, A., Gottesman, I., Bolton, P., Simonoff, E., Yusda, E. and Rutter, M. (1995) Autism/Asperger syndrome: a strongly genetic disorder: evidence from a twin study, *Psychological Medicine*, 25: 63–77.

Baron-Cohen, S. (2003) *The Essential Difference: Men, Women and the Extreme Male Brain*. London: Allen Lane.

Bauman, M. L. and Kemper, T. L. (1994) *Neurobiology of Autism*. Baltimore: Johns Hopkins University Press.

Blackburn, R. (2000) Within and without autism, *Good Autism Practice*, 1: 2–8

Crawford, J. (2003) The National Literacy strategy: teacher knowledge, skills and beliefs and impact on progress, *Support for Learning*, 18: 71–6.

Cumine, V., Stephenson, G. and Leach, J. (1997) *Asperger Syndrome: A Practical Guide for Teachers*. London: David Fulton.

Department of Health (2001) *Valuing People: A New Strategy for Learning Disability for the 21st Century*. Norwich: HMSO.

Fombonne, E. (1999) The epidemiology of autism: a review, *Psychological Medicine*, 29: 769–86.

Fombonne, E. (2002) Epidemiological trends in rates of autism, *Molecular Psychiatry*, 7(Supplement 2): S4–6.

Frosh, S., Phoenix, A. and Pattman, R. (2003) The trouble with boys, *Psychologist*, 16: 84–7.

Gillberg, C. and Coleman, M. (2001) *The Biology of the Autistic Syndromes*, 2nd edn. Cambridge: Cambridge University Press.

Hobson, R. P. (1993) *Autism and the Development of Mind*. London: Erlbaum.

Hobson, P. (2002) *The Cradle of Thought: Exploring The Origins of Thinking*. London: Macmillan.

Howlin, P. (1998) *Autism and Asperger Syndrome*. Chichester: Wiley.

Innes and Van Berckelaer-Onnes, I. (in press) *Autism: The International Journal of Research and Practice*.

Iovannone, R., Dunlap, G., Huber, H. and Kincaid, D. (2003) Effective educational practices for students with autistic spectrum disorders, *Focus on Autism and Other Developmental Disabilities*, 18: 150–65.

Jones, G. E. (2002) *Educational Provision for Children with Autism and Asperger Syndrome*. London: David Fulton.

Jordan, R. (1996) Teaching communication to individuals within the autistic spectrum, *REACH: The Journal of Special Educational Needs in Ireland*, 9: 95–102.

Jordan, R. (1999a) *Autistic Spectrum Disorders: An Introductory Handbook for Practitioners*. London: David Fulton.

Jordan, R. (1999b) Evaluating interventions in ASDs: problems and possibilities, *Autism: The International Journal of Research and Practice*, 3: 411–34.

Jordan, R (2001) *Autism with Severe Learning Difficulties*. London: Souvenir Press.

Jordan, R. (2002) *Autistic Spectrum Disorders in the Early Years*. Lichfield: QED.

Jordan, R. and Jones, G. (1996) *Review of Provision for Children with Autism in Scotland: Report of Research for the Scottish Office*. Birmingham: School of Education, University of Birmingham.

Jordan, R. and Jones, G. (1999) *Meeting the Needs of Children with Autistic Spectrum Disorders*. London: Fulton.

Jordan, R., Jones, G. and Murray, D. (1998) *Educational Interventions for Children with Autism: A Literature Review of Recent and Current Research*. Norwich: DfEE.

Jordan, R., Jones, G. and Morgan, H. (2001) *Children with Autistic Spectrum Disorders: A Guide for Service Providers*. London: Mental Health Foundation.

Jordan, R., Macleod, C. and Brunton, L. (1999) Making special schools 'specialist': a case study of the provision for pupils with autism in a school for pupils with severe learning difficulties, in G. Jones (ed.) *Good Autism Practice*. Birmingham: University of Birmingham.

Jordan, R. and Powell, S. (1994) Whose curriculum? Critical notes on integration and entitlement, *European Journal of Special Needs Education*, 9: 27–39.

Jordan, R. and Powell, S. (1995) *Understanding and Teaching Children with Autism*. Chichester: Wiley.

Kanner, L. (1943) Autistic disturbances of affective contact, *Nervous Child*, 2: 217–50.

Klin, A. (1991) Young autistic children's listening preferences in regard to speech: a possible characterisation of the symptoms of social withdrawal, *Journal of Autism and Developmental Disorders*, 23: 1–5–35.

Lewis, A. and Norwich, B. (2001) A critical review of systematic evidence concerning distinctive pedagogies for pupils with learning disabilities, *Journal of Research in Special Educational Needs*, 1(1): 1–13.

Lindsay, G. (2003) Inclusive education: a critical perspective, *British Journal of Special Education*, 30: 3–12.

Lotter V. (1966) Epidemiology of autistic conditions in young children: prevalence, *Social Psychiatry*, 1: 124–37.

Medical Research Council (2000) *A Framework for the development and Evaluation of RCTs for Complex Interventions to Improve Health*. London: MRC.

Medwell, J., Wray, D., Poulson, L. and Fox, R. (1998) *Effective Teachers of Literacy*. Exeter: University of Exeter Press.

Mesibov, G. and Howley, M. (2003) *Accessing the Curriculum for Pupils with Autistic Spectrum Disorders: Using the TEACCH Programme to Help Inclusion*. London: David Fulton.

National Initiative for Assessment, Screening and Education in Autism (2003) *National Plan for Autism*. London: National Autistic Society.

Noens, I. and van Berckelaer-Onnes, I. (in press) Making sense in a fragmentary world: communication in people with autism and learning disability, *Autism: The International Journal of Research and Practice*.

Norwich, B. (1996) Special needs education or education for all: connective specialisation and ideological impurity, *British Journal of Special Education*, 23, 100–4.

Norwich, B. and Lewis, A. (2001) Mapping a pedagogy for special educational needs, *British Educational Research Journal*, 27: 313–30.

Odom, S. L., Brown, W. H., Frey, T., Karasu, N., Smith-Canter, L. L. and Strain, P. (2003) Evidence-based practices for young children with autism: contributions for single-subject design research, *Focus on Autism and Other Developmental Disabilities*, 18: 166–75.

Oliver, M. (1992) Intellectual masturbation: a rejoinder to Soder and Booth, *European Journal of Special Needs Education*, 7: 20–8.

Peeters, T. and Jordan, R. (1999) What makes a good practitioner in autistic spectrum disorders?, in G. Jones (ed.) *Good Autism Practice 1: First Collection of Papers*. Birmingham: School of Education, University of Birmingham.

Powell, S. and Jordan, R. (1993) Diagnosis, intuition and autism, *British Journal of Special Education*, 20: 26–9.

Powell, S. and Jordan, R. (1997) Rationale for the approach, in S. Powell and R. Jordan (eds) *Autism and Learning: A Guide to Good Practice*. London: David Fulton.

Rogers, S. J., Hepburn, S. L., Stackhouse, T. and Wehner, E. (2003) Imitation performance in toddlers with autism and those with other developmental disorders, *Journal of Child Psychology and Psychiatry*, 44: 763–81.

Rutter, M. (1999) Autism: two-way interplay between research and clinical work, *Journal of Child Psychology and Psychiatry*, 40: 169–88.

Rutter, M., Andersen-Wood, L., Beckett, C., Bredenkarrp, D., Castle, J., Groothues, C., Kreppner, J., Keaveney, L., Lord, C. and O'Connor, T.G. (1999) Quasi-autistic patterns found following severe early global deprivation, *Journal of Child Psychology and Psychiatry*, 40: 537–50.

Scheuermann, B., Webber, J., Beutot, E. A. and Goodwin, M. (2003) Problems with personnel preparation in Autism Spectrum Disorders, *Focus on Autism and other Developmental Disabilities*, 18: 197–206.

Seach, D., Lloyd, M. and Preston, M. (2002) *Supporting Children with Autism in Mainstream Schools*. Birmingham: Questions Publishing.

Shea, V. and Mesibov, G. (1985) The relationship of learning disabilities and higher-level autism, *Journal of Autism and Developmental Disorders*, 15: 425–35.

Sherratt, D. and Peter, M. (2002) *Developing Play and Drama in Children with Autistic Spectrum Disorders*. London: David Fulton.

Skrtic, T. M. (1999) Learning disabilities as organisational pathologies, in R. J. Sternberg and L. Spear-Swirling (eds) *Perspectives on Learning Disabilities*. New York: Westview Press.

Teacher Training Agency (1999) *National Special Educational Needs Standards for Teachers*. London: TTA.

Trevarthen, C., Aitken, K., Papoudi, D. and Robarts, J. (1996) *Children with Autism: Diagnosis and Intervention to Meet Their Needs*. London: Jessica Kingsley.

Ward, M. and Alar, N. (2000) Being autistic is part of who I am, *Focus on Autism and Other Developmental Disabilities*, 15: 232–5.

Williams, D. (1996) *Autism: An Inside Out Approach*. London: Jessica Kingsley.

Wing, L. (1981) Asperger's syndrome: a clinical account, *Psychological Medicine*, 11: 115–29.

Wing, L. (1996) *Autistic Spectrum Disorders: A Guide for Parents and Professionals*. London: Constable.

Wing, L. and Gould, J. (1979) Severe impairments of social interaction and associated abnormalities in children: epidemiology and classification, *Journal of Autism and Developmental Disorders*, 9: 11–29.

World Health Organization (1992) *International Classification of Diseases, IX*. Paris: WHO

Wragg, E. C., Wragg, C. M., Haynes, G. S. and Chamberlin, R. P. (1998) *Improving Literacy in the Primary School*. London: Routledge.

CHAPTER TEN

AD/HD
Paul Cooper

Overview

The structure of this chapter is dictated by a particular view of pedagogy that builds on the definition provided by the book's editors. The concept of teachers' professional 'craft knowledge' is central to this expanded view. After a brief description and discussion of craft knowledge, the possibility of incorporating research-based theoretical knowledge into teachers' craft knowledge is considered. This is followed by an account of AD/HD as a bio-psycho-social phenomenon, and the contribution to teachers' craft knowledge that can be gained from this. The distinctiveness of the impact of this knowledge on teachers' pedagogy is considered in the conclusion to the chapter.

What is 'Pedagogy' and what do we know about how teachers think?

The editors of this book define 'pedagogy' usefully and succinctly as: 'The broad cluster of decisions and actions taken in classroom settings that aim to promote school learning.' The words 'decisions' and 'aim' are most important here because they indicate that we must attach central importance to the thinking that lies behind the teacher behaviour that we might see in the form of pedagogic strategies and teacher activity. The problem of seeking insight from a focus on behaviour alone (in almost any context), however, always resides in the difficulty of separating the causes and effects of behaviour from the myriad of contextual variables that surround any behavioural act.

Central to the teacher as craftsperson analogy is the idea that teaching expertise develops through practice. This means that teaching is not theory-led;

the common-sense theories that all teachers have about why particular pedagogical decisions are taken are usually based on experience of what has worked
in the past. Teachers refine their teaching repertoires and routines through
processes of reflection that can be understood in terms of Donald Schon's
(1983) model of the 'reflective practitioner'. In the initial stages of a teaching
career, the teacher will often engage in practices that are an imitation of the
behaviours of expert teachers they have observed during their own experience
as a school student, or those they have encountered during their training and
initial teaching experience (Morrison and McIntyre 1968). These approaches
may also be accompanied by hypothesis testing, by which trainees and newly
qualified teachers try out different approaches to facilitating learning of particular content. By the time teachers have reached the stage of being 'expert',
they have accumulated a complex repertoire of teaching skills that enable
them to manage a bewildering number and range of classroom variables and to
make on the spot decisions.

When it comes to research evidence on how teachers think about pupils we
find studies suggesting that teachers' pedagogical decision-making is strongly
influenced by teachers' perceptions of pupils that are based on fairly limited
interaction with, and observation of, pupils (Brown and McIntyre 1993). A
study of teachers in English secondary schools found that, after only seven
weeks of Year 7, teachers came to apparently stable decisions about the characteristics of their pupils in terms of pupils' levels of ability, while strong specula-
tions were being made about pupils' behaviour, motivation and personal
attributes (Cooper and McIntyre 1996: 133). These decisions can be understood in terms of Hargreaves *et al.*'s (1975) theory of 'typing', by which the
teacher places pupils into ready-made categories relating to pupils' perceived
ability, behaviour and motivation, and other personal attributes (appearance,
gender etc.) (Cooper and McIntyre 1996). These studies suggest that this 'typing' process is an important element in expert teachers' professional craft
knowledge, enabling them to make speedy sense of complex circumstances
and conditions in busy classroom settings in which there is a limited time for
extended reflection and analysis.

Typing teachers' knowledge of effective pedagogy

The dangers of the typing process, identified by Cooper and McIntyre as a
component of teachers' pedagogical decision-making, are well rehearsed in
the sociological literature on education and special education (e.g. Hargreaves
et al. 1975). Typing can lead to self-fulfilling prophecies. In the field of special
educational needs this concern has been voiced in relation to the phenomenon
of attention deficit/hyperactivity disorder (AD/HD). AD/HD has been dismissed
by some commentators as a medical construct that individualizes educational
failure and disruptive behaviour and thus contributes to the social construction
of learning and behavioural problems (e.g. Slee 1995).

It would be wrong to ignore negative possibilities suggested by the practice
of typing. However, it would be equally wrong to assume that the only way to

avoid such negative consequences would be to abandon the practice of typing. It can be argued forcefully that if we are to influence teachers' practice in ways that exploit the best research evidence on effective teaching we must do so by exploiting teachers' existing patterns of professional thinking (Monro 1999). The AD/HD diagnostic criteria, it is argued, and the research that supports and flows from them, can be utilized to great effect in this endeavour.

Theory and pedagogy

A number of important points follow from this discussion. The first point is that teaching can be usefully understood as a theory-driven process. However, there is a difference between the practical theorizing of professional teachers and the scientific theorizing of professional psychologists. Practical theories are not necessarily articulated explicitly, and are not necessarily falsifiable (and, therefore, testable) in the way that scientific theories are required to be. The second point is that it is entirely wrong to dismiss the practical theorizing of teachers, simply because it is 'unscientific' (see O'Connor, 1973). Practical theorizing is at the heart of expert teaching. It is a central component in the professional development of teachers and a major source of insight into the nature of effective teaching. Furthermore, it is a key factor in justifying the current renewed interest in teacher autonomy as an important basis for the future development of the teaching profession in complex and fast moving advanced economies (Johnson and Hallgarten 2002). Finally, practical theorizing does not preclude scientific theorizing. It is suggested that the processes of teaching become more available to scrutiny and purposive development when (a) practical theorizing is shifted from the tacit to the explicit realm and (b) opportunities are sensitively created for teachers to incorporate scientific understandings into their reflections on their practical theories. The rest of this chapter deals with the contribution that various aspects of the theoretical construct of AD/HD can make to the development of teachers' pedagogical decision-making processes. Before we can develop this line of discussion further, however, it is necessary to provide a brief account of AD/HD, its nature and antecedents.

AD/HD: its nature, origins, correlates and evolution

AD/HD is a diagnosis of the American Psychiatric Association (APA 1994). It describes behavioural symptoms of inattention and/or impulsiveness/ hyperactivity that are presented to a degree that significantly interfere with a person's family and peer relations as well as their educational and/or occupational functioning.

International estimates suggest that between 2 and 6 per cent of school aged children and young people are affected by AD/HD, with males out-numbering females by a ratio of 3:1 (Tannock 1998). Current estimates place the prevalence rate in the UK at between 2 and 5 per cent for school aged children (NICE 2000). This accords closely with US prevalence rates (APA 1994), making AD/HD one of the most commonly diagnosed childhood disorders (Greenhill 1998). The developmental course of AD/HD usually begins between the ages of three and four, though some children show evidence of the disorder in early infancy, and others not until the ages of five or six years (Anastopoulos 1999). The APA diagnostic criteria requires the presence of symptoms before the age of seven years.

There are many seriously debilitating social, emotional and behavioural correlates of AD/HD. Individuals with AD/HD are more likely than the general population to experience social isolation, accidental injury and psychological disturbance (Tannock 1998). People with undiagnosed AD/HD are often dismissed as incompetent, disorganized, aggressive, disruptive, lazy, untrustworthy, neglectful, selfish, accident prone, antisocial and/or asocial. Pupils with AD/HD are prone to poorer academic performance than their scores on standardized tests of cognitive ability predict (Barkley 1990; Hinshaw 1994). In the UK, Hayden (1997) found the symptoms of hyperactivity to be one of a range of correlates of formal exclusion from school among children of primary school age.

This is consistent with the findings of prevalence studies carried out in special schools for children with emotional and behavoural difficulties. For example, Place et al. (2000) found an AD/HD prevalence rate of 70 per cent there, while Vivian (1994) found a HD rate of 40 per cent. Other studies have found the symptoms of AD/HD to be associated in adults with serious relationship problems, marital breakdown, employment difficulties (Hinshaw 1994) and imprisonment (Farrington 1990; Weiss and Hechtman 1993). In addition to these problems AD/HD is found to co-occur with a wide range of other difficulties at rates of between 25 and 60 per cent, including specific learning difficulties (SpLD/dyslexia) (Richards 1995), conduct disorder (CD), oppositional defiant disorder (ODD), depression (DD) and anxiety disorder (AD) (Angold et al. 1999; Barkley 1990). The emotional and behavioural 'co-morbid' disorders (CD, ODD, DD, AD) tend to emerge during the adolescent years, giving rise to the hypothesis that these are socially induced problems that occur as a result of the misunderstanding and mismanagement of the primary AD/HD symptoms. Having said this, the finding of high rates of co-morbidity between AD/HD and CD/ODD may indicate the existence of an additional major sub-type of AD/HD and an externalizing behavioural disorder (Angold et al. 1999).

The long evolution of the clinical and scholarly treatment of the AD/HD diagnosis has reached a point where educational implications are clearly evident. The 1968 DSM II criteria (hyperkinetic reaction of childhood) mark, to a considerable degree, a shift away from an emphasis on neurobiological causation (e.g. minimal brain dysfunction) to a continuing emphasis on behavioural symptoms as the defining characteristics of the condition (Anastopoulos 1999). This shift is reflected in the alternative diagnosis of hyperkinetic disorders (HD) (World Health Organization 1990).

Executive functions and the evidence base for AD/HD

A definitive account of the causes of AD/HD is not available. However, AD/HD has become one of the most widely researched disorders in the psychological and psychiatric literature. Three major areas of theoretical exploration of AD/HD have been identified (Tannock 1998): cognitive research, neurobiological research and genetic research. Evidence from studies in these areas creates a compelling argument for AD/HD as a bio-psycho-social phenomenon and provides a sound base for a multimodal approach to intervention that combines medical, psycho-social and educational dimension.

Cognitive research has increasingly focused on impulsiveness as the central feature of AD/HD, and the possibility that a dysfunctional response inhibition system is the neuropsychological mechanism, largely located in the physiology of the frontal lobes of the brain, underlying this problem. This neurobiological explanation is supported by a number of neuro-imaging studies (Tannock 1998) as well as by neuro-chemical studies, which have detected dysfunctions in certain neuro-transmitter systems implicated in the regulation of attention and behaviour (McMullen *et al.* 1994). That neurobiological mechanisms are implicated in the aetiology of AD/HD is further supported by findings from genetic studies that have shown a much greater incidence of AD/HD among identical (i.e. monozygotic) twins than among non-identical (dizygotic) twins, and among children who are biologically related as opposed to adopted. Molecular genetic research has identified abnormalities in the dopamine system (McMullen *et al.* 1994). Dopamine is a neuro-transmitter that is found in systems of the brain concerned with, among other things, the regulation of movement (Thompson 1993). These findings suggest that children with AD/HD are biologically predisposed to experience significantly greater problems than most in inhibiting or delaying a behavioural response. The nature of the dysfunction in this system is described alternatively in terms of a failure of the inhibitory control system to become activated (Barkley 1997) or as extreme delay in the activation of this system (Sergeant 1995; van der Meere 1996).

Barkley (1997) proposes an integrated model that suggests that neurologically based problems of response inhibition lead directly to problems in four major 'executive functions' of the brain that are essential to effective self-regulation. The first executive function is working memory, impairment of which makes it difficult for individuals to retain and manipulate information for purposes of appraisal and planning. The second function is internalized speech. It is suggested that self-control is exerted through a process of self-talk, during which possible consequences and implications of behaviours are weighed up and internally 'discussed'. The third executive function is motivational appraisal. This system enables us to make decisions by providing us with information about the emotional associations generated by an impulse to act and the extent to which the impulse is likely to produce outcomes we find desirable. The final executive function is reconstitution, or behavioural synthesis. The role of this function is to enable us to plan new and appropriate behaviours as an outcome of deconstructing and analysing past behaviours.

In addition to the cognitive–neuroscientific evidence, there are data from a number of studies to suggest that factors in the family environment may be implicated in the development of AD/HD. Family factors include parenting skills (Taylor *et al.* 1991), disorderly home environments (Cantwell 1996), marital discord between parents (Barkley 1990), maternal mental health and paternal personality factors (Nigg and Hinshaw 1998). These findings combined with the neuro-physiological research suggest that AD/HD is a bio-psycho-social phenomenon; that is, a behavioural manifestation with its origins in a biologically based predisposition. The biological predisposition and the behavioural outcomes, however, are mediated by environmental and experiential factors (Frith 1992; Rutter 2002).

Once we move into this bio-psycho-social territory the unhelpful polarity that is sometimes stated in terms of biological versus social explanations for learning and behavioural problems (e.g. Slee 1995; Visser 1997; Booth and Aimscow 1998) becomes redundant. It is clear that AD/HD is influenced by both biology and the social environment. AD/HD is, indeed, 'socially constructed' (Purdie *et al.* 2002), but certain individuals, by virtue of their biological inheritance and social circumstances, are more prone to being constructed as being 'disordered' in this way than others. The school is a major site where this process of social construction takes place, and it is through the patterns of institutional controls and pedagogical practices that such construction is implemented. These also provide the means by which deconstruction can take place.

The pedagogical implications of understanding AD/HD as a bio-psycho-social phenomenon

A key problem with the DSM diagnostic criteria is that they harbour taken for granted assumptions about the kinds of pupil behaviours that are to be expected in properly functioning classrooms. Pupils from an early age are expected to internalize and behave in accordance with a set of rules that derive from constraints imposed by a teacher-centred, curriculum-focused method of teaching pupils in age-related groups. Teacher–pupil ratios create potential problems of social disorder that are met with rules of conduct designed to regulate pupil movement around the classroom and interactions between peers. Externally imposed curricula, as opposed to negotiated curricula, assuming a tight relationship between pupil age and cognitive functioning, tend to be managed by teachers in ways that require pupils to follow a lineal programme of tasks at predetermined times and within strict time limits. It follows from this that teachers often fulfil the role of 'instructors', providing an estimated 80 per cent of the talk that goes on in classrooms (Sage 2002). Pupils, therefore, are required to be expert in following complex instructions and internalizing behavioural and cognitive routines that, in turn, are intended to establish patterns of self-regulation that become increasingly important as pupils pass through the higher realms of the curriculum and schooling process. It has long been noted that this factory model of education is by no means the only, or even the most desirable, model of schooling. At its worst it rewards conformity and passivity at the expense of intellectual curiosity, critical debate and creativity (Silberman 1971). At its best it favours pupils whose cognitive styles favour systematic reflection and abstract lineal thinking. This makes schooling a problematic experience for many contemporary pupils and provides a major, relatively new source of stress to pupils with attention and activity problems.

Cognitive strategies

The pedagogical task of the teacher is to mediate between these ever-present forces that socially construct problems and exacerbate existing problems for the learner in order to achieve desired forms of pupil participation that are calculated to produce desired learning outcomes. The pedagogical thinking of the teacher knowledgeable about AD/HD will be significantly influenced by the knowledge that an appropriately diagnosed individual will have been judged to demonstrate specific cognitive deficiencies in relation to executive functions. Broswell (1995) contrasts cognitive distortions – that is, problems of understanding – with cognitive deficits that are processing difficulties. This distinction can be used to inform pedagogical decision-making by directing the teacher towards strategies designed to 'train or reinforce his or her use of the "missing pieces" in his or her cognitive repertoire' (Braswell 1991). Cognitive behavioural therapy (CBT) (Meichenbaum 1997), sometimes referred to as cognitive behaviour modification (CBM), provides the basis for classroom interventions that can be used by teachers. These commonly involve teaching pupils to use internal dialogue in order to regulate their thinking and behaviour through self-reinforcement of desired behaviours, self-instruction techniques and problem-solving routines (Ervin et al. 1996; Royer 1999). Self-monitoring strategies have been found to increase pupils' attention to task and reduce the core symptoms of AD/HD (Lerner et al. 1995). However, evidence for the overall efficacy of CBT for AD/HD is far from conclusive. Reviews by Purdie et al. (2002), Royer (1999) and Ervin et al. (1996) report mixed findings, though school-based programmes tend to be more effective than clinic-based approaches in promoting behavioural change (Ervin et al. 1996). This change, however, is not often generalized to settings outside the training situation, though Royer (1999) asserts that generalization can be achieved if it is systematically programmed.

It has been suggested by Ervin et al. (1996) that some of the disappointing research evidence in relation to CBT in relation to AD/HD is possibly the result of a failure of some of the interventions to distinguish effectively between cognitive deficits and cognitive distortions (see above). Ervin indicates that many CBT interventions are based on the erroneous assumption that children with AD/HD lack cognitive strategies, rather than the more persuasive view (proposed by Barkley 1997) that dysfunctions in the operation of their executive functions make it difficult for them to perform the strategies, even when they know them. This suggests that CBT techniques will be more successful if they focus on providing pupils with techniques that enable them to delay and inhibit their responses.

Educational strategies

'Educational' approaches 'reframe' AD/HD as a particular cognitive style, rather than a 'deficit' (Cooper and Ideus 1996; Cooper and O'Regan 2001). They are pedagogical strategies designed to exploit, rather than inhibit, some of the characteristics associated with AD/HD; for example, through the use of visual-motor tasks (Zentall *et al.* 1993; DuPaul and Stoner 1995; Zentall and Stormont-Spurgin 1995; Purdie *et al.* 2002). Evidence from studies reviewed by DuPaul and Stoner (1995) supports this view that pupils with AD/HD respond well to feedback and reinforcement when the frequency of these interventions is greater than for 'regular' students. Interventions based on the belief that students with AD/HD tend to have an active ('kinaesthetic') learning style have been shown to increase levels of attention to tasks and reduce disruptive and impulsive behaviours (Hinshaw *et al.* 1984). Related to this is the insight that pupils with AD/HD are particularly prone to the negative consequences of 'recess deprivation' (Zentall and Stormont-Spurgin 1995). Pelligrini and Horvat (1995) found that disruptive behaviour decreased and on-task behaviour increased when periods of 'seatwork' were punctuated by frequent periods of structured physical activity. This implies that the redistribution of such time throughout the day at regular intervals will produce positive outcomes.

A classroom problem associated with AD/HD, talking at inappropriate times, can be exploited by increasing opportunities for on-task verbal participation (Zentall 1995). Studies have found that pupils with AD/HD perform better on reading comprehension tasks when they are required to read comprehension passages aloud, rather than silently (Dubey and O'Leary 1975). Zentall (1995) also suggests that seating pupils in a semi-circle around the teacher or in small groups produces more on-task verbal participation and more appropriate hand raising behaviours during whole-class teaching episodes. Furthermore, there is evidence to support the conclusion that reducing the teacher–pupil ratio, in situations involving teacher–group verbal interaction, improves the quality of engagement of pupils with AD/HD (Zentall 1995). This effect is enhanced when teachers provide behavioural models for active listening strategies.

The twin pedagogical strategies of behavioural modelling and teacher direction are strongly associated with a reduction in pupil inattentiveness and impulsiveness in the classroom and positive academic outcomes. These effects are most powerful when teacher direction involves clear and distinct information about performance, behavioural expectations and expected outcomes. Optimal pupil performance is associated with brevity and clarity of sequences of instruction, the accompaniment of verbal instructions with visual cues and the availability of resources that pupils can refer to for reminders of direction and expectations (DuPaul and Stoner 1995; Zentall 1995). The use of pupils as behavioural and academic models through the careful programming of inter-action between the pupil with AD/HD and preferred role models is also found to be an effective pedagogical tool, though it is important that the opportun-ities for disruption created by such pupil interaction are controlled by the teacher's use of positive reinforcement for task appropriate and socially desir-able behaviour (Zentall 1995). In accordance with these findings, Cooper and O'Regan (2001) provide case study material indicating that pupils with AD/HD can benefit from taking on the role of peer tutors with younger, less competent pupils.

In a classroom environment in which extraneous stimuli, such as irrelevant noise and other distractors, are limited, and where pedagogical strategies of the type described above are in use, opportunities are created to enable the pupil with AD/HD to practise self-pacing. Self-pacing, as opposed to external (i.e. teacher directed) pacing, is associated with greater accuracy (Zentall 1995) and pupil self-reported satisfaction (Cooper and Shea 1999) with learning tasks. This can usefully extend to providing pupils with AD/HD with opportunities to remove themselves from classroom situations that they find stressful to a predetermined quiet area (DuPaul and Stoner 1995; Zentall 1995).

In their meta-analysis of interventions for AD/HD, Purdie *et al.* (2002) found that, in comparison to clinic-based interventions, educational interventions of the type described above were most effective in promoting positive cogni-tive outcomes (defined in terms of non-specified academic performance, lan-guage and reading skills, mathematical skills, IQ and memory functions). Although the overall mean effect size was small (28), it was concluded that educational interventions were the most effective in producing cognitive improvements. School-based cognitive interventions were also more effective than clinic-based cognitive interventions. This highlights the central import-ance of pedagogical approaches to the amelioration of the negative outcomes of AD/HD. Multimodal approaches (combining medical, psycho-social and educational interventions) were found to be second only to medication in achieving improvements in behaviour, and superior to medication in producing improvements in social functioning.

The focus of this chapter on pedagogy has meant that the issue of medica-tion has not been dealt with. This might be seen as an omission by some readers. Medication is seen by many commentators as the single most import-ant feature of the AD/HD phenomenon (Slee 1995; Baldwin 2000). The irony of this position is that it assumes a bio-medical definition of AD/HD. On the other hand, viewing AD/HD from an educational perspective enables us to envision what is possible when schools and teachers adopt AD/HD as an edu-cational issue. It has already been suggested in this chapter that AD/HD as a debilitating problem is at least in part constructed by the uncritical acceptance of certain assumptions about what the demands of schooling are and should be. It is suggested that the concept of AD/HD illuminates these assumptions and thus leads us to important pedagogical insights. It may well be the case that were these insights to be widely incorporated into the craft knowledge of teachers then the use of medication for pupils with AD/HD could be less necessary than currently assumed, as a means of enabling pupils with AD/HD to participate in educational settings.

Having said this, significant obstacles remain. For reasons already outlined, AD/HD cannot be dealt with simply through reference to a recipe book. Some of the educational implications of what the evidence base tells us about appropriate pedagogy for pupils with AD/HD may well be seen to challenge approaches to teaching and the organization of schools that are well established and underpinned by statutory accountability structures. For example, approaches to pacing and the role of pupil self-direction described above might be seen to be in conflict with Ofsted criteria. Suggestions relating to staff–pupil ratios are bound to strike fear into the heart of fiscally prudent politicians and the managers of LEA budgets. Furthermore, the role of 'typing' in teachers' pedagogical decision-making is problematic. If AD/HD is construed as a bio-medical issue then its function may be to encourage teachers to abdicate responsibility for adapting their practice in favour of expecting (or even demanding) medication to be applied in order to adapt the pupil to an unsuitable learning environment. These challenges can only be met through creative ways of educating teachers about AD/HD, and enabling them to assimilate knowledge about it into their craft knowledge.

Conclusion: what, if anything, is distinctive about pedagogy for pupils with AD/HD?

Pupils with AD/HD do well in classroom environments that are managed in ways that acknowledge involuntary difficulties they may have with regulating their attention, motor activity and tendency towards impulsiveness. This could be said of virtually all pupils in most schools throughout the world. When we look at schooling from the perspective of the individual with AD/HD we find fault lines that, when addressed, benefit all pupils. The particular problem here, however, is that the surface difficulties posed by the child with AD/HD, which tend to be behavioural, are easily and effectively addressed by medication alone (Purdie *et al.* 2002). They are also rendered more amenable to the kinds of pedagogical practices described in this chapter (Barkley 1990). However, it may be the case that in the mainstream classroom the absence of a disruptive behavioural presence may make it unnecessary for the teacher to adapt her pedagogical practices in order to promote the optimal educational engagement of the pupil with AD/HD. After all, while the majority of pupils might benefit from AD/HD-friendly pedagogy, they do not necessarily demand it. The majority of pupils, it seems, are able to tolerate classrooms that fall short of the requirements demanded by the unmedicated child with AD/HD. We return, therefore, to a central theme of this chapter: AD/HD is to a significant degree constructed by assumptions about what a mainstream classroom and school are meant to look like. The strategies described above will be rendered 'generic' only when these assumptions are firmly challenged at the policy level.

Summary

Nature of the group

- AD/HD is a psychiatric condition that interferes with educational and other functioning.
- It co-occurs with other conditions covered in this book.
- It is a bio-psycho-social condition that undercuts the dichotomy between social and biological causation; some individuals are more prone to being socially constructed this way than others.

Pedagogy

- Professional craft knowledge is important.
- Thinking lies behind teacher actions; practical theorizing is at the heart of teaching.
- Scientific theories can be incorporated into teacher reflections on their practices.
- Pedagogy is strongly influenced by teachers' perceptions of pupil characteristics, the use of ready-made categories and the typing process.
- Typing can have negative and positive potentials, where knowledge about conditions like AD/HD is central.
- The school, as the site for this social process through current institutional and pedagogic practices, partly produces and exaggerates problems.
- Cognitive behavioural interventions inform pedagogic strategies. AD/HD is a cognitive style rather than a deficit. The strategy is to exploit the AD/HD characteristics rather than suppress them. There are implications for the organization of classroom setting and scheduling.
- Use of these strategies is likely to reduce teacher abdication of responsibility and decrease the need for medication.

Curriculum

- Curriculum structure and product orientation are implicit in the construction of AD/HD, implicating national strategies.
- There is a need for curriculum implementation and organizational arrangements that are more geared to pupil learning styles.

Knowledge

- Knowledge about AD/HD is relevant to practical theorizing.
- Knowledge of AD/HD as bio-psycho-social versus a bio-medical condition is central to educational strategies.

Unique versus general differences position as pedagogic base

- The general difference position is implicit in the case for incorporating insights about AD/HD into teachers' practical theorizing and teaching.

- Generalized pedagogic strategies are seen as benefiting non-AD/HD pupils.

Notable aspects introduced

- Teachers' pedagogy based on craft knowledge and practical theorizing is central.
- Teacher decision-making involves typing; this needs to be harnessed in positive ways.
- The factory model/instruction style of schooling is critiqued.

References

Anastopoulos, A. (1999) AD/HD, in S. Netherton, C. Holmes and C. Walker (eds) *Child and Adolescent Psychological Disorders: A Comprehensive Textbook*. Oxford: Oxford University Press.

Angold, A., Costello, E. and Erkanli, A. (1999) Comorbidity, *Journal of Child Psychology and Psychiatry*, 40(1): 57–88.

American Psychiatric Association (1968) *Diagnostic and Statistical Manual of Mental Disorders*, 2nd edn. Washington, DC: APA.

American Psychiatric Association (1980) *Diagnostic and Statistical Manual of Mental Disorders*, 3rd edn. Washington, DC: APA.

American Psychiatric Association (1987) *Diagnostic and Statistical Manual of Mental Disorders*, 3rd rev. edn. Washington, DC: APA.

American Psychiatric Association (1994) *Diagnostic and Statistical Manual of Mental Disorders*, 4th edn. Washington, DC: APA.

Booth, T. and Aimscow, M. (1998) *From Them to Us*, London: Routledge

Barkley, R. (1990) *AD/HD: A Handbook for Diagnosis and Treatment*. New York: Guilford.

Barkley, R. (1997) *AD/HD and the Nature of Self Control*. New York: Guilford.

Braswell, L. (1991) *Cognitive-Behavioural Therapy with ADHD Children: Child, Family, and School Interventions*. New York, Guilford Press.

British Psychological Society (1996) *AD/HD: A Psychological Response to an Evolving Concept*. Leicester: BPS.

British Psychological Society (2000) *AD/HD: Guidelines and Principles for Successful Multi-agency Working*. Leicester: BPS.

Brown, S. and McIntyre, D. (1993) *Making sense of teaching*. Buckingham, Open Universtiy Press.

Cantwell, D. (1996) 'Attention deficit disorder: A review of the past 10 years', *Journal of the Academy of Child and Adolescent Psychiatry*, 35, 978-987.

Carter, R. (1998) *Mapping the Mind*. London: Weidenfeld and Nicolson.

Cooper, P. (1997a) Biology, behaviour and education: AD/HD and the bio-psycho-social perspective, *Educational and Child Psychology*, 14(1): 31–8.

Cooper, P. (1997b) The reality and hyperreality of AD/HD: an educational and cultural analysis, in P. Cooper and K. Ideus (eds) *Attention Deficit/Hyperactivity Disorder: Medical, Educational and Cultural Issues*, 2nd edn. East Sutton: Association of Workers for Children with Emotional and Behavioural Difficulties.

Cooper, P. and Idedus, K. (1996) *ADHD: A Practical Guide for Teachers*. London: David Fulton.

Cooper, P. and McIntyre, D. (1996) *Effective teaching and learning: teachers' and students' perceptions*. Buckingham, Open University Press.

Cooper, P. and O'Regan, F. (2001) Ruby Tuesday: A student with ADHD and learning difficulties, *Emotional and Behavioural Difficulties*. 6, 4: 265–269.

Detweiler, R., Hicks, M. and Hicks, A. (1999) A multimodal approach to the assessment of ADHD, in P. Cooper and K. Bilton (eds) *ADHD: Research, Practice and Opinion*. London: Whurr.

Dubey, D. R. and O'Leary, S. G. (1975) Increasing reading comprehension of two hyperactive children: Preliminary investigation. *Perceptual and Motor Skills*, 41(3): 691–694.

DuPaul, G. and Stoner, G. (1995) *ADHD in the Schools*. New York: Guilford.

Ellis, A. and Young, A. (1988) *Human Cognitive Neuropsychology*. Hove: Lawrence Erlbaum.

Ervin, R. A., Bankert, C. L. and DuPaul, G. J. (1996) Treatment of attention-deficit hyperactivity disorder, in M. A. Reinecke and F. M. Datillo (eds.) *Cognitive-therapy with children and adolescents: a casebook for clinical practice* (38–61). New York: Guilford Press.

Farrington, D. (1990) Implications of criminal career research for the prevention of offending, *Journal of Adolescence*, 13: 93–113.

Frith, U. (1992) Cognitive development and cognitive deficit, *The Psychologist*, 5: 13–19.

Greenhill, L. (1998) Childhood ADHD. pharmacological treatments, in X. P. Nathan and M. Gorman (eds) *A Guide to Treatments that Work*. Oxford: Oxford University Press.

Hargreaves, D., Hester, A. and Mellor, F. (1975) *Deviance in classrooms*. London: Routledge.

Hayden, C. (1997) Exclusion from primary school: children in need and children with special educational need, *Emotional and Behavioural Difficulties*, 2(3): 36–44.

Hill, P. and Cameron, M. (1999) Recognising hyperactivity: a guide for the cautious clinician, *Child Psychology and Psychiatry Review*, 4(2): 50–60.

Hinshaw, S. (1994) *Attention Deficits and Hyperactivity in Children*. London: Sage.

Hinshaw, S., Klein, R. and Abikoff, H. (1998) Childhood ADHD: non pharmacological and combination treatments, in X. P. Nathan and M. Gorman (eds) *A Guide to Treatment That Works*. Oxford: Oxford University Press.

Hughes, L. (1999) Professionals' perceptions of AD/HD, in P. Cooper (ed.) *AD/HD Research, Practice and Opinion*. London: Whurr.

Ideus, K. (1997) A sociological critique of an American concept, in P. Cooper and K. Ideus (eds) *Attention Deficit/Hyperactivity Disorder: Medical, Educational and Cultural Issues*, 2nd edn. East Sutton: Association of Workers for Children with Emotional and Behavioural Difficulties.

Johnson, M. and Hallgarten, J. (2002) *From Victims of change to agents of change: the future of the teaching profession*. London: Institute of Public Policy Research.

Kewley, G. (1998) Medical aspects of assessment and treatment of children with ADHD, in P. Cooper and K. Ideus (eds) *ADHD: Educational, Medical and Cultural Issues*. East Sutton: Association of Workers for Children with Emotional and Behavioural Difficulties.

Lahey, B., Waldman, I. and McBurnett, K. (1999) The development of antisocial behaviour: an integrative and causal model, *Journal of Child Psychology and Psychiatry*, 40(5): 669–682.

Levy, F. and Hay, D. (eds) (2001) *Attention, Genes and ADHD*. London: Brunner-Routledge.

McMullen, G., Painter, D. and Casey, T. (1994) Assessment and treatment of AD/HD in children, in L. VendeCreek, S. Knapp and T. Jackson (eds.) *Innovations in Clinical Practice*. Sarasotat, FL: Professional Resource Press.

Meichenbaum, D. (1977) *Cognitive-behaviour modification: an integrative approach*. New York: Plenum Press.

Morrison, A. and McIntyre, D. (1993) *Teachers and teaching*. Harmondsworth: Penguin.

Munden, A. and Arcelus, J. (1999) *The AD/HD Handbook*. London: Jessica Kingsley.

Munro, J. (1999) Learning more about learning improves teacher effectiveness, *School Effectiveness and School Improvement*, 10(2), 151–171.

National Institute of Clinical Excellence (2000) *Guidance on the Use of Methyphenidate for AD/HD*. London: NICE.

Neill, A. S. (1968) *Summerhill*. Harmondsworth: Penguin.

Nigg, J. and Hinshaw, S. (1998) Parent personality traits and psycho pathology associated with antisocial behaviors in childhood AD/HD, *Journal of Child Psychology and Psychiatry*, 39(2): 145–59.

O'Connor, D. (1973) The Nature and scope of education theory, in G. Langford and D. O'Connor, (eds.) *New essays in the philosophy of education*. London: Routledge.

Pellegrini, A. and Horvat, M. (1995) A developmental contextualist critique of AD/HD, *Educational Researcher*, 24(1): 13–20.

Place, M., Wilson, J., Martin, E. and Hulsmeier, J. (2000) The frequency of emotional and behaviour disturbance in an EBD School, *Child Psychology and Psychiatry Review*, 5(2): 76–80.

Purdie, N., Hattie, J. and Carroll, A. (2002) A review of the research on interventions for attention deficit hyperactivity disorder: what works best?, *Review of Educational Research*, 72(1): 61–99.

Richards, I. (1995) ADHD, ADD and Dyslexia, in P. Cooper and K. Ideus (eds.) *Attention Deficit Hyperactivity Disorder: Educational, medical and cultural Issues*, 2nd edition, East Sutton: AWCEBD (SEBDA).

Rutter, M. and Smith, D. (eds) (1995) *Psychosocial Disorders in Young People*. Chichester: Wiley.

Rutter, M. (2002) Child psychiatry in the era following sequencing the genome, in F. Levy and D. Hay (eds.) *Attention, Genes and ADHD*. London: Routledge.

Sage, R. (2002) Start talking and stop misbehaving: teaching pupils to communicate, think and act appropriately, *Emotional and Behavioural Difficulties*, 7, 2: 85–96.

Schon, D. (1983) *The reflective practitioner: How professionals think in action*. London: Basic Books.

Schostak, J. (1982) *Maladjusted Schooling*. Lewes: Falmer.

Sergeant, J. (1995) Hyperkinetic disorder revisited, in J. Sergeant (ed.) *Eunythydis: European Approaches to Hyperkinetic Disorder*. Amsterdam: Sergeant.

Silberman, C. (1971) *Crisis in the Classroom*. New York: Random House.

Slee, R. (1995) *Changing theories and practices of discipline*. London: Falmer Press.

Sonuga-Barke, E., Taylor, E. and Hepenstall, E. (1992) Hyperactivity and delay aversion II: the effects of self versus externally imposed stimulus presentation periods on memory, *Journal of Child Psychology and Psychiatry*, 33: 399–409.

Sonuga-Barke, E., Williams, E., Hall, M. and Saxton, T. (1996) Hyperactivity and delay aversion III: the effects on cognitive style of imposing delay after errors, *Journal of Child Psychology and Psychiatry*, 37: 189–94.

Tannock, R. (1998) AD/HD: advances in cognitive, neurobiological and genetic research, *Journal of Child Psychology and Psychiatry*, 39, 1: 65–99.

Taylor, E., Sandberg, S., Thorley, G. and Giles, S. (1991) *The Epidemiology of Childhood Hyperactivity*. Oxford: Oxford University Press.

Thompson, R. (1993) *The Brain: A Neuroscience Primer*, 2nd edn. New York: Freeman.

van der Meere, J. (1996) The role of attention, in S. Sandberg (ed.) *Monographs in Child and Adolescent Psychiatry: Hyperactivity Disorders of Childhood*. Cambridge: Cambridge University Press.

Visser, J. (1997) The myth of the myth of Attention Deficit Disorder . . .", *Education Section Review*, Vol.21, 1: 97, 23–25.

Vivian, L. (1994) The changing pupil population of schools for pupils with emotional and behavioural difficulties, *Therapeutic Care and Education*, *3* (3), 218–231.

Weiss, G. and Hechtman, L. (1993) *Hyperactive Children Grown Up*, 2nd edn. New York: Guilford Press.

World Health Organization (1990) *International Classification of Diseases*, 10th edn. Geneva: WHO.

Zentall, S. S. and Stormont-Spurgin, M. (1995) Educator Preferences of Accommodations for Students with Attention Deficit Hyperactivity Disorder. *Teacher Education and Special Education*, 18, 2: 115–23.

Zentall, S. S., Hraper, G. and Stormont-Spurgin, M. (1993) Children with Hyperactivity and Their Organizational Abilities, *Journal of Educational Research*, *87*, 2: 112–17.

CHAPTER ELEVEN

Dyslexia

Gavin Reid

Introduction

This chapter examines pedagogical approaches in the area of dyslexia and relates these to the 'unique differences' position indicated by Norwich and Lewis (Chapter 1). It suggests that pedagogical approaches aimed at dyslexic children require a recognition of general teaching principles, informed through a 'specialized' knowledge base.

It can be suggested that 'dyslexia' is one of the best known, but least understood, 'disabilities'. The term dyslexia is frequently used in the popular press. There is often reference in publicity campaigns and other literature on dyslexia to famous and successful personalities who are dyslexic. Yet although the label may be known to many, it can be argued that the term dyslexia is not necessarily fully understood. There can be a gap between the use of the term 'dyslexia' on the one hand and a conceptual understanding of its defining features, characteristics and the implications of these for pedagogy on the other. This is a consequence of the longstanding and ongoing debate and controversies surrounding the nature of dyslexia, and how the label 'dyslexia' is used, or indeed misused, in practice.

The debate

There is ongoing debate relating to the nature of dyslexia and the particular neurological structures and cognitive processes that contribute to dyslexia (Snowling 2000; Fawcett 2002; Knight and Hynd 2002; Reid 2003). There is also debate on the nature of the reading difficulties experienced by children with dyslexia, particularly concerning the qualitative differences between dyslexic readers and 'garden variety poor readers' (Stanovich 1988: 96).

Similarly, some frequently applied assessment measures, particularly on the use of IQ and discrepancy criteria, in an assessment for dyslexia have been subjected to criticism (BPS 1999; Burden 2002; Reid 2003).

This was one of the aspects discussed in the working party enquiry (BPS 1999) into dyslexia and psychological assessment. The working party report suggested that 'statistically unexpected contrasts between individual norm-referenced reading test scores and those predicted on the basis of IQ scores (discrepancy criteria of dyslexia) can be criticised on theoretical grounds' (BPS 1999: 63). The working party report provided no fewer than ten different hypotheses that can be associated with dyslexia. This gives some indication of the measure of the potential confusion about the nature of dyslexia and underlines the need for a specialized knowledge base.

In relation to definitions of dyslexia the picture can also be conflicting and confusing. In the United States there is a clear focus on word decoding: 'Dyslexia is a specific learning disability that is neurobiological in origin. It is characterized by difficulties with accurate and/or fluent word recognition and by poor spelling and decoding abilities' (IDA 2003). In the UK, however, the British Dyslexia Association (BDA) provides a broader definition that focuses on visual and organizational factors, and attention, cognitive and coordination difficulties, as well as literacy difficulties (http://www.bda-dyslexia.org.uk). The definition of dyslexia in the BPS working party report also generated discussion. The report suggested that 'dyslexia is evident when accurate and fluent word reading and/or spelling develops very incompletely or with great difficulty . . . it provides the basis for a staged process of assessment through teaching' (BPS 1999: 11). This has generated considerable debate because it seems to blur any distinction, if one does exist, between dyslexic and poor readers. This would therefore imply that pedagogical approaches suitable for dyslexic children would be suitable for all children with reading difficulties, whether dyslexic or not.

Although there has been a greater emphasis on defining dyslexia there is also debate about the effectiveness of different teaching approaches (Norwich and Lewis 2001; Reid 2003). This debate has focused on phonological approaches, process-based interventions, literacy teaching (including top-down approaches), self-esteem and parental support.

One of the key aspects of the debate on dyslexia has in fact centred on the notion that children with dyslexia need different teaching and in some cases different provision. This is encapsulated in the statement that 'The growing consensus that there are common approaches to teach literacy for the diversity, including those with specific learning difficulties and the view that something different is needed that is additional [and] is not needed by most pupils' (Norwich and Lewis 2001: 321). This is further fuelled by the controversies surrounding the range of difficulties associated with dyslexia (Nicolson 2001) and the notion of dyslexia as a continuum and an umbrella or 'convenience term' (Burden 2002).

Origins of the pedagogical approaches

The 'causal modelling framework' (Morton and Frith 1995; Frith 2002) can provide a theoretical framework for conceptualizing dyslexia and therefore for understanding the origins and principles for current pedagogical approaches. Frith (2002) asserts that the definition and explanation of dyslexia has long been problematic. She suggests that a causal modelling framework involving three levels of description – behavioural, cognitive and biological – can help to clarify some of the issues relating to the concept of dyslexia.

The three levels suggested by Frith can provide a useful guide because different professionals will have different priorities and interests; for example, the teacher and psychologist will be interested in the behavioural and cognitive dimensions, while the neuro-psychologist will be interested in the neurological and biological factors. The important point is that, at all three levels, interactions with cultural and environmental influences occur. It is therefore crucial that any evaluation of pedagogical approaches should be considered within this frame of reference. This would also indicate that it is unlikely that any one approach would be successful for all children diagnosed as having dyslexia.

Phonological awareness and multisensory programmes

Most of the research and the definitions of dyslexia appear to point to the important role of phonological programmes for children with dyslexia. These usually have a prominent bottom-up phonic element and are normally linked, to a lesser degree, to top-down approaches (Connor 1994; Reid 2003). These may also be integrated with visually based approaches. Vellutino and Scanlon (1986) claim that teaching both sight and phonic strategies leads to the flexible application of these strategies in the acquisition of reading.

In the UK there has been considerable activity in the study of phonological awareness and the use of phonological approaches in assessment and teaching in relation to dyslexia. This is reflected in the development of assessment and teaching materials such as the Phonological Abilities Test (Muter *et al.* 1997), the Phonological Assessment Battery (Fredrickson *et al.* 1997), the Dyslexia Screening Tests (Fawcett and Nicolson 1996), the Listening and Literacy Index (Weedon and Reid 2001) and the Special Needs Assessment Profile (Weedon and Reid 2003). Additionally, there are many phonological teaching approaches such as Sound Linkage (Hatcher 1994), the Phonological Awareness Training Programme (Wilson 1993), the Hickey Multisensory Teaching System (Combley 2001), Phonic Code-cracker (Russell 1992), the Teaching of Handwriting, Reading and Spelling (THRASS, Davies 1998), Toe by Toe (Cowling and Cowling 1998) and the Multisensory Teaching System for Reading (Johnson *et al.* 1999), all of which have been developed and claim to be successful for children with dyslexia.

Wise *et al.* (1999) conducted a large-scale study using different forms of 'remediation' and found that the type of phonological awareness training was less important than the need to embed that training within a well structured and balanced approach to reading. Adams (1990) argues that combining phonological and 'whole language' approaches to reading should not be seen as incompatible. Indeed, it is now well accepted that poor readers rely on context more than do good readers. Language experience is therefore as vital to the dyslexic child as is a structured phonological awareness programme. This is particularly important in the secondary education sector, where it may be inappropriate to provide a phonological based programme for a dyslexic student (Nation and Snowling 1998). In the secondary sector the priority may be on language experience, print exposure and comprehension activities (Peer and Reid 2001).

The key question for the purpose of this chapter is whether these approaches need to be any different for children with dyslexia. There is evidence that the key factor for children with dyslexia is in fact how the materials and programmes are presented and how the learning outcomes are assessed (Reason 1998; Peer and Reid 2001). This would imply that the pedagogy is in fact an adaptation of class teaching.

Review and evaluation of pedagogical approaches

There is a plethora of teaching programmes that claim to be successful for children with dyslexia (see Reid 2003 for a detailed description of and comment on these). Many of these are essentially bottom-up programmes and are characterized by the following factors:

- multisensory, indicating that the programme involves visual, auditory, kinaesthetic and tactile involvement;
- sequential, involving a step-by-step approach;
- cumulative, indicating a progression, with the previous step providing a foundation for the next step;
- over-learning, a series of repetitive activities to help the learner to achieve mastery.

Walker (2000) discusses an evaluation study using the structured, cumulative, mutisensory teaching formula (Rack and Walker 1994) and shows that the pupils who were taught in this way for one to two hours a week for just over two years doubled their rate of progress in spelling and did even better in reading. According to Walker (2000) this emphasizes some key factors in developing a programme for children with dyslexia. Principally this includes the view that the student with dyslexia may need more input and a different structure of teaching from other children. It also presupposes that the teacher should be aware of (a) the factors associated with the acquisition of literacy, (b) the particular difficulties in literacy that can be noted in dyslexic children, (c) the principles of multisensory teaching, (d) the importance of selecting clear and coherent teaching aims and (e) an awarenesss of the important role played by both pre-reading strategies and proofreading, as a post-writing strategy, in the teaching of students with dyslexia.

Reason (1998) also indicated that children with dyslexia, compared with other readers, learn more slowly and need more time to learn. Fawcett (1989, 2002) suggests that the dyslexia automatization deficit hypothesis might explain this factor. She suggests that children with dyslexia have a difficulty in acquiring automaticity and need more time, through over-learning, to achieve this. It can be argued that these are underlying principles for teaching dyslexic children. These principles can also be found in many other reading and teaching programmes that can benefit all children. This would imply, therefore, that these approaches are not dyslexia-distinctive, although they may have to be applied with more intensity with dyslexic children.

Programmes and approaches

Reid (2003) has subdivided pedagogical approaches that can be used for children with dyslexia into the following categories:

- *Individualized programmes.* These are usually programmes that are highly structured. These can be seen as essentially free-standing and can form a central element of the overall strategy for teaching children with dyslexia.
- *Support approaches and strategies.* These may utilize the same principles as some of the individual programmes, but can be used more selectively by the teacher. This makes it possible to integrate them more easily into the normal activities of the curriculum.
- *Assisted learning techniques.* These strategies utilize different (and a variety of) methods but a central and essential component is the aspect of learning from others. Therefore, these programmes could involve either peer or adult support and interaction, as well as utilizing some of the principles of modeling.
- *Whole-school approaches.* These approaches recognize that dyslexia can be a whole-school concern and not just the responsibility of individual teachers. Such approaches require an established and accessible policy framework for consultancy, whole-school screening and monitoring of children's progress. Early identification is a further key aspect of a whole-school approach.

These approaches can also be viewed as incorporating the debate that forms the focus of this book. This is highlighted in Table 11.1, which suggests that the specialized and support approaches are those described in the opening chapter as 'high density' teaching and specialized adaptations. The assisted learning approaches and whole-school approaches are those that can be considered within the 'unique differences' position and the common perspectives of all learners. This implies that these approaches utilize common pedagogic principles.

Table 11.1 highlights how some established teaching programmes and strategies can be broadly categorised into the general (or group) differences position and the unique differences position. Some individualized approaches, which may require specific training to use and are generally seen as one-to-one teaching programmes, can be categorized within the general differences position. These programmes can also be supplementary to the other work taking

Table 11.1 Pedagogical approaches

General differences position	
Individualized programmes	*'Continua' of specialized approaches*
Alphabetic Phonics	Aston Portfolio
Alpha to Omega	Simultaneous oral spelling
Bangor Dyslexia Teaching System	Counselling approaches
Hickey Language Course	Visual acuity activities
Reading Recovery Programme	Word games
Toe by Toe	
THRASS	
Units of Sound	
Slingerland Orton-Gillingham Method	
Sound linkage	
Unique differences position	
Assisted learning	*Whole-school approaches*
Apprenticeship approach	Counselling strategies
Paired reading	Literacy projects
Peer tutoring	Study skills programmes
Reciprocal teaching	Thinking skills
Cued spelling	Consultancy

place within the curriculum and therefore may be seen as an 'add-on'. These individualized approaches can be supported by those under the category 'continua of specialized approaches' because the latter can link with the type of intensive input from the individualized approaches. For example, the Hickey language course can be enriched by some of the approaches in the 'continua' section, such as word games and counselling approaches. These approaches can be seen to be located within the general differences position.

The unique differences position relates to approaches that are intended for all children as a means of accessing literacy. For example, paired reading and peer tutoring can be beneficial to all readers. However, at the same time there is evidence that they can help 'reading delayed' children (Topping 2000). Similarly, whole-school approaches, which are essentially aimed at all children irrespective of whether they have literacy difficulties or not, may also benefit children with reading difficulties. This was noted, for example, in some of the reading projects reported in Reid (1998) that took place in Sunderland, Knowsley and Newcastle. For example, in the Knowsley project the evaluation cited an average 20 month improvement in reading over a one-year period (Brooks et al. 1996).

Many of the evidenced-based approaches for dyslexia are principally based on evaluation studies of individual programmes, examining gains in reading and spelling over an identified period of time. Some of the individual programmes have been evaluated positively. Hornsby and Miles (1980) conducted a series of investigations examining 'dyslexia-centred teaching' programmes with the aim of evaluating how effective these programmes were in alleviating dyslexia. This study and a follow-up study (Hornsby and Farmer 1993) indicate that the programmes did result in an improvement in terms of pupils' reading and spelling ages. Additionally, other programme providers have published reports on the effectiveness of particular programmes, as well as independent evaluations. For example, Johnson (1999) reported on the Multisensory Teaching Scheme for Reading and Moss (2000) on Units of Sound and other programmes, such as Bangor Dyslexia Teaching System (Turner 2002) and the teaching of reading through spelling.

Underlying principles/learning strategies

Snowling (2000) reports on a number of phonological intervention studies. One of particular interest is that conducted by Wise *et al.* (1999). They used a range of phonological interventions with three groups of children, all with severe reading deficits, and compared three different interventions, all of which related to phonological acquisition. It was concluded that, overall, there was little evidence that the type of phonological training mattered. Wise *et al.* suggest that their findings lend support to the view that work on phonological awareness, prior to and integrated within a well structured approach to reading, is helpful for children with specific reading difficulties.

According to Townsend (2000), an effective teaching programme for dyslexic children should include, apart from phonological aspects, other factors such as the promotion of attention and listening, the development of spoken language, the development of fine motor skills and handwriting, sequencing and directionality and the development of short- and long-term memory skills. It has been well documented that the principles of a teaching programme for dyslexic children include multisensory, structured, cumulative and sequential aspects. Additionally, it is likely that the programme will also have a phonic emphasis even though a number of dyslexic children may present with more pronounced visual difficulties, rather than those of a phonic nature (Everett 2002). One of the important points to be considered is the view that each dyslexic child should be viewed as an individual and therefore any pedagogical programme should not be overly prescriptive because adaptations will have to be made to accommodate to the individual's needs.

Critique and evaluation of practice

Pumfrey and Reason (1992: 113) recognize the potential difficulties in evaluating pedagogical approaches for dyslexia when they suggest that 'The key issue is whether the considerable range of teaching/learning methods, techniques and materials currently available are differentially effective with pupils having identifiably different learning characteristics.' They also suggest that one of the important aspects of pedagogical approaches for children with dyslexia is the quality of teaching. They state that 'one important aspect of teaching quality is the knowledge, ability and willingness to look critically at the evidence . . . in support of particular methods' (*ibid.*: 125). The view held by Pumfrey and Reason in 1992 still holds good today; they suggest that, for conceptual reasons, there is unlikely ever to be a panacea for dyslexia. This is worthy of consideration in the light of the aim of this chapter to examine the evidence for specific pedagogical approaches for dyslexia. It can be argued that while the evidence may support one approach over another, crucial aspects such as the quality of teaching, the resources available and the nature and availability of training programmes need to be considered and weighed against environmental considerations. There is, however, no evidence that the implementation of these approaches represents an 'alternative' classroom pedagogy.

International dimension

It is acknowledged in the BPS (1999) report that dyslexia can occur across languages, cultures, socio-economic status, race and gender. However, while dyslexia is recognized in most countries, there are still across-cultural differences in perceptions and definitions of dyslexia. These perceptions can be a result of policy differences or factors attributed to the language of the country. In the UK, it is estimated that there are two million severely dyslexic individuals, including 375,000 school children (Smythe 2002). In contrast, there are no such estimates in China. Whether this reflects perceived importance or differences in incidence is as yet unknown; however, it is known that differences in awareness will lead to variations in provision. For example, Wydell (2003) argues that phonological processing deficits, which are a common indicator of dyslexia in most countries, do not necessarily impede the acquisition of reading in Japanese. This is because the units of writing are larger than the phoneme unit and the language has perfect symmetry between letters and sounds. Goswami (2000) proposes that the phonological representations hypothesis 'offers a unifying causal framework at the cognitive level for many of the difficulties faced by dyslexic children in different languages'. She suggests that orthographic transparency together with within-child speech processing factors will influence the speed and efficiency of representations at the phonemic level. She also suggests that children who are learning to read in non-transparent languages will acquire reading and spelling more slowly than do children who are learning to read and spell in transparent orthographies.

Goulandris (2003: 12) suggests, in relation to dyslexia in different languages, that there is a recurrent theme, such as the view that 'language specific differences account for significant individual differences in performances in phonological awareness and reading and spelling ability'. She also suggests that the evidence points to difficulties in phonological processing as the core difficulty in dyslexics in all countries. This was so even though in some languages (such as German, Greek and Dutch) the dyslexics were able to perform many of the simpler tasks with ease, but when they were faced with more challenging tasks, such as 'spoonersims', phonological memory tasks or rapid naming, performance deficits were reported. Therefore, it follows that if dyslexic children are required to learn irregular languages (such as English and French), reading, spelling and phonological difficulties will be evident. If they are exposed to regular orthographies (such as Italian or Spanish) 'the underlying impairments will be masked by their apparently proficient literacy skills' (*ibid.*: 13). It has been noted above that there is a generic element to the underlying principles suggested for pedagogy for dyslexic children and this would imply that there is not a distinctive 'dyslexia' curriculum, as these principles would benefit all learners. This view appears also to be supported by the international studies because the specific approaches would vary depending on the attributes and characteristics of the language used in each country, although the underlying principles indicated earlier in this chapter may still be valid.

Conclusion

This chapter has sought to highlight the view that an understanding of the various aspects that contribute to dyslexia, through reference to a framework, such as the casual modelling framework (Morton and Frith 1995), is necessary in order to guide and monitor the progress of children identified as dyslexic. While it is recognized that a cluster of characteristics may contribute to dyslexia, it is also understood that there will be differences in the nature and extent of these in individual children. For that reason, it is futile to talk of a distinctive dyslexia pedagogy; we need to view the teaching of dyslexic children within a framework that incorporates specialized knowledge of the child together with the application of a range of teaching principles and learning approaches.

It is also noted in this chapter that the conceptual understanding of dyslexia may be a matter of some controversy, particularly in relation to the identification criteria. The notion of focusing on the 'barriers to learning' may be a more helpful way of identifying and planning intervention. In relation to the underlying conceptual framework of this book, it is suggested in this chapter that the pedagogical approaches for dyslexia are essentially 'adaptations of common teaching approaches' and these adaptations can vary in density depending on individual needs. This, as indicated in Chapter 1 of this book, can have significant implications for inclusive practices.

Summary

Nature of the group

- There is ongoing debate about the nature of dyslexia, regarding differences between dyslexic and garden variety readers, and identification models.
- Potential confusion underlines the need for specialized knowledge.
- A causal modelling framework (biological, cognitive, behavioural interacting with environment) is needed as the basis for considering pedagogic issues.

Pedagogy

- Many teaching approaches are claimed to be successful for this group – these are usually bottom-up programmes.

- Underlying principles can be found in other teaching programmes for other children – when applied to this group it is question of intensity.
- There are difficulties in evaluating pedagogical approaches.
- The quality of teaching, resources and training is also important.

Curriculum

- Not addressed as relevant.

Knowledge

- There is a need for approaches that include specialized knowledge about the child and the condition, despite confusion about the nature of dyslexia.

Individual versus general differences as pedagogic base

- There is support for the unique differences position. General teaching principles are informed through a specialized knowledge base; there is no 'alternative classroom pedagogy'.

Notable aspects introduced

- The BPS definition of dyslexia blurs the distinction between dyslexic and other poor readers, leading to support for the unique differences position.
- Analysis of different approaches: individualized, support approaches, assisted learning and whole school approaches
- Individualized approaches can be seen as adopting the general differences position, though this is not justified.
- Focussing on barriers to learning is useful for identifying and planning intervention.

References

Adams, M. J. (1990) *Beginning to Read: The New Phonics in Context*. Oxford: Heinemann.

British Psychological Society (1999) *Dyslexia, Literacy and Psychological Assessment*. Leicester: British Psychological Society.

Brooks, G., Cato, V., Fernandes, C. and Tregenza, A. (1996) *The Knowsley Reading Project: Using Trained Reading Helpers Effectively*. London: NFER.

Burden, R. (2002) A cognitive approach to dyslexia; learning styles and thinking skills, in G. Reid and J. Wearmouth (eds) *Dyslexia and Literacy, Theory and Practice*. Chichester: Wiley.

Combley, M. (2001) *The Hickey Multisensory Language Course*, 3rd edn. London: Whurr.

Connor, M. (1994) Specific learning difficulty (dyslexia) and interventions, *Support for Learning*, 9: 114–19.

Cowling, H. and Cowling, K. (1998) *Toe by Toe, Mutlisensory Manual for Teachers and Parents*. Bradford.

Davies, A. (1998) *Handwriting, Reading and Spelling System* (THRASS). London: Collins Educational.

Everett, J. (2002) Visual processes, in G. Reid and J. Wearmouth (eds) *Dyslexia and Literacy, Theory and Practice*. Chichester: Wiley.

Fawcett, A. (1989) Automaticity: a new framework for dyslexic research. Paper presented at the First International Conference of the British Dyslexia Association, Bath.

Fawcett, A. (2002) Dyslexia and literacy: key issues for research, in G. Reid and J. Wearmouth (eds) *Dyslexia and Literacy, Theory and Practice*. Chichester: Wiley.

Fawcett, A. J. and Nicolson, R. I. (1996) *The Dyslexia Screening Test*. London: The Psychological Corporation Europe.

Frederickson, N., Frith, V. and Reason, R. (1997) *Phonological Assessment Battery*. London: NFER/Nelson.

Frith, U. (2002) Resolving the paradoxes of dyslexia, in G. Reid and J. Wearmouth (eds) *Dyslexia and Literacy, Theory and Practice*. Chichester: Wiley.

Goswami, U. (2000) Phonological representations, reading development and dyslexia: towards a cross-linguistic theoretical framework, *Dyslexia*, 6: 133–251.

Goulandris, N. (ed.) (2003) *Dyslexia in Different Languages: Cross-linguistic Comparisons*. London: Whurr.

Hatcher, P. (1994) *Sound Linkage. An Integrated Programme for Overcoming Reading Difficulties*. London: Whurr.

Hornsby, B. and Farmer, M. (1993) Some effects of a dyslexia centred teaching programme, in P. D. Pumfrey, and C. D. Elliott (eds) *Children's Difficulties in Reading, Spelling and Writing*. London: Falmer Press.

Hornsby, B. and Miles T. R. (1980) The effects of a dyslexic-centred teaching programme, *British Journal of Educational Psychology*, 50(3): 236–42.

International Dyslexia Association (2003) *Perspectives, Volume 29*. Baltimore: IDA (http://www.interdys.org).

Johnson, M., Philips, S. and Peer, L. (1999) *Multisensory Teaching System for Reading*. Manchester: Special Educational Needs Centre, Didsbury School of Education, Manchester Metropolitan University.

Knight, D. F. and Hynd, G. W. (2002) The neurobiology of dyslexia, in G. Reid and J. Wearmouth (eds) *Dyslexia and Literacy, Theory and Practice*. Chichester: Wiley.

Morton, J. and Frith, U. (1995) Causal modelling: a structural to a developmental psychopathology, in D. Cicchetti and D. J. Cohen (eds) *Manual of Developmental Psychopathology*. New York: Wiley.

Moss, H. (2000) Using literacy development programmes, in J. Townend and M. Turner (eds) *Dyslexia in Practice: A Guide for Teachers*. New York: Kluwer Academic.

Muter, V., Hulme, C. and Snowling, M. (1997) *Phonological Abilities Test*. London: Psychological Corporation.

Nation, K. and Snowling, M. J. (1998) Individual differences in contextual facilitation; evidence from dyslexia and poor reading comprehension, *Child Development*, 69: 996–1011.

Nicolson, R. I. (2001) Developmental dyslexia: into the future, in A. Fawcett (ed.) *Dyslexia, Theory and Good Practice*. London: Whurr.

Norwich, B. and Lewis, A. (2001) Mapping a pedagogy for special educational needs, *British Educational Research Journal*, 27(3): 313–31.

Peer, L. and Reid, G. (eds) (2001) *Dyslexia: Successful Inclusion in the Secondary School*. London: David Fulton.

Pumfrey, P. (2001) Specific developmental dyslexia: 'basics to back' in 2000 and beyond?, in M. Hunter-Carsch (ed.) *Dyslexia, A Psychosocial Perspective*. London: Whurr.

Pumfrey, P. D. and Reason, R. (1992) *Specific Learning Difficulties (Dyslexia) Challenges and Responses*. Windsor: NFER/Nelson.

Rack, J. P., Snowling, M. J. and Olson, R. K. (1992) The non-word reading deficit in dyslexia: a review, *Reading Research Quarterly*, 27: 29–53.

Rack, J. and Walker, J. (1994) Does dyslexia institute teaching work?, reprinted from *Dyslexia Review*, 6(2).

Reason, R. (1998) Does the 'specific' in specific learning difficulties make a difference to the way we teach?, *Educational and Child Psychology*, 15(1): 71–83.

Reid, G. (1998) *Dyslexia: A Practitioners Handbook*, 2nd edn. Chichester: Wiley.

Reid, G. (2003) *Dyslexia: A Practitioners Handbook*, 3rd edn. Chichester: Wiley.

Russell, S. (1992) *Phonic Code Cracker*. Glasgow: Jordanhill College.

Smythe, I. (2002) Cognitive factors underlying reading and spelling difficulties: a cross-linguistic study, Unpublished PhD thesis, University of Surrey.

Snowling, M. J. (2000) *Dyslexia*, 2nd edn. Oxford: Blackwell.

Stanovich, K. E. (1988) Explaining the difference between the dyslexic and the garden-variety poor readers: the phonological core model, *Journal of Learning Disabilities*, 21(10): 590–604.

Stanovich, K. E. (1996) Towards a more inclusive definition of dyslexia, *Dyslexia*, 2(3): 154–66.

Topping, K. (2000) Parents and peers as tutors for dyslexic children, in G. Reid (ed.) *Dimensions of Dyslexia, Volume 2, Literacy, Language and Learning*. Edinburgh: Moray House.

Townend, J. (2000) Phonological Awareness and Other Foundation Skills of Literacy, in J. Townend and M. Turner (eds) *Dyslexia in Practice: A Guide for Teachers*. New York: Kluwer Academic.

Turner, E. (2002) Multisensory teaching and tutoring, in *The Dyslexia Handbook 2002*. Reading: BDA.

Vellutino, F. R. and Scanlon, D. M. (1986) Experimental evidence for the effects of instructional bias on word identification, *Exceptional Children*, 53(2): 145–55.

Walker, J. (2000) Teaching basic reading and spelling, in J. Townend and M. Turner (eds) *Dyslexia in Practice: A Guide for Teachers*. New York: Kluwer Academic.

Weedon, C. and Reid, G. (2001) *Listening and Literacy Index*. London: Hodder and Stoughton.

Weedon, C. and Reid, G. (2003) *Special Needs Assessment Profile (SNAP)*. London: Hodder and Stoughton.

Wilson, J. (1993) *Phonological Awareness Training Programme*. London: University College London Educational Psychology Publishing.

Wimmer, H. (1993) Characteristics of developmental dyslexia in a regular writing system, *Applied Psycholinguistics*, 14(1): 1–33.

Wise, B. W., Ring, J. and Olson, R. (1999) Training phonological awareness with and without explicit attention to articulation, *Journal of Experimental Child Psychology*, 72: 271–304.

Wydell, T. N. (2003) Dyslexia in Japanese and the 'hypothesis of granularity and transparency', in N. Goulandris (ed.) *Dyslexia in Different Languages: Cross-linguistic Comparisons*. London: Whurr.

CHAPTER TWELVE

Dyspraxia

Madeleine Portwood

Introduction

For decades, the development of language and literacy skills has been a focal issue of the teaching profession. The acquisition of these skills is measured as an indicator of 'good teaching' even in children with significant special educational needs. However, not all educational practice is developed from research-based theory. The idea that teachers teach and children learn is a curriculum model that has not acknowledged many studies of pedagogy and child development and their contributions to our understanding of teaching and learning.

Grinder (1989) notes that 'The process of education is determined by the process of communication'. Children with dyspraxia have difficulty communicating, especially when there is a requirement to produce handwritten work. The focus of this chapter is to identify the characteristics of this neurodevelopmental disorder and review published research into the development of language and literacy skills in children with dyspraxia to determine whether there is evidence to support the idea that they need a special and distinct kind of teaching or whether it is the teachers' knowledge of the learning difficulty that best directs strategy.

Defining the focal pupil group

Children who have problems planning and executing tasks with a motor-skill component are evident in every classroom. They are described as having 'perceptual motor dysfunction', 'sensory integrative dysfunction', 'deficits in attention, motor control and perception (DAMP)', 'developmental dyspraxia', 'clumsy child syndrome' (Missiuna and Polatajko 1995). Although the condition was first recognized in the early twentieth century, increasing awareness has provided evidence that demonstrates prevalence in 5 per cent of primary-aged schoolchildren (Gubbay 1975; Henderson and Hall 1982; Kadjeso and Gillberg 2001). This prompted recognition by the American Psychiatric Association (1994) and the World Health Organization of a distinct movement-skill syndrome classified as 'developmental coordination disorder' (DCD). At an international consensus meeting held to debate these different labels, the definition of DCD was accepted by researchers and clinicians (Polatajko *et al.* 1995).

Diagnostic features of developmental coordination disorder

The essential feature of DCD (see DSM-IV 1994) is a marked impairment in the development of motor coordination (criterion A). The diagnosis is made only if this impairment significantly interferes with academic achievement or activities of daily living (criterion B). The diagnosis is made if the coordination difficulties are not due to a general medical condition (e.g. cerebral palsy, hemiplegia or muscular dystrophy) and the criteria are not met for pervasive developmental disorder (criterion C). If mental retardation is present, the motor difficulties are in excess of those usually associated with it (criterion D). The manifestations of this disorder vary with age and development. For example, younger children may display clumsiness and delays in achieving development motor milestones (e.g. walking, crawling, sitting, tying shoe-laces, buttoning shirts, zipping trousers). Older children may display difficulties with the motor aspects of assembling puzzles, building models, playing ball and printing or writing.

Associated features and disorders

Problems commonly associated with DCD include delays in other non-motor milestones; associated disorders may include phonological disorder and expressive language disorder. The prevalence of DCD has been estimated to be as high as 6 per cent for children in the age range of five to eleven years. Recognition of DCD usually occurs when the child first attempts such tasks as running, holding a knife and fork, buttoning clothes or playing ball games. Its progression is variable. In some cases, lack of coordination continues through adolescence and adulthood.

Differential diagnosis

DCD must be distinguished from motor impairments that are due to a general medical condition (see Chapter 8). Problems in coordination may be associated with specific neurological disorders (e.g. cerebral palsy, progressive lesions of the cerebellum), but in these cases, there is definite neural damage and abnormal findings on neurological examination. If mental retardation is present, DCD can be diagnosed only if the motor difficulties are in excess of those usually associated with the mental retardation. A diagnosis of DCD is not given if the criteria are met for a pervasive developmental disorder. Individuals with attention deficit/hyperactivity disorder may fall, bump into things or knock things over, but this is usually due to distractibility and impulsiveness rather than to a motor impairment. If criteria for both disorders are met, both diagnoses can be given.

Summary of diagnostic criteria for DCD

A Performance in daily activities that require motor coordination is substantially below that expected given the person's chronological age and measured intelligence. This may be manifested by marked delays in achieving motor milestones (e.g. walking, crawling, sitting), dropping things, 'clumsiness', poor performance in sports or poor handwriting.
B The disturbance in criterion A significantly interferes with academic achievement or activities of daily living.
C The disturbance is not due to a general medical condition (e.g. cerebral palsy, hemiplegia or muscular dystrophy) and does not meet criteria for a pervasive developmental disorder.
D If mental retardation is present, the motor difficulties are in excess of those usually associated with it.

DCD and co-occurring neurodevelopmental disorders

Although childhood developmental disorders are classified into discrete categories, in many cases children display the characteristics of several: comorbidity is widespread (Dewey *et al.* 2000). Research evidence suggests that between 50 and 80 per cent of children with a diagnosis meet the criteria for at least two disorders (Biederman *et al.* 1990). Children with coordination difficulties commonly have other conditions, such as attention deficit/hyperactivity disorder (AD/HD; see Chapter 10), dyslexia (see Chapter 11) and speech and language impairments (see Chapter 8; COT/NAPOT 2003).

Substantive research connecting dyslexia with deficits in motor skills was published by Duffy and Geschwind (1985). Denckla *et al.* (1985) reported that dyslexic children showed impaired development in tests relating to speed of movement, balance and coordination.

The acquisition of motor skills, more specifically the 'automaticity of motor development', has been the focus of much research undertaken by Fawcett and Nicolson since the early 1990s. They discovered that children with dyslexia put more effort into 'planning' sequential movements when compared with 'controls' matched for age and ability. Further research showed a relationship between deficits in motor skills and speed of articulation and processing of sound sequences in children and adults with dyslexia (Fawcett and Nicolson 1999).

Wolff (1999) also links impaired motor skills with language delay. In this study of dyslexic children 90 per cent of those with motor coordination deficits also had motor speech deficits measured by a task involving repetitious syllable production. He concludes: 'the detailed analysis of co-articulation in speech production may be one pathway by which impaired timing precision in motor action impinges on reading and writing deficits in Developmental Dyslexia'.

Ramus *et al.* (2003), reporting on a study into motor control and phonology in dyslexic children, suggest that part of the discrepancy in their motor skills is due to dyslexic individuals who had the additional disorders AD/HD and DCD. The purpose of this study was to attempt to replicate the findings of Fawcett and Nicolson: that dyslexic children are impaired on a range of tasks involving manual dexterity, balance, coordination and that motor dysfunction might be the cause of dyslexia. Wimmer *et al.* (1998) suggested that the presence of AD/HD in any study sample of dyslexic children would account for the variance in the percentage of individuals identified with coordination difficulties. Kaplan *et al.* (1998) reported that 63 per cent of the dyslexic children in their study also had DCD. Research involving more than 600 school-aged children with dyspraxia indicated that there was a co-occurrence with dyslexia in more than 50 per cent of those studied (Portwood 1999, 2000).

Silver (1992) and Dewey *et al.* (2000) reported that many children with generalized learning difficulties display DCD. Kaplan *et al.* (2000) reported Canadian research showing that 58 per cent of the sample of children with AD/HD displayed reading disabilities and 27 per cent of these children with AD/HD had DCD. Moreover, 82 per cent of the children with DCD displayed some other co-morbid disorder. They conclude by stating: 'this research suggests that the co-morbidity of developmental disorders appears to be the rule rather than the exception'. In addition, Gillberg and colleagues have described autistic features, behavioural problems and depression/anxiety as co-occurring with DCD (Klin *et al.* 1995; Gillberg 1998; Rasmussen and Gillberg 2000).

Do studies of DCD consider that it is an homogeneous group?

The literature describing DCD includes wide-ranging terminology and criteria. Sugden and Keogh (1990) found that the characteristics of children diagnosed with DCD depended upon the source of referral, the professional background of the assessor and the type of assessment used.

Interpretation of the literature on DCD is further compounded by the lack of inclusion criteria. Geuze *et al.* (2001) reviewed 164 publications on the study of DCD and found that only 60 per cent were based on objective criteria, as there is no 'generally accepted' level of motor proficiency (Sugden and Keogh 1990) to define clumsiness. As a result, Geuze *et al.* (2001) recommended that a child scoring below the fifteenth percentile on standardized tests of motor skill (Henderson and Sugden 1992) and having an IQ score above 69 (Wechsler Intelligence Scales) would qualify for a diagnosis of DCD. Missiuna (1996) concludes that all children with DCD have some impairment of motor skill, in the absence of other physical and intellectual disorders. However, they are certainly not an homogenous group: 'this is why many treatment methods have been largely ineffectual'.

DCD and associated learning difficulties

Support is given to children with DCD who have difficulties accessing the curriculum but provision shows great variation between settings, which is unsurprising, given this lack of homogeneity. Learning difficulties and DCD may be caused by the same underlying mechanism; learning difficulties may coexist in some children who have DCD; or learning difficulties may develop as secondary complications when a child has DCD.

Learning difficulties and DCD

Although the literature in this area is inconclusive, children with DCD appear to experience a particular cluster of learning difficulties described as 'non-verbal learning disabilities' (NLD), and intervention should address the academic difficulties that a child is actually experiencing (Missiuna 1996).

Rourke (1989, 1995) described two types of learning difficulty: individuals with a basic phonological processing disorder (BPPD) who were assessed as having lower verbal than performance IQs and those characterized as having non-verbal learning disability (NLD) had lower performance IQs. NLD was characterized by evidence of poor performance on tasks requiring visual-spatial organisation together with poor psycho-motor, tactile perceptual and conceptual skills and abilities.

Rourke *et al.* (1986) compared the performances of children identified with NLD and a group of adults who on assessment using the Wechsler Scales had greater verbal IQ than performance IQ. The patterns of age-related performances of the adults and children identified through neuropsychometric assessment were almost identical. Portwood (1999) replicated the results obtained by Rourke (1995) in a study of UK children aged three to 16.

In younger pupils verbal scores are generally within the average range, but the non-verbal (performance) sub-test scores show difficulties in the perceptual component: geometric design, block design and mazes. Difficulties with perception persisted in older pupils (coding, block design) and additional problems were found with short-term memory. The pattern of strengths and weaknesses, it can be argued, gives some insight into the children's learning difficulties (Rourke 1998). Such knowledge could provide the 'key to effective teaching strategies'.

Translating this information into classroom behaviour, the child struggles to achieve a perceptual understanding of mathematics. Spatial and perceptual problems make abstract thinking difficult. This has a profound effect on organizational skills. Maintaining attention and translating thoughts into actions are also problematic. The combination of perceptual and motor-planning difficulties makes handwriting very difficult, a factor that impacts greatly on the communication of ideas. Children with DCD rely heavily on language to supplement their learning. However, it is suggested that 82 per cent of teacher-communicated information is non-verbal (Grinder 1989). This impacts greatly on children with non-verbal learning disabilities.

Ozols and Rourke (1988) suggested that children with NLD, besides having a particular configuration of academic learning difficulties, also exhibit severe psychosocial disturbance, which becomes more evident over time: children with the NLD profile are usually described by parents as emotionally or behaviourally disturbed. In contrast, children with dyslexia are identified with behavioural difficulties at a much lower frequency (Rourke *et al.* 1986). A screening of 69 juveniles (aged from 15 years 2 months to 16 years 11 months) at Deerbolt Young Offenders Institute (Portwood 1999), where inmates were assessed using the Weschler Intelligence Scales for Children III, identified:

- 13 young people with generalized learning difficulties (19 per cent);
- 41 young people with coordination and non-verbal learning difficulties (dyspraxia) (61 per cent);
- 19 of these (41) young people also had symptoms of dyslexia, suggesting that the co-occurrence of dyslexia and dyspraxia in this sample was 46 per cent;
- 34 young people had a reading ability of nine years or less (52 per cent).

It seems evident from this study that young offenders are more likely to have NLD than to have other specific learning difficulties. However, are these emotional and behavioural problems characteristic of the DCD profile, or the result of a social/educational system that fails to meet their needs? Children with DCD may develop secondary complications (Missiuna 2003).

Identifying the child in the classroom

There is a wealth of information listing the problems faced by children with DCD in the nursery school environment. The Dyspraxia Foundation leaflet 'Dyspraxia in Primary/Secondary Schools' describes these observed behaviours:

- high levels of motor activity;
- delayed acquisition of language;
- problems with tasks involving a perceptual component;
- immature social skills;
- literal use of language;
- poor listening skills;
- handwriting difficulties with both style and speed;
- poor visual and auditory memory;
- poor organizational skills;
- poor body posture and difficulties coordinating movement.

Do observed behaviours inform strategy?

Strategies are specific techniques for solving problems and there are many different strategies. Working forward to reach a solution or backward from an assumed solution are strategies. Which strategy is more efficient depends on the nature of the problem (Williams 1986).

The 'strategies' to support the dyspraxic/DCD child summarized below are presented in numerous publications (Ripley et al. 1997; Portwood 1999; Kirby and Drew 2002; Dyspraxia Foundation, www. dyspraxiafoundation. org.uk):

- Seating should be comfortable, ensuring that the child is able to rest both feet flat on the floor and maintain an upright posture.
- The desk should be at elbow height with a facility to use a sloping surface for reading.
- The child should be able to view the teacher without turning round.
- Attach paper to the desk to avoid the necessity of having to hold it in position.
- Use paper that matches the child's handwriting difficulties:

  (a) Widely spaced lines for a child who writes very large.
  (b) Raised, lined paper for a child who has trouble writing within the lines.
  (c) Graph paper for a child whose writing is too large or improperly spaced.
  (d) Graph paper with large squares for a child who has trouble keeping numbers aligned in mathematics.

- Try to reduce the amount of handwriting required.
- Teach children specific handwriting strategies that encourage them to print or write letters in a consistent manner. Use thin magic markers or pencil grips if they seem to help the child to improve pencil grasp or to reduce pencil pressure on the page.
- Focus on the target of the activity: judge content rather than presentation.
- Explore alternate methods of recording, e.g. drawings, mind maps, tape recorder.
- Break down activities into small achievable targets.
- Repeat verbal instructions and reinforce with a visual cue.
- Provide opportunities for the child to access a higher level of adult support.
- Give praise and positive feedback.
- Allow extra time for the completion of a task.

These listed recommendations provide little direction for teachers to help them to understand the underlying principles of a strategy supposedly directed to extend the child's thinking and learning.

To achieve this, it is important to identify a relationship between the particular neurological pattern of non-verbal learning difficulties evident in children with DCD and their learning style. However, there is also considerable overlap with the presenting behaviours associated with other neurodevelopmental disorders, which will necessarily affect teaching and learning. So, while a neurodevelopmental profile supports the notion that children with DCD can be categorized into a specific special educational needs sub-group, effective teaching strategies could apply equally to groups of learners classified by learning style. An example would be to consider gender ratios in this 'specific' group. The pedagogic needs of boys and the requirement of the National

Curriculum with particular regard to literacy have raised many concerns among educationalists.

Many children with DCD exhibit competencies in language tasks, particularly poetry (Portwood 2000). Indeed, it is an area in which they can excel if the teacher is able to find a means of overcoming the speed of information processing difficulties, handwriting problems and distractibility when there are additional factors, such as sound or movement in the classroom.

In one learning environment, Jonathan, aged six, had work differentiated to 'meet the needs' of the lower set of eight pupils (six boys, two girls) with behavioural/learning difficulties in a Year 2 class. He spent much of his time under the table seeking his broken pencil and making 'clicking' noises. His concentration on written tasks was described as less than 30 seconds. However, it was acknowledged that his verbal skills could be improved if he could remain focused. He had a measured reading age of 12+ years.

The following term Jonathan changed schools and was allowed, through negotiation with the class teacher, to sit in the cupboard at the side of the classroom (door open) when he needed to write. He was unable to use lined paper. To sequence his thoughts, he preferred to draw boxes and write his sentences inside them. When describing the structure for his poem, he said, 'I knew that if I made five marks down and wrote on either side, that would give me six lines. I did it four times because I wanted to write four verses.' Jonathan was six years seven months old when he wrote 'Once upon a wintertime'. It was word-processed by his teacher, and displayed, with the original alongside, on the classroom wall (Figure 12.1).

Returning to the discussion paper produced by HMI (2000: para. 23), there are obvious concerns about the teaching of boys: 'There is clearly no simple answer to the challenge how to raise the achievement of boys – especially in writing.' Reference is then made to the HMCI (1999) report: 'Boys respond particularly well to direct interactive teaching. There are important implications here for raising their achievement.' Clearly the suggestion is that boys need distinct kinds of teaching strategies and as they comprise the greater proportion of pupils identified with learning and behavioural difficulties, published research should inform the decisions and actions of teachers working with all groups of pupils with SEN.

However, in published literature on SEN-specific pedagogy for pupils with DCD, there is very little empirical evidence to support the persistent claims that specialist teaching improves learning outcomes. Many currently used interventions have not been experimentally evaluated. While there is evidence of improved reading scores and reductions in excitability in children who have accessed a range of motor-skill interventions, few make comparisons with randomized controls. Good intentions do not necessarily ensure good outcomes (Fitz-Gibbon 2000). Many studies reporting the effects of specific educational interventions are based on subjective impressions and informal observations. This does not, however, suggest that change/improvement has not occurred, but objective research is necessary.

An explanation as to the lack of empirical data on studies of educational interventions was suggested by Prideaux (2002). Well controlled, randomized trials are difficult because 'while randomisation is theoretically possible in educational research, it is often not feasible or justifiable. A second issue is the control of variables. The intervention itself may be variable. The process of education depends on the context and a myriad of factors including facilities and resources, teacher and student maturation, individual expectation and institutional ethos affect the process.' Despite the absence of empirical evidence relating to studies of children with DCD, it is still possible to comment as to whether a system (school/teaching) should be adapted to meet their individual needs, or whether they, as a specific SEN group, should adapt to a system.

Children with DCD generally have a preferred learning style but, with the majority having co-occurring disorders, they will also display unique differences. In the classroom, it is difficult to meet the needs of all the pupils all of the time, but there can be an accommodation of individual differences as was the case with Jonathan; he was not alone in requiring a distraction-free environment for part of the school day.

The awareness of DCD in the teaching profession is relatively new, when compared with other learning difficulties. There are now numerous research projects being carried out in the UK, Holland, Sweden, Australia, Canada and the USA, but it may be some time before there is sufficient substantive evidence supporting a specific pedagogical approach. Targets within the National Curriculum apply to pupils with DCD but there should be some accommodation regarding the completion of the task (this allows for problems with speed of information processing) and the method of communication, i.e. is it possible to give a verbal rather than handwritten response?

Currently the support given to children in this specific SEN group is dependent upon the teacher's knowledge and understanding of the associated learning difficulties. The children are therefore most likely to access teaching from within the continuum of common teaching strategies, which apply to all learners. With increasing awareness of the visual/perceptual and organizational problems experienced by these children, teachers would be able to assume the general (group) differences position and utilize specific teaching strategies in the classroom to accommodate this defined group of learners.

Barnhart *et al.* (2003) specify that the directions for research into DCD should include determining:

- the most appropriate level of intervention intensity;
- which interventions provide results that generalize to the environment;
- the effect environmental adaptations have on performance;
- whether improved motor skills lead to improved learning and, if so, the process involved that leads to the improvement.

Education is a discipline that is rich in theory. One of the functions of this theory is to make predictions about outcomes that can be tested empirically. With DCD, there clearly is a need to research the effects of educational interventions, but the research must be designed so that the findings can be truly ascribed to the strategy (Prideaux 2002).

Figure 12.1 A poem by Jonathan, aged 6 years 7 months

Once Upon a Wintertime

The south wind will rest and the north
wind will blow
Crashes of mountains all full with snow
Nothing will crash, nothing will float
Nothing's exciting, nothing like boat
I heard a sound, first a crash
Then was a clatter, last was a smash

700 years or so
7000 years ago
Windows, curtains, chimney, roof
It's Christmas time, I'm telling the truth
I have made a little rhyme
Once upon a wintertime

No candle, no light, no dirt, no bin
No sparrows, no birds, no robins they sing
All of the pigeons have gone to their nest
The children are sleeping; they're doing
their best
Now every time I read a book
The faster I ran, the candle I shook

I marked my hand with biro or pen
It's Christmas time, now and then
Sing and sing, song and song
Learning you were right, learning you were
wrong
All is right, no not crime
Once upon a wintertime

Summary

Nature of the group

- Varied terms are used to describe the group; DCD is the favoured one.
- Some reflect overlaps with other areas of difficulties, or are associated with other difficulties (dyslexia and AD/HD are the rule rather than the exception).
- DCD differential diagnosis is in terms of a specific difficulty relative to age and cognitive abilities that impacts on school learning, not general medical condition. If mental retardation is present, motor difficulties are in excess of this.
- DCD is not a homogeneous group; there is great variation within the group, linked to why many interventions are not effective.
- DCD is associated with non-verbal learning disabilities (NLD), where verbal abilities are significantly greater than performance abilities.
- The author's work confirms these US findings about DCD-associated learning difficulties.
- NLD is also found to be associated with severe psycho-social disturbance, and the author's work confirms this.

Pedagogy

- One approach translates the DCD performance profile into implications for pedagogy.
- Teaching approaches for DCD/dyspraxia are recommended, which is in line with the general differences position, but these strategies could equally apply to other children with other kinds of difficulties.
- As more boys than girls have DCD/dyspraxia, it may be relevant to consider teaching approaches relevant to gender-based pedagogic strategies.
- Some children with DCD have competencies in language area, and this can be built on.

Curriculum

- Not covered.

Knowledge

- It is implied that teachers need to understand the underlying principles of any teaching strategy they adopt.
- Knowledge should be based on understanding of the DCD/dyspraxia condition, e.g. visual, perceptual and organizational problems.

Unique versus general differences position as pedagogic base

- There is little research that supports DCD/dyspraxix specific pedagogy.
- Most recommended interventions have not been experimentally evaluated.
- Most reports of interventions are based on subjective impressions and informal observations.

- This supports the unique difference position – teaching draws on a continuum of common teaching strategies.

Notable aspects introduced

- The significance of an underlying cluster of learning difficulties defined in terms of the pattern of cognitive strengths/difficulties (NLD).
- The significance of potential areas of strength in DCD. The language area has relevance to the teaching approach.
- Support for the unique difference position and teaching strategies being a matter of degree along a continuum of common strategies. This may change with further evaluation studies to indicate a general differences position.

References

American Psychiatric Association (1995) *Diagnostic and Statistical Manual of Mental Disorders: DSM-IV. International Version with ICD-10 Codes*, 4th edn. Washington, DC: APA.

Barnhart, R. C., Davenport, M. J., Epps, S. B. and Nordquist, V. M. (2003) Update: developmental coordination disorder, *Physical Therapy*, 83: 722–31.

Biederman, J., Faraone, S. V., Kennan, K., Knee, D. and Tsuang, M. T. (1990) Family-genetic and psychosocial risk factors in DSM-III attention deficit disorder, *Journal of the American Academy of Child and Adolescent Psychiatry*, 29: 526–33.

Byers, R. (1994) Providing opportunities for effective learning, in R. Rose, A. Fergusson, C. Coles, R. Byers and D. Banes (eds) *Implementing the Whole Curriculum for Pupils with Learning Difficulties*. London: David Fulton.

Coleman, R., Piek, J. P. and Livesey, D. J. (2001) A longitudinal study of motor ability and kinaesthetic acuity in young children at risk of developmental coordination disorder, *Human Movement Science*, 20(1/2): 95–110.

College of Occupational Therapists, National Association of Paediatric Occupational Therapists (2003) *Children with Developmental Coordination Disorder*. London: COT.

Cooper, P. and McIntyre, D. (1996) *Effective Teaching and Learning*. Buckingham: Open University Press.

Denckla, M. B. (1985) Motor co-ordination in dyslexic children: theoretical and clinical implications, in F. H. Duffy and N. Geschwind (eds), *Dyslexia: A Neuroscientific Approach to Clinical Evaluation*. Boston: Little Brown.

Denckla, M. B., Rudel, R. G., Chapman, C. and Kreiger, J. (1985) Motor proficiency in dyslexic children with and without attentional disorders, *Archives of Neurology*, 42(3): 228–31.

Dewey, D., Wilson, B., Crawford, S. G. and Kaplan, B. J. (2000) Comorbidity of developmental coordination disorder with ADHD and reading disability, *Journal of the International Neuropsychological Society*, 6: 152.

Dewey, D. and Wilson, B. N. (2001) Developmental coordination disorder: what is it?, *Physical and Occupational Therapy in Pediatrics*, 20: 5–27.

DfEE (1998) *National Literacy Strategy: Additional Guidance. Children with Special Educational Needs*. London: DfEE.

DfEE (1999) *National Learning Strategy: Additional Literacy Support (ALS)*. London: DfEE.

Duffy, F. H. and Geschwind, N. (eds) (1985) *Dyslexia: A Neuroscientific Approach to Clinical Evaluation*. Boston: Little Brown.

Ellison, D. G. (1976) Tutoring, in N. Gage (ed.) *The Psychology of Teaching Methods.* Chicago: University of Chicago Press.

Fawcett, A. J., and Nicolson, R. I. (1999) Performance of dyslexic children on cerebellar and cognitive tests, *Journal of Motor Behaviour*, 31: 68–78.

Fitz-Gibbon, C. R. (2000) Cross age tutoring: should it be required in order to reduce social exclusion?, in G. Walraven, C. Parson, D. van Veen and C. Day (eds) *Combating Social Exclusion through Education: Laissez-faire, Authoritarianism or Third Way?* Leuvan: Grant.

Geuze, R. H., Jongmans, M. J., Schoemaker, M. M. and Smits-Engelsman, B. C. (2001) Clinical and research diagnostic criteria for developmental coordination disorder: a review and discussion, *Human Movement Science*, 20(12): 7–47.

Gillberg, I. C., Winnergard, I. and Gillberg, C. (1993) Screening methods: epidemiology and evaluation of intervention in DAMP in pre-school children, *European Child and Adolescent Psychiatry*, 2: 121–35.

Gillberg, I. C. (1998) Neuropsychiatric disorders, *Current Opinion in Neurology*, 11(2): 109–14.

Grinder, M. (1989) *Righting the Educational Conveyor Belt.* Portland, Oregon: Metamorphis Press.

Grissmer, D. (1999) Conclusion: class size effects. Assessing the evidence, its policy implications and future research agenda, *Educational Evaluation and Policy Analysis*, 21(2): 231–48.

Gubbay, S. S. (1975) Clumsy children in normal schools, *Medical Journal of Australia*, 1: 223–6.

Hamilton, S. S. (2002) Evaluation of clumsiness in children, *American Family Physician*, 66(8): 1435–40.

Hellgren, L., Gillberg, C., Gillberg, I. C. and Enerskog, I. (1993) Children with deficits in attention motor control and perception (DAMP) almost grown up: general health at 16 years, *Developmental Medicine and Child Neurology*, 35(10): 881–92.

Henderson, S. E. and Hall, D. (1982) Concommitants of clumsiness in young school children, *Developmental Medicine and Child Neurology*, 24: 448–60.

Henderson, S. E. and Sugden, D. (1992) *Movement Assessment Battery for Children.* New York: Harcourt Brace/The Psychological Corporation.

HMCI (1999) Annual Report of HMCI: Standards and quality in education 1997–98. London: OFSTED.

HMI (2000) Teaching of writing in primary schools: could do better – a discussion paper by HMI. London: OFSTED.

Hulme, C., Biggerstaff, A., Morann, G. and McKinlay, L. (1982) Visual, kinaesthetic and cross-modal judgements of length by normal and clumsy children, *Developmental Medicine and Child Neurology*, 24: 461–71.

Kadjeso, B. and Gillberg, C. (2001) The comorbidity of ADHD in the general population of Swedish school age children, *Journal of Child Psychology and Psychiatry*, 42: 487–92.

Kaplan, B. J., Crawford, S. G., Wilson, B. N. and Dewey, D. (2000) Does pure ADHD exist?, *Journal of the International Neuropsychological Society*, 6: 153.

Kaplan, B. J., Wilson, B. N., Dewey, D., and Crawford, S. G. (1998) DCD may not be a discrete disorder, *Human Movement Science*, 17: 471–90.

Kirby, A. and Drew, S. (2002) *Guide to Dyspraxia and Developmental Coordination Disorders.* London: David Fulton.

Klin, A., Sparrow, S. S., Volkmar, F., Cicchetti, D. V. and Rourke, B. P. (1995) Asperger syndrome, in B. P. Rourke (ed.) *Syndrome of Non-verbal Learning Disabilities: Neurodevelopmental Manifestations.* New York: Guilford Press.

Levin, H. M., Glass, G. V. and Meister, G. R. (1984) *Cost Effectiveness of Four Educational Interventions*. Project report no. 84-A11. Stanford, CA: Stanford Institute for Research on Educational Finance and Governance.

Lewis, A. and Norwich, B. (2000) *Mapping a Pedagogy for Learning Difficulties*. Exeter: University of Exeter and University of Warwick.

Losse, A., Henderson, S. E., Elliman, D., Hall, D., Knight, E. and Jongmans, M. (1991) Clumsiness in children: do they grow out of it? A 10-year follow-up study, *Developmental Medicine and Child Neurology*, 33: 55–68.

Mandich, A. D., Polatajko, H. J., Macnab, J. J. and Miller, L. T. (2001) Treatment of children with developmental coordination disorder: what is the evidence?, *Physical and Occupational Therapy in Pediatrics*, 20(2/3): 51–68.

Missiuna, C. (1996) *Keeping Current on Developmental Coordination Disorder*. Hamilton, Ont: Centre for Childhood Disability Research.

Missiuna, C. (2003) *Children with Developmental Coordination Disorder: At Home and in the Classroom*. Hamilton, Ont: Centre for Childhood Disability Research.

Missiuna, C. and Polatajko, H. (1995) Developmental dyspraxia by any other name: are they all just clumsy children?, *American Journal of Occupational Therapy*, 49: 619–27.

Miyahara, N. and Mobs, I. (1995) Developmental dyspraxia and developmental coordination disorder, *Neuropsychology Review*, 5: 245–68.

Nye, B., Hedges, L. V. and Konstantopoulos, S. (1999) The long-term effects of small classes: a five year follow-up of the Tennessee Class Size Experiment, *Educational Evaluation and Policy Analysis*, 21(2): 127–42.

Ofsted (1999) *Pupils with Specific Learning Difficulties in Mainstream Schools*. London: Ofsted.

Ozols, E. J. and Rourke, B. P. (1988) Characteristics of young children with learning disabilities classified according to patterns of academic achievement: auditory-perceptual and visual-perceptual disabilities, *Journal of Clinical Child Psychology*, 17: 44–52.

Peters, J. M., Barnett, A. L. and Henderson, S. E. (2001) Clumsiness, dyspraxia and developmental coordination disorder: how do health and educational professionals in the UK define the terms?, *Child Care, Health and Development*, 27: 399–412.

Polatajko, H. J., Fox, M. and Missiuna, C. (1995) An international consensus on children with developmental coordination disorder, *Canadian Journal of Occupational Therapy*, 62: 3–6.

Polatajko, H. J., Macnab, J. J. and Anstett, B. (1995) A clinical trial in the process-oriented treatment approach for children with developmental coordination disorder, *Developmental Medicine and Child Neurolology*, 37: 310–19.

Portwood, M. M. (1999) *Developmental Dyspraxia: Identification and Intervention. A Manual for Parents and Professionals*, 2nd edn. London: David Fulton.

Portwood, M. M. (2000) *Understanding Developmental Dyspraxia. A Textbook for Students and Professionals*. London: David Fulton.

Portwood, M. M. (2003) *Dyslexia and PE*. London: David Fulton.

Prideaux, D. (2002) Researching the outcomes of educational interventions: a matter of design, *British Medical Journal*, 32(4): 126–7.

Ramus, F., Pidgeon, E. and Frith, U. (2003) The relationship between motor control and phonology in dyslexic children, *Journal of Child Psychology and Psychiatry and Allied Disciplines*, 44, 712–722.

Rasmussen, P. and Gillberg, I. C. (2000) Natural outcome of ADHD with developmental coordination disorder at age 22 years: a controlled, longitudinal, community-based study, *Journal of American Academy of Child and Adolescent Psychiatry*, 39(111): 1424–31.

Ripley, K., Daines, B. and Barrett, J. (1997) *Dyspraxia: A Guide for Teachers and Parents*. London: David Fulton.

Rourke, B. P. (1989) *Nonverbal Learning Disabilities: The Syndrome and the Model*. New York: Guilford Press.

Rourke, B. P. (ed.) (1995) *Syndrome of Nonverbal Learning Difficulties: Neurodevelopmental Manifestations*. New York: Guilford Press.

Rourke, B. P. (1998) Significance of verbal-performance discrepancies for subtypes of children with learning disabilities, in *WISC-III Clinical Use and Interpretation*. San Diego: Academic Press.

Rourke, B. P., Fisk, J. L. and Strang, J. D. (1986) *Neurodevelopmental Assessment of Children: A Treatment-oriented Approach*. New York: Guilford Press.

Schoemaker, M. M., Hijlkema, M. G. J. and Kalverboer, A. F. (1994) Physiotherapy for clumsy children: an evaluation study, *Developmental Medicine and Child Neurology*, 36: 143–55.

Silver, L. B. (ed.) (1992) *The Misunderstood Child*. Blue Ridge Summit: Tab Books.

Sugden, D. A. and Keogh, J. F. (1990) *Problems in Movement Skill Development*. Columbia: University of South Carolina.

Wechsler, D. (1992) *WISC-III, WPPSI-R UK*. New York: The Psychological Corporation/ Harcourt, Brace.

Williams, L. V. (1986), *Teaching for the Two-sided Mind*. New York: Touchstone.

Wimmer, H., Mayringer, H. and Landerl, K. (1998) Poor reading: a deficit in skill-automatization or a phonological deficit?, *Scientific Studies of Reading*, 2(4): 321–40.

Wolff, P. H. (1999) A candidate phenotype for familial dyslexia, *European Child and Adolescent Psychiatry*, 8(7): S021–7.

Wright, H. C. Sugden, D. A. (1996) A two-step procedure for the identification of children with developmental coordination disorder in Singapore, *Developmental Medicine and Child Neurology*, 38: 1099–105.

CHAPTER THIRTEEN

Social, emotional and behavioural difficulties

Tim O'Brien

In this chapter I consider existing research regarding pedagogy and learners who experience social and emotional and behavioural difficulties (SEBD) and relate this to my research into teacher constructions of pedagogy in settings for learners who experience SEBD. My intention is to consider empirical evidence regarding pedagogy for this learner group. I propose that pedagogy is fundamentally ideational and thus its psychological construction is prior to pedagogic application (O'Brien 2001). I also propose that a person's individual disposition – cognitive, social and emotional – creates sensitivity to different aspects of the pedagogic environment (O'Brien 2000). Thus, learners may experience SEBD because they find themselves in situations that they perceive as intolerable.

This chapter mainly considers whether teachers construct pedagogy differently for learners who experience SEBD and for learners who are not identified as experiencing SEBD. When the term 'construction of pedagogy' is used it refers to psychological construction (Kelly 1955), not organizational design. The term 'learners who experience SEBD' is used throughout the chapter in order to avoid within-child deficit labelling, to place a focus on learning, to highlight alterability of learning need and to indicate that SEBDs are socially constructed through interaction between a learner and their environment. SEBD has replaced the previous category that was applied to learners who experience emotional and behavioural difficulties (EBD) (DfES 2001). Both descriptors are used in this chapter in keeping with how they are applied in the literature that is referenced.

Navigation and destination

The ontological vagueness and fragility of the categories EBD and SEBD limits the potential for the analysis of whether pedagogy for this group is, or can be, specialized. EBD and SEBD can be conceptualized as constructs that are culturally defined and redefined by understandings that are shared or contested by different groups in different locations and contexts. This has implications for identifying and understanding how teachers construct pedagogy for learners who experience SEBD in mainstream and special settings as well as how they construct it for learners who are not categorized by these descriptors. It also has implications for how teachers conceptualize a relational connection between social factors and their interaction with emotional and behavioural factors and its influence upon pedagogical construction. The orienting nature of the categories SEBD and EBD make it a complex task to discover if there is a pedagogy that is specific or specialized to individuals within this group.

Most UK government definitions identify EBD, and latterly SEBD, as existing along a continuum ranging from short-term reactive difficulties, which produce degrees of disruptive and challenging behaviour, to serious mental health problems (DfE 1994; DfES 2001). This is supported by literature in the field (Weare 2000; Atkinson and Hornby 2002). Defining EBD is further problematized because of the historical and cultural perceptions and assumptions inherent in, or implied by, the terms used to describe learners who experience EBD. Examples of the variety of terms include 'maladjustment' (Laslett 1983), a reference to deviation from a perceived consensus regarding social norms requiring modes of intervention with aims related to social, emotional and educational readjustment. Other terms include 'troubled' (Bennathan 1992; Cambone 1994), often referring to unhappiness and failure in personal and social relationships, and 'conduct disordered' (Loeber and Keenan 1994; Mandel 1997). Medical descriptors such as 'disturbed' are still prevalent and relate to biologically based perspectives for understanding EBD, which imply that causation relates to neurological and neurochemical dysfunction (Rutter and Taylor 2002).

Thomas and Loxley (2001) propose that the EBD label has a powerful subtext regarding child defiance. This conveniently distracts thinking away from pedagogical processes on to individual learner deficit. To be pedagogically relevant at this level the label should aim to explain emotional and behavioural difficulties in relation to the individual disposition of a person in the context of the environment in which they learn at a particular time (O'Brien 2002). The label should direct thinking towards pedagogy, not perceived treatment of pathology. However, EBD is a generic descriptor of difficulty and the term SEBD simply highlights additional social dimensions from a generic positioning. Pedagogically it softens rather than sharpens focus: it creates further distance from individuality. The terms EBD and SEBD are generalized umbrella terms that point in the direction of particular outcomes. They take the teacher on a conceptual pedagogical journey that is navigated via group-referenced thinking. The generalized nature of these terms does not support the teacher in constructing or applying pedagogy that is particular to individuality within the SEBD label.

Defining SEBD is also complex because the process of defining involves exclusionary thinking: generating meaning about what something is by establishing what it is not. This process influences provision and raises tensions between pedagogical and therapeutic practice for this group – dichotomised as a 'teaching' versus 'treatment' debate based upon interpretations of the onto-logical nature of SEBDs. Multiple conditions and multiple factors can create the context for a learner being described as experiencing SEBD. Therefore, SEBD, however it is defined, is likely to be a descriptor that indicates interconnections with other areas of special educational needs (SEN). This is critical in considering whether a specialized pedagogy exists for this group, or for individuals within the group. It highlights the limitations of the SEBD label and also offers insight into tensions that are inherent in the application of generalized special educational needs labelling to particular groups. Such a process results in labels – and related short- and long-term social and educational processes and goals – that contain limited meaning when they are applied to individuals. Therefore, 'SEBD', like the term 'inclusion', becomes a navigating term related to broad processes and goals but does not focus upon individualized factors in order to direct pedagogical decisions to meet additional need. Nor does it provide clarity of focus upon pedagogical processes that may become exclusionary for particular individuals. One proposition for promoting a greater pedagogical focus upon individual need is to conceptualize learning difficulties as emanating from an interaction between psychological, biological and social factors (Norwich 1990). The psycho-bio-social model, with its opportunity to build on the strengths of each model (Blamires 2001), could be a more effective way of moving beyond group-referenced navigation in order to meet additional individual pedagogical needs. It provides an interactional approach and combats the tendency to over-individualize the causation of difficulty.

Pedagogy and SEBD

Identifying a pedagogical approach for individuals who experience SEBD that is supported by empirical research is problematic because of the limited availability of empirically generated and validated writing about pedagogy and SEBD – especially by practitioners. The literature regarding pedagogy and SEBD includes value positioning, practice-focused strategies and case studies. These are based upon theoretical and sometimes pragmatic models that relate to the distinct nature of the SEBD group and often include behavioural and cognitive–behavioural interventions. Thankfully, the literature has helped teachers to move on in complexity beyond Laslett's (1983) four-stage model for teaching maladjusted pupils: get them in, get on with it, get on with them, get them out. The emphasis in the literature tends to be upon the 'how' of teaching rather than the 'why', the 'why' being an area for this group of learners where there is a dearth of empirical evidence and thus areas of beneficial pedagogical practice may remain unknown (Cooper 1999; Simpson 1999). Whether beneficial practice incorporates specialized pedagogy remains unknown too. The teacher who works with learners who experience SEBD is assumed to need to develop particular practical skills and to be able to implement behaviourally oriented interventions. There is also an assumed need to enhance the emotional development of learners and to develop personal qualities, such as resilience, due to the lack of compliance that they encounter from learners (Thacker *et al.* 2002). Research illustrates that teachers view personal and professional characteristics as being key to successful intervention for learners who experience EBD (Garner 1999). I challenge the complexity-made-simple approach that is prevalent in some SEBD literature. This assumes that there is a need for the teacher to focus on quick-fix, on-your-feet strategies for managing behaviour rather than analysing the formulation of their own constructions of pedagogy and the epistemological orientations, dominant discourses and ideologies and taken-for-granted explanatory frameworks that influence formulation. I propose that you cannot have the former without the latter.

Researching constructions of pedagogy

Much of the literature in the SEBD field relates to the application rather than the construction of pedagogy. As stated at the outset, my assumption is that construction of pedagogy influences application. A logical proposition from this standpoint is that if there is a specialized pedagogy for learners who experience SEBD, relevant aspects of its origins might be gained through eliciting personal constructs relating to how teachers construct pedagogy for this group in comparison to other learners. I shall now highlight some findings from a research study that I conducted that elicited and analysed constructions of pedagogy for learners who experience EBD (O'Brien 2003). The criterion for the selection of participants for the study was that they currently worked in EBD settings and were qualified teachers who had two years' or more experience of mainstream education and two years' or more experience of special education in an EBD setting. In the study they use mainstream teaching as a reference point for making meaning out of teaching in an EBD setting. The ontological orientation of the study was realist, the epistemological orientation was constructivist and the theoretical perspective was premised upon the phenomenological proposition that human feelings and thoughts present to consciousness and thus it is possible to gain insight into how humans construct reality. Insight was gained through a series of in-depth semi-structured interviews (Kvale 1996). While theoretical propositions generated in the study do not purport to contain explanatory power beyond the study, they do illuminate where further research might identify areas for inquiry relating to whether there is a specialized pedagogy for learners who experience SEBD.

In the study, teachers constructed pedagogy through a preferred learner-centred pedagogical route in an EBD setting. By 'pedagogical route' I am referring to the conceptual starting point that teachers use when constructing pedagogy. The focus of pedagogic thinking and curricular decisions in a learner-centred route is learner need. A curriculum-centred route, where curriculum need is the starting point of construction, was seen to produce contexts in which curriculum coverage and delivery, rather than individual need, influenced teaching approaches. This route was seen to be more prevalent in a mainstream setting. I do not wish to dichotomize these 'routes' as inevitably they do interact with each other – it is the starting point for pedagogic routes that I wish to emphasize. In an EBD setting, with learner need as a conceptual starting point, teachers adopted a pedagogy that was dialogic, placing an emphasis upon intersubjectivity. Knowledge was conceptualized as participatory rather than acquired (Sfard 1998). This epistemic stance was assumed to support those who were coming to terms with previous failure and who might resent teacher intervention. In an EBD setting fewer assumptions were made than in a mainstream setting about how learners acquire and apply knowledge, learner disposition and temperament, the pace at which learning takes place and the nature of the life experiences of learners. Fewer assumptions led to a greater consideration of adaptation, producing a prioritized focus upon emotional (rather than cognitive) processes and goals.

Joyce *et al.* (1997) propose that pedagogical models, whether they are directive or non-directive, always have 'nurturant' and 'instructional' dimensions. Nurturant factors aim at increasing the emotional health and growth of individuals through pedagogy that reduces anxiety, improves relationships and develops self-worth. Instructional factors aim to provide increased cognitive performance related to particular aspects of curriculum knowledge. Presumably, nurturant and instructional factors vary in different settings. In this study nurturant factors were given higher priority than instructional factors when teachers constructed pedagogy for individuals within the EBD group. This was seen as a necessary response to learner characteristics. Teachers also emphasized that the small scale of the school community (class and school size) in a specialist setting enabled their pedagogy to become more nurturant and learner-focused and to influence school aims and development. Pedagogical knowledge within EBD settings could be conceptualized as anti-foundational and constantly evolving.

The style of pedagogy that teachers adopted for learners who experience EBD was flexible, interactive and mediatory. This is consistent with the research of Cole *et al.* (1998) and Daniels et al. (1999). In the research of Cole *et al.* (1999), involving the application of an expansive model of pedagogy (Engestrom *et al.* 1999), it was noted that in relation to EBD in mainstream schools, discourse among teachers about relationships and identity was subsumed by instructional discourse about curriculum content. This was not so in my study. Regulative discourse, about the emotional, social, cognitive and behavioural needs of the learners, was central to constructing pedagogy. The needs of the learners were not submerged by the need to deliver the curriculum. Regulative discourse was also central to the construction, circulation and interpretation of community-based knowledge (Wenger 1998; Anderson 1999). Fundamentally, pedagogy was based upon the interaction between the mind of the teacher and the mind of the learner, with emotional difficulties taken into account. Premised upon intersubjectivity, teachers adopted a pedagogical style that actively responded to the needs of the EBD group. It is a different style from one in which the teacher is the locus of epistemic power and where pedagogy is based upon strict subject/object formulations. This results in a didactic model of broadcast and reception (O'Brien and Guiney 2001).

Difference makes a difference

Pedagogy in an EBD setting was also constructed through a greater focus upon individual difference than in a mainstream setting. Construction of difference depends upon commonality as difference is generated according to implied structures of sameness. Difference can be constructed differently within different frameworks. It could exist within a framework where difference points to variability along a continuum: differences of degree. It could also refer to variety within particular categories: differences of kind. Identifying difference can be seen as emancipatory or discriminatory. In relating teacher constructions to a conceptual framework I shall refer to the unique and general differences position (Lewis and Norwich 2000).

All teachers in the study adopted a general (group) differences perspective when constructing pedagogy. Teachers referenced majority, minority and individual needs: common, exceptional/distinct and individual needs (Norwich 1996). Most began by foregrounding distinct group-based needs. A small proportion of teachers adopted a lower order interpretation by foregrounding distinct needs and recognizing individual needs without making reference to common needs. This variant within a general differences perspective illuminates how a sub-group can be potentially outgrouped or stereotyped by conceptual reference to unique needs within the distinct group but not to commonality. There are implications when pedagogic inclusion is conceptualized from this positioning. The EBD category was relevant to the construction of pedagogy and pedagogic decision-making for every teacher in the study. This suggests that it may be possible to ascertain whether pedagogy for learners who experience SEBD is specialized or not, by detailing the specificity of constructions within the foregrounding of distinct needs and then relating these to pedagogic decisions. One assumption that underpins such a view is that it is both valuable and possible to identify similarities between learners in the SEBD group, and differences between those learners and learners in other groups and sub-groups, and to associate this identification with a pedagogic need for specialized teaching. Further research that engages with the social reality of those who are involved in the construction of pedagogy for such learners could offer insight into whether this assumption is valid.

Regarding inclusion in education, due to pragmatics rather than political ideology, specialist provision for the SEBD group is still seen as being required (Cole et al. 2003). The adoption of a differences position regarding learners who experience SEBD raises further questions about their inclusion. Does highlighting the distinct needs of the SEBD group require increased adaptation or stratification of additional provision? If so, institutional disposition will have to alter if it is to authenticate and accommodate individual disposition through pedagogic inclusion as well as placement inclusion. A focus upon placement and space may consider minority group representation and distribution but the erroneous assumption is that it will meet individual need. A focus upon pedagogic inclusion can do this by enabling broad common goals and principles for all to be pursued in different ways within associated systems – including different curriculum content for some that is not necessarily required by all (O'Brien and Guiney 2004).

Being-with

Another theme, which emerged from data analysis, I refer to as 'being-with'. It relates to teacher adaptation to the EBD context and offers insight into an ontological focus upon 'being' (existence and experience), rather than 'doing' (observable practice and competencies). Figure 13.1 is a visual data network (Miles and Huberman 1994) that is a composite for all the teachers in the study in relation to this theme. The network illustrates relationships within and between theme-related phenomena. I shall select two dimensions of this theme in order to raise questions about constructions of pedagogy for learners who experience SEBD that illuminate positioning on difference and issues regarding pedagogic specialisation.

Teachers referred to the differences between a mainstream and an EBD context, such as increased unpredictability, vulnerability, changeability, variability of need and intensity in the latter. These are identified as features relating to learner characteristics (LC). Teacher characteristics (TC) were perceived as being context-responsive too. This included increased levels of tension and anxiety when compared to teaching in a mainstream setting. The two dimensions of 'being-with' that I discuss briefly are 'self' and 'fear'.

'Self' and 'other'

When referring to self I mean an alterable self that can be strengthened or fragmented by context and culture, rather than an absolutist universal self. Teachers in this study claim that the EBD context brings the teacher more in touch with who they are as a person as well as who they are as a teacher. Teacher experiences were processed subjectively and provided particular forms of feedback to consciousness that caused teachers to ask questions about their own concept of self and personal/professional identity. Identity was a key factor in the construction and application of pedagogy in an EBD setting and seen to be less so in a mainstream setting. I am not conceptualizing identity in terms of an externally created and validated construct of professional identity. I conceptualize it in relation to a complex and reflexive process that is responsive to a teacher's day-to-day and minute-by-minute self-witnessing and self-referential thinking and experience. Creation of identity is contextual (Gergen 1991). It is also mediated by context. Grasping and grappling with notions of 'self' and 'other', in a context that can include hostile, aggressive and chaotic

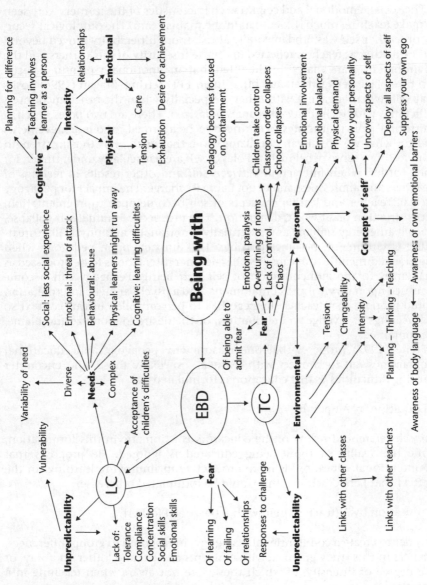

Figure 13.1 Being-with (LC, learner characteristics; TC, teacher characteristics)

presentations, was at the core of the meaning-making process that influenced intentional action by teachers towards learners in an EBD setting. As one teacher states, 'In mainstream, I never let myself be who I was . . . in EBD, the teacher *has* to be who they are.'

The social, emotional and cognitive characteristics of the learners were seen to make teaching much riskier than in the mainstream. The ontological security of teacher self was fundamentally at risk too. Vulnerability moved beyond self into other as teachers reflected upon the insecurity of the learners and the environment. Data analysis highlighted that an emotionally painful dialectic can take place between self and other in an EBD setting. Bragan (1996) posits that self, when engaging with other – especially when the other encounters difficulties with reciprocity – becomes polarized. There are two poles of self: a 'mirroring' pole that relates to our need to be affirmed for our achievements and for what we do and an 'idealizing' pole that enables us to gain strength from feeling a sense of belonging. Poles of self are particularly under threat, for both parties, when interaction between self and other results in feelings of weakness and aimlessness and of not being in charge. The impact for pedagogy is clear. Teacher and learner concepts of self become open to fragmentation, deconstruction or, at worst, demolition. The prospect of mutual self-collapse, in such an energy sapping and potentially emotionally and physically threatening environment, becomes possible. This impacts upon pedagogy when emotional difficulties can cause teacher–learner interactions to be processed as challenges to the authentication of self and being. Pedagogy can become premised upon survival and containment, and a psychoanalytic interpretation would propose that teacher superego has to be controlled in this context so that feelings of revenge and retribution, or the desire to moralize and blame, are contained.

Freire (1997) proposes that one reason why pedagogy and educational programmes fail to connect with learners, especially those who encounter learning difficulties, is that education is formulated as:

Education by A upon B

The self-referenced reality of the educators is axiomatic in this formulation, while the reality of those being educated is ignored. He proposes that 'co-intentional education' is more productive in improving learning. In the context that I am describing this would be formulated otherwise:

Education by A (teacher) [self] with B (learners) [other]

In order to create a co-intentional pedagogy, in response to group differences, teachers in this study grappled with concepts of 'self' and 'other' in a way, or at a degree of intensity, of which they were not aware when teaching in a mainstream setting.

Being with fear

Teachers in the study described being more anxious in an EBD setting than they were in a mainstream setting. For many, anxiety over time became fear: fear of unwanted and threatening challenges to teacher as person as well as to teacher as teacher. Some talked of the fear of losing self-control and fear of the collapse of expected teaching norms that can result in learners trying to take control of the classroom. The existence or intensity of this fear was not seen to be present in a mainstream setting and the management of fear was perceived as being relevant to the construction of pedagogy in an EBD setting. Some teachers proposed that for the teacher, perhaps like the learner, there might also be a fear of being able to admit that you are frightened. One teacher explained:

> teaching in an EBD school you deal with an unspeakable fear . . . a fear that relationships or lessons that you have put so much into can break down, go pear-shaped . . . fall apart in seconds. Fear affects what you do, but most people don't talk about it.

The experience of fear may be a stress-related reaction. However, fear also related to moments when teachers felt a sense of worthlessness in a context where powerlessness replaced power and where learners overturned the planned and ethically justifiable actions of the teacher. The fundamental values, beliefs, assumptions and skills of the teacher are under threat. This type of fear could be more connected to existential angst and dread (Heidegger 1968). Some teachers identified this fear-driven response producing a pedagogy that was focused upon containment of learners and survival of teachers. Fear was also identified as a learner-referenced characteristic. Not only do teachers confront their own fear but they also have to confront fear as a characteristic of those whom they teach, particularly in relation to fear of learning and fear of proximity within relationships. The acknowledgement, acceptance, holding and managing or transcendence of fear – both teacher and learner fear – was an influential factor in constructing pedagogy for teachers in EBD settings in this study. The sense of vulnerability of self and the experience of fear may not be particular to EBD settings – the proposition is that they are experienced differently in an EBD setting compared with a mainstream setting. The difference is a matter of degree because, in relation to the personal and emotional aspects of teaching in EBD settings, the process is amplified and the intensity of the experience occurs at a higher or deeper level.

Concluding comments

SEBD and EBD function as generalized umbrella concepts that are relevant in all aspects of teaching. They serve legislative, political, resource-driven and bureaucratic purposes but in themselves they do not possess sufficient meaning for teachers to make pedagogic decisions at a level of individuality. While they raise important questions about the goals of education for learners who experience SEBD they only serve a general orienting pedagogic purpose. This chapter has navigated within the territory of specialized pedagogy for learners who experience SEBD, highlighting the role of learner-centredness, co-intentionality and the prioritizing of emotional goals in constructions of pedagogy in one research study. It has indicated that teachers in this study do construct pedagogy differently for learners who experience SEBD through a typified concept of group disposition. Pedagogic adaptation is relevant too because construction of pedagogy is prior, context-responsive and informs practice. The chapter may seem to assert the ultimate importance of a general (group) differences position. Instead, I propose that a central concept in constructing pedagogy in this study was the existence of a continuum of constructs across settings – as illuminated by the theme 'being-with'. Moreover, the intensity of subjective experience and amplification of emotional processes were not qualitatively different between mainstream and EBD settings. What is critical is that they are different in relation to the degree to which they are processed, experienced and understood. This highlights the importance of a unique differences position and illuminates how a difference of degree is determinate in the construction and application of pedagogy for this learner group.

Summary

Nature of the group

• EBD and SEBD has within-child deficit labelling implications: the preferred phrase is 'experiencing SEBD'.
• These categories are fragile and vague and function only as orienting concepts.

Pedagogy

• Pedagogy is treated as a construction, which is seen to be prior to and influencing of application/practice.
• The general nature of SEBD/EBD does not support the construction or application of a pedagogy that can relate to individual need.
• There are limited empirical bases about SEBD and pedagogy. The literature is value positioning, case studies and practice focused.
• It is assumed that teachers of children with SEBD need particular practical skills, behaviourally oriented.
• The chapter reports the study of constructions of teaching in EBD and mainstream settings.
• In EBD settings, the learner-centred route (more flexible, interactive, mediatory, nurturant) is used, as opposed to curriculum-centred/instructional in mainstream settings.
• Teachers in the study adopted a general difference position, foregrounding distinct group needs.
• The theme of 'being-with' emerged from constructions of EBD settings focusing on two dimensions.

- Regarding self and others, teachers need to be in touch with who they are as persons and as teachers: co-intentional pedagogy. The pedagogic relation is self with other, not self on other.
- Being with fear means anxiety in EBD settings, fear of losing control.

Curriculum

- It is assumed that teaching aims to enhance emotional development/personal qualities: SEBD raises questions about educational goals, but only in an orienting way.

Knowledge

- This is not covered but the author does discuss the epistemological position, with knowledge conceptualized as intersubjective, participatory and anti-foundational.

Unique versus general differences position as pedagogic base

- All teachers in the study seemed to adopt a general differences position but this is interpreted in terms of a unique differences position.

Notable aspects introduced

- Quick fix strategies are critiqued for managing behaviour in this field, and not on the basis of a pedagogy.
- SEBD serves legislative and administrative purposes, not pedagogic ones.
- The central construct in the study of pedagogic constructions was the continuum of constructs across emotional and behavioural difficulties and non-EBD settings.
- In the being-with theme, the intensity of experience and amplification of process are not qualitatively different across settings, but a matter of degree.

References

Anderson, H. (1999) Collaborative learning communities, in S. McNamee and K. Gergen (eds) *Relational Responsibility*. Thousand Oaks, CA: Sage.

Atkinson, A. and Hornby, G. (2002) *Mental Health Handbook for Schools*. London: RoutledgeFalmer.

Bennathan, M. (1992) The care and education of troubled children, *Therapeutic Care and Education*, 1(1): 37–9.

Blamires, M. (2001) Is a social model sufficient to enable inclusive educational practice?, in T. O'Brien (ed.) *Enabling Inclusion: Blue Skies . . . Dark Clouds?* London: The Stationery Office.

Bragan, K. (1996) *Self and Spirit in the Therapeutic Relationship*. London: Routledge.

Cambone, J. (1994) *Teaching Troubled Children*. New York: Teachers College Press.

Cole, T., Daniels, H. and Visser, J. (2003) Patterns of provision for pupils with behavioural difficulties in England: a study of government statistics and behaviour support plan data, *Oxford Review of Education*, 29(2): 197–205.

Cole, T., Visser, J. and Daniels, H. (1999) A model explaining effective EBD practice in mainstream schools, *Emotional and Behavioural Difficulties*, 4(1): 12–18.

Cole, T., Visser, J. and Upton, G. (1998) *Effective Schooling for Pupils with Emotional and Behavioural Difficulties*. London: David Fulton.

Cooper, P. (1999) Changing perceptions of EBD: maladjustment, EBD and beyond, *Emotional and Behavioural Difficulties*, 4(1): 3–11.

Daniels, H., Visser, J., Cole, T. and Reykebill, N. (1999) *Emotional and Behavioural Difficulties in Mainstream Schools*. London: DfEE.

Department for Education (1994) *The Education of Children with Emotional and Behaviour Difficulties: Circular 9*. London: DfE.

Department for Education and Skills (2001) *Special Educational Needs: Code of Practice*. London: DfES.

Engestrom, Y., Miettinen, R. and Punamaki, R. L. (eds) (1999) *Perspectives on Activity Theory*. Cambridge: Cambridge University Press.

Freire, P. (1997) *Pedagogy of Hope: Reliving Pedagogy of the Oppressed*. New York: Continuum.

Garner, P. (1999) *Pupils with Problems: Rational Fears . . . Radical Solutions?* Stoke-on-Trent: Trentham Books.

Gergen, K. (1991) *The Saturated Self: Dilemmas of Identity in Contemporary Life*. New York: Basic Books.

Heidegger, M. (1968) *What Is Called Thinking?* New York: Harper & Row.

Joyce, B., Calhoun, E. and Hopkins, D. (1997) *Models of Learning: Tools for Teaching*. Buckingham: Open University Press.

Kelly, G. (1955) *The Psychology of Personal Constructs*. New York: Norton.

Kvale, S. (1996) *InterViews: An Introduction to Qualitative Research Interviewing*. London: Sage.

Laslett, R. (1983) *Changing Perceptions of Maladjusted Children: 1945–1981*. London: AWMC.

Lewis, A. and Norwich, B. (2000) *Mapping a Pedagogy for Special Educational Needs*. Exeter: University of Exeter and University of Warwick.

Loeber, R. and Keenan, K. (1994) Interactions between conduct disorder and its comorbid conditions: effects of age and gender, *Clinical Psychology Review*, 14: 497–523.

Mandel, H. P. (1997) *Conduct Disorder and Underachievement: Risk Factors, Assessment, Treatment and Intervention*. New York: Wiley.

Miles, M. and Huberman, A. (1994) *Qualitative Data Analysis: An Expanded Sourcebook*, 2nd edn. Thousand Oaks, CA: Sage.

Norwich, B. (1990) *Reappraising Special Needs Education*. London: Cassell.

Norwich, B. (1996) Special needs education or education for all? Connective specialisation and ideological impurity, *British Journal of Special Education*, 23(3): 100–4.

O'Brien, T. (2000) Providing inclusive differentiation, in P. Benton and T. O'Brien (eds) *Special Needs and the Beginning Teacher*. London: Continuum.

O'Brien, T. (2001) Learning from the hard cases, in T. O'Brien (ed.) *Enabling Inclusion: Blue Skies . . . Dark Clouds?* London: The Stationery Office.

O'Brien, T. (2002) As chaotic as a box of frogs? Teaching learners who experience emotional and behavioural difficulties, in B. Rogers (ed.) *Teacher Leadership and Behaviour Management*. London: Paul Chapman.

O'Brien, T. (2003) Teacher constructions of pedagogy in settings for learners who experience emotional and behavioural difficulties. Unpublished PhD thesis, University of London.

O'Brien, T. and Guiney, D. (2001) *Differentiation in Teaching and Learning: Principles and Practice*. London: Continuum.

O'Brien, T. and Guiney, D. (2004) The problem is not the problem: hard cases in modernist systems, in P. Garner, P. Clough, T. Pardeck and F. Yuens (eds) *The International Handbook of Emotional and Behavioural Difficulties*. London: Sage.

Sfard, A. (1998) On two metaphors for learning and the dangers of just choosing one, *Educational Researcher*, 27(2): 4–13.

Rutter, M. & Taylor, E. (2002) *Child and Adolescent Psychiatry* (ed.) Fourth edition. Oxford: Blackwell Science.

Simpson, R. L. (1999) Children and youth with emotional and behavioural disorders: a concerned look at the present and a hopeful eye for the future, *Behavioural Disorders*, 24: 284–92.

Thacker, J., Strudwick, D. and Babbedge, E. (2002) *Educating Children with Emotional and Behavioural Difficulties: Inclusive Practice in Mainstream Schools*. London: Routledge Falmer.

Thomas, G. and Loxley, A. (2001) *Deconstructing Special Education and Constructing Inclusion*. Buckingham: Open University Press.

Weare, K. (2000) *Promoting Mental, Educational and Social Health*. London: Routledge.

Wenger, E. (1998) *Communities of Practice: Learning, Meaning and Identity*. Cambridge: Cambridge University Press.

CHAPTER FOURTEEN

Moderate learning difficulties
Felicity Fletcher-Campbell

Introduction

There is some evidence that the cohort broadly categorized as pupils 'with moderate learning difficulties' represents the largest within the totality of students 'with special educational needs', although, unlike in other European countries (see, for example, OECD 2001), data with respect to different categories of need are not presently available within England on a national level – though data will emerge with the accumulation of Pupil-Level Annual Schools Census data. Quantification is often possible at the level of the local educational authority but definitional problems abound, as discussed below, so that the mere application of a category may give only a broad indication of need. Similarly, a crude quantification of places at schools nominally for pupils with moderate learning difficulties is unreliable because there is case study evidence that these schools educate pupils with a wide range of levels of ability and additional needs (see, for example, Lee and Wright 2001).

Definition: to whom are we referring?

The question remains as to whether quantification is of any value given the definition problems surrounding 'moderate learning difficulties'. Quantification might indicate the degree of the issue, where there is to be evidence that special pedagogies apply to this cohort, but if, as studies suggest, there are so many variable profiles within the cohort nominally referred to as 'with moderate learning difficulties', this value diminishes.

Williams's (1993) review of the integration of pupils with moderate learning difficulties a decade ago encountered problems of definition and used the earlier description of Buckland and Croll (1987). Very broadly, these pupils were distinguished from their peers with severe learning difficulties by the fact that their needs were identified at school: that is, once they had engaged upon formal, structured learning and been exposed to the regular curriculum it became clear that they had the relatively greater difficulty in learning that defines a special educational need. (The needs of pupils with severe learning difficulties in the UK are normally identified and assessed via health routes prior to the child registering at school.) Williams (1993) points out that pupils with moderate learning difficulties are distinguishable from those whose needs are identified through 'sensory, physical or behavioural considerations' and that their difficulties are general rather than specific to a curriculum area. While these descriptions help us to 'label' a pupil as 'having moderate learning difficulties' – rather than something else – they do not give any indication of intervention or of where on the continuum between 'average ability' and 'severe learning difficulty' any different pedagogy might be deployed.

Using an IQ score range as a criterion produces a clear definition according to one parameter but ignores the nature of individual profiles, in which range of learning difficulty and extent of other special educational needs (Crowther *et al.* 1998) are critical. Moderate learning difficulties are increasingly associated with other special educational needs; indeed, one of the challenges for those who teach these pupils is to identify the profile of need and, in particular, to understand the interrelationship of the different 'sources' of difficulty. From case studies, Johnston (1998) points out that 'deficiencies in cognition, memory and language, short attention span, inadequate achievement, social skills deficits and emotional problems' collectively characterize both students who are diagnosed as having mild/moderate learning difficulties and those who are 'at risk' on account of contextual features such as low socio-economic status (see also Williams 1993). This has implications for the evaluation of interventions: Johnston suggests that interventions for students with mild–moderate learning difficulties should be interdisciplinary and focused on prevention.

At a mundane level, the label 'moderate learning difficulties' elicits responses different from those elicited by 'autistic spectrum disorders' or 'specific learning difficulties' categories that are treated elsewhere in this volume (see Chapters 9 and 11 respectively). It is not insignificant that pupils with moderate learning difficulties were considered one of the 'easiest' groups to integrate; as an indication of the changes in perception about the integration of this group of pupils, see Williams (1993). This is not a little to do with perceptions of needs and of appropriate responses to those needs. Most teachers feel able to accommodate pupils with moderate learning difficulties in their classroom because they recognize the nature of their difficulties (slowness of response, difficulties in recognizing similar concepts, for example) in a way that they may not recognize the rather 'different' difficulties of a pupil with specific learning difficulties or autistic spectrum disorders whose perceptions of the world and that being presented in the classroom or in school are very different (because there is evidence that their cognitive responses are different). It may be that there have been advances in this respect so that the child with autistic spectrum disorders is no longer shrugged off as 'eccentric' or the one with dyspraxia as 'lazy'. None the less, teachers can feel in control of the situation *vis-à-vis* a pupil with moderate learning difficulties because their perception is that they have a good idea, from general teaching skills, of how to address these difficulties. These pupils are similar to other low achievers who have not been identified as having special educational needs. Dyson *et al.* (1994) commented that this group has tended to have been exposed to general intervention strategies and argued for a reconceptualization of educational interventions in order to deconstruct the general categorical responses that take minimal account of individual profiles of need (see also Chapter 15 in this volume). This is in line with the approach of Skrtic (1999), who considers that teachers should respond to unique learning needs rather than categories.

Intervention

The question remains – as originally posed by Lewis and Norwich (2001) – as to the uniqueness of responses. The thinking behind this question is not new. Fish (1989) addressed the question of 'what is special education?' over a decade ago, suggesting that it be located in a framework of 'dimensions' and perceiving it as fluid, logically dependent on 'ordinary' education and 'special' insofar as it required resources additional to those generally available. Fish's framework offers a means of describing 'special education' – something which he perceived to be done inadequately within other parameters such as location or pupil grouping. The main 'dimensions' that he considers are the curriculum (and differentiation within this, which can include selective involvement, various types of support to ensure full access, modification and additional objectives), 'contact type' (which includes how the differentiated curriculum is delivered; for example, in a segregated setting, via consultation or collaborative teaching), 'time intensity', which assesses the intensity and duration of interventions, and environment. Other dimensions include those of technology, type of knowledge and parental involvement. Arguably, these dimensions are contingent and, conceptually, could have been designed differently. Some are independent, while others seem to cluster. However, their value is the way in which they challenge assumptions about provision. For example, should interventions necessarily be 'intensive' in a 'segregated' environment (small classes in a special school, for example) or should pupils in special schools sometimes learn in much larger than normal groups even if the outcomes of this may be unpredictable. What is the relationship between 'intensity' of teaching (one pupil having to concentrate on his or her own for an hour a week) and 'drip-feed' exposure to a mathematical process in a regular class setting twice a day for five days a week?

Aubrey (1995: 25), albeit discussing providing for all learning difficulties, calls for 'more and better teaching . . . more time and more high quality forms of instruction, which is teacher intensive, more deliberate in planning and tighter in its methods of monitoring and reviewing'. In some ways, this contention is disquieting, for it suggests that what may be needed is more a refocusing/re-enlivening of teacher skills and attention to good management, which may, perhaps, have been neglected, rather than anything qualitatively new. While evidence from pupils is qualitative, telling us about their emotional response to various interventions, rather than quantitative, specifying actual progress made, it nevertheless suggests something of the contrast between situations where the pupil feels that his or her needs are being met and those where they are not. It is worth noting that when pupils are interviewed about differences between educational placements and/or teachers, they frequently comment to the effect that a particular special education teacher or assistant 'explains things' or 'does not shout at you', or that they prefer learning in a small group because help is more readily available: that is, they are contrasting their preferred placement with another situation, the characteristics of which are contingent rather than inevitable. This again raises questions about whether the pedagogy is different *per se* or whether it is delivered in a package more amenable to the recipients in 'social' terms. There is no evidence that the delivery is affected by categories of location – what is important is the ethos within that location. This can have a more theoretical basis as it resonates with the emphasis, in inclusive schools, on 'ethos' and strong interpersonal relationships not only among students but between students and adults.

Students with moderate (and severe) learning difficulties are customarily regarded as needing a 'small steps' curriculum (see, for example, Fletcher-Campbell and Lee 1996), in which the focus is on the presentation of the content (using scaffolding, for example). However, the literature suggests that this, alone, is inadequate and, if the sole approach, may be unhelpful. Goddard (1997: 170) offers a critique of a curriculum purely based on a behavioural model as being 'reductionalist, adopting a step-by-step approach to learning and embracing a product ideology'. He sees a danger in individual education plans encouraging this approach and points out that 'although [students] are learning small tasks, their overall functioning is not appreciably improving in school or life'. Goddard favours a process model that allows for problem-solving and interaction (see also the work of Nind and Hewett (1988, 1994) with respect to work for pupils with severe learning difficulties).

While differentiation is widely accepted as the critical approach to providing for pupils with any type of need, and, arguably, is expected of all teachers in England under the criteria required for Qualified Teacher Status, this does not get us very far. Studies (e.g. Stradling *et al.* 1992) give a descriptive account of good practice but do not link that practice to individual profiles of need or give clear accounts of how decisions are made in the light of needs. For example, Spillman's (1995) 'differentiation checklist' embraces the whole range of teaching strategies and approaches – including the use of resources, questioning techniques, use of language and cooperative pupil work – suggesting that differentiation involves the whole craft of teaching and the whole of teachers' *modi operandi*. Similarly, in the UK there has emerged a fairly extensive literature on classroom management but this is not always related to particular strategies within that framework. The literature advocates attention to:

- student groupings (Spillman 1995; Lewis and Norwich 2001);

- the use of support assistants (Aubrey 1995; Lewis and Norwich 2001);
- applied behaviour analysis techniques to allow appropriate target-setting, the reinforcement of desired response and the elimination of undesired responses (Aubrey 1995);
- strategies for teaching basic skills (Aubrey 1995; Fletcher-Campbell 2000);
- individual programmes based on Vygotskian analysis (Aubrey 1995).

However, again, all this happens in a context and begs the question of the effective learning environment; Hegarty (2001) makes the point that criteria for effective special education closely resemble criteria for effective general education.

Specific approaches for which there is offered a rationale related to pupils' cognitive processes are rare and, interestingly, often located in subject specialist journals and aimed at teachers in general, rather than in the general special education literature and aimed at pupils with learning difficulties. One such example is the discussion of ways of helping children to acquire a concept of number via visual aids (Clausen-May 2003). Brooks (2002), reviewing the available British research on intervention schemes designed to raise the reading attainment of lower-achieving but non-dyslexic pupils in Years 1–4, concluded that 'normal schooling' (i.e. no particular intervention) does not allow slow readers to catch up and that other factors, such as self-esteem, may be influential. Again, this gives credence to a focus on 'ethos', which is related to location of intervention rather than the 'content' (or pedagogy) of the intervention. The latter is also related to Fish's argument that the whole learning environment and the profile of intervention must be discussed. Other points that emerged from Brooks's review are related to very obvious 'management' issues: interventions are only effective if they are highly targeted and accompanied by appropriate staff training and support. Interestingly, there was evidence that most of the literacy interventions reviewed were effective for pupils with moderate learning difficulties but not for those with severe learning difficulties, suggesting that there are pedagogical reasons for distinguishing between these two groups.

Within Europe, a study (of which the primary school phase has been published (Meijer 2001) and the secondary school phase is in preparation) gave similar evidence that there is a dearth of detailed pedagogic studies in relation to teaching pupils with learning difficulties. However, there was broad agreement that a clutch of strategies was widely used throughout European classrooms. All these were generic: cooperative teaching, cooperative learning, individual planning, collaborative problem-solving and heterogeneous pupil grouping (see literature review in Meijer 2001).

It may be that the trend in the inclusion literature towards considering the social mileau and ensuring inclusivity in all aspects of school life (the approach is epitomized in CSIE (2002), a document that has been translated into other languages and is widely used internationally) is limited. There needs to be an integration of this literature with that of the highly individualized pupil-level studies that are part of the US 'psychological' tradition, which, in its own way, is limited in that it tends to neglect the wider learning context.

One way of addressing the issue of special pedagogies or, at least, effective provision – which, clearly, may or may not be the same thing – would be to look at different effects/outcomes of different provisions. It is interesting that, in the UK, there have been few studies comparing provision for a particular profile of need in different settings. Exceptions are studies that follow pupils between institutions (for example, Bennett and Cass 1988; Thomas *et al.* 1997) but these do not study provision in parallel so that they cannot look at comparable progress in the different environments and, arguably, pupil needs may change at key transfer/transition points anyway and so the same profile may not be presenting itself in the different environments. Ofsted (1993) studied about 300 lessons involving pupils with moderate learning difficulties, half of these in special schools and half in mainstream schools. While the study represents a rather different policy context from that of today (for example, it noted the greater curricular opportunities for pupils in mainstream schools at a time when the National Curriculum was not fully operational in special schools), the findings are transferable insofar as HMI found better progress where the general learning environment was favourable. There was minimal reference to 'special pedagogy'. For example:

> Where pupils were taught by teachers interested in them and with work prepared to meet their needs, they were secure, confident, well behaved and achieved encouraging standards. If low ability groups were taught by specialist with neither expertise or insight into special educational needs and the work was not planned or matched to their needs, the quality of their work was poor and achievements were minimal
>
> Overall, integrated pupils did not always show a gain in academic standards achieved. Where they did the gain often reflected higher expectations in terms of both pace and achievement and also access later to examination courses with some notable successes.
>
> (Ofsted 1993: paras 35, 42)

Outcome studies generally are not definitive and different studies have opposing findings. A decade ago, Williams (1993) contended that reviewers agreed that there was no appreciable difference between the academic achievements of integrated and segregated pupils, although US studies tend to suggest advantage for placement in a regular class but with individual attention. Again, this begs the question of what the 'individual attention' looked like. Crowther *et al.*'s (1998) review, which informed a UK study on costs and outcomes of provision for pupils with moderate learning difficulties, relied heavily on US literature, which they found did not withstand scrutiny in terms of methodological rigour (e.g. small and 'impure' samples and invalid comparisons). There is negligible literature giving evidence on the long-term efficacy of interventions, although Brooks (2002) found that literacy interventions generally maintained their effect. The available studies are uninformative about the effects of pedagogy (Farrell 2000 questions much of the inclusion debate in terms of pupil progress). Data are lacking and relate outcomes to economic realities. For example, Hornby and Kidd (2001) followed up students with moderate learning difficulties whom they originally studied ten years previously (Kidd and Hornby 1993). There is also a relevant series of Scottish studies (Riddell *et al.* 1997, 1998, 1999; Baron *et al.* 1999).

The study of Lamb *et al.* (1997) is unusual within the literature, focusing as it does on a specific intervention designed to promote the communication skills of a group of pupils with moderate learning difficulties on the grounds that these skills would then equip them to approach their learning more effectively. Notable is its aim to encourage a particular strategy rather than task practice. The study was small and highly focused, so it could hardly be deemed a 'special pedagogy'. Nevertheless, the interventions were at a strategic level and the principles of, and rationale for, the study are worth considering, particularly as the outcomes were encouraging: 'By the end of the intervention the children were talking more, responding to ambiguous instructions more effectively and asking more appropriate types of question' (Lamb *et al.* 1997: 273).

That individualized learning can inhibit interactive learning, which is a vital part of any learning, has been highlighted in specific studies (e.g. Goddard 1997). However, this is closely related to general, rather than special, pedagogy and is, furthermore, not new. For example, in the seminal study following the implementation of the Education Act 1981, Croll and Moses (1985) found that group work was effective, and Carpenter (1997) points out that individual work does not have to be 'isolated'. As greater understanding of the benefits of small group work and interactive learning has developed in response to the National Curriculum, so has understanding of providing for individual needs within group learning situations in both special and mainstream schools; that is, with different 'baselines' of ability (Watson 1999). This is something that was, oddly, largely ignored in the initial articles following the implementation of the National Curriculum in special schools: Costley (1996), for example, considers the appropriateness of the *content* of the National Curriculum for pupils with moderate learning difficulties rather than its pedagogic opportunities.

It is interesting that pupils' views on the pedagogy offered to them are rarely sought – or, more accurately, reported in the literature. Norwich and Kelly (2004) and Fletcher-Campbell (forthcoming) are exceptions: both pieces of research found that pupils were generally positive about their present situation. However, they differed in that, where pupils were able to compare their experiences in special and in mainstream schools, a significant minority of those in special schools interviewed by Norwich and Kelly preferred the mainstream setting while in Fletcher-Campbell's work, albeit in a different educational system, they preferred the special school setting. Clearly, further work needs to take place to extract exactly what pupils prefer in different settings and whether, first, these preferences can be reproduced in other contexts and, second, they enhance their learning, broadly understood (see also Chapter 13).

Conclusions

How is the cohort of students regarded as having moderate learning difficulties positioned within Lewis and Norwich's framework? It is somewhat disappointing that the literature is non-committal rather than confirmatory. There is evidence that:

- This group of learners can follow a programme of work broadly similar to their age-peers: for example, they have access to written language, can record their own work in conventional ways, can manipulate numeric symbols.
- This group of learners can follow a common programme without particular technical aids: for example, the benefits of drafting work on a computer will be qualitatively similar to the benefits for other pupils in an age-related teaching group.
- Differentiation for these learners as a group rests on focusing on earlier stages of the learning path which their peers have travelled rather than traversing a different path. Thus, these learners will have less complex texts and tasks, and be required to engage in more straightforward analysis of situations (for example, in history) than their peers.
- These pupils do not need a supplementary curriculum (unlike, for example, those needing mobility training; see Chapter 3) unless they have associated learning difficulties in another area.
- These pupils, as a group, are rarely discussed in terms of benefiting from other specific therapies, interventions or medication even if these may benefit individual pupils within the group and the group may benefit to a similar extent to any group of age-related peers.

Differentiation at the level of the individual will be similar in nature: that is, in a group of pupils with moderate learning difficulties, there will be different profiles of attainment within areas of the curriculum (e.g. numeracy, literacy) and also within an individual learner (so one pupil's mathematical skills may be in advance of his or her reading skills), but this is exactly the same as for any group of learners of any ability. There is no evidence, for example, that, as a group, all will find the same task or skill difficult, or all will be similarly delayed because of their particular experience of the world.

In essence, their careers are similar but delayed (as, indeed, some may have been diagnosed as having 'developmental delay') and ceilings will look the same as for other pupils but will be lower. However, this is very much a presentation of the accepted way of working with this group and available descriptions of it: and it is a way within which, certainly, many have thrived. The literature does not yield a corpus of recorded research evidence of radically different approaches to the formal education of this cohort: for example, starting formal education at a later age, and hence delaying the demand to acquire reading skills (a well designed comparative study would be useful here), or a meticulously controlled environment so that 'failure' in literacy was never experienced. That these pupils seem to benefit from smaller classes, more individual attention and a slower pace of learning may be largely because these conditions may be preferable to those obtaining in a regular classroom, and it does not necessarily mean that they could not learn as effectively by other means: for example, by being taught by a distinctive approach within a large group.

At present, there is no evidence for particular learning characteristics – other than a very generalized difficulty – for this group. It is not unlikely that the difference among the group in terms of learning styles, preferences and abilities is greater than the generalized difficulty that they have in common. Whether the particular label of moderate learning difficulties is attributed for administrative convenience (related to resource allocation) rather than for a type of provision is debatable. This is not to deny that the label forms a recognizable group but, once initial recognition is made or membership of the group identified (for example, by response to an artifice such as an intelligence test), it is not, on present evidence, clear what further purpose the label serves. For if designation is related to resource allocation, there is the prior question of what resources need allocating and in what form (recall the contention that allocation to a set 'provision' is inadequate if the nature of that provision is assumed rather than crafted on the evidence of its effectiveness with respect to particular learners: Fish 1989, for example). If the group name thus serves no useful function, arguably, and, again, returning to Lewis and Norwich's framework, there seems to be no role for the dimension of a pedagogy for the group, then interventions are properly made with respect to the individual. While this raises questions about the conditions that best support such interventions, it does not predetermine the way in which these conditions may be produced. There is, thus, a challenge to all those educating pupils regarded as having moderate learning difficulties.

Summary

Nature of the group

- There are many definitional problems – the category gives only a broad indication of need.
- So many variables profiles are found in the group that no special pedagogies can be identified.
- The group is mainly identified during schooling, has general rather than specific difficulties and is associated with other difficulties, and it is hard to differentiate between MLD and the at-risk group.

Pedagogy

- There are calls for more intensive and deliberate teaching for this group.
- Pedagogy is not affected by location, and has more to do with the ethos in the location.
- There is a dearth of detailed pedagogic studies; outcome studies are not definitive.
- Where there are studies, they point to generic strategies useful for others without MLD.

Curriculum

- The group is usually seen as needing a small steps curriculum.
- Some argue that this is inadequate alone, and there is also a also need for problem-solving and interaction.
- The group can follow similar programmes without aids to non-MLD group; there is no need for a supplementary curriculum.
- Differentiation is focused on earlier stages of the learning path, not different paths.

Knowledge

- Not addressed.

Unique versus general differences position as pedagogic base

- Supportive of the unique differences position.

Notable aspects introduced

- The inclusion literature focuses on ethos/milieu, and this needs integrating with a pupil-level studies approach.
- It is not clear what the purpose of the category is. If it has no pedagogic function, what future has it?

References

Aubrey, C. (1995) Quality teaching, *Special Children*, 88: 22–6.

Baron, S., Riddell, S. and Wilson, A. (1999) The secret of eternal youth: identity, risk and learning difficulties, *British Journal of Sociology of Education*, 20(4): 483–99.

Bennett, N. and Cass, A. (1989) *From Special to Ordinary Schools: Case Studies in Integration*. London: Cassell.

Brooks, G. (2002) *What Works for Children with Literacy Difficulties? The Effectiveness of Intervention Schemes*. DfES Research Report 380. London: DfES.

Buckland, M. and Croll, P. (1987) Classroom organisation and interactions of pupils with moderate learning difficulties in mainstream and special schools, *European Journal of Special Needs Education*, 2(2): 75–87.

Carpenter, B. (1997) The interface between curriculum and the code. *British Journal of Special Education*, 24(12), 18–20.

Centre for the Study of Inclusive Education (2002) *Index for Inclusion: Developing Learning and Participation in Schools*. Bristol: CSIE.

Clausen-May, T. (2003) Seeing numbers at work, *TES Teacher*, October: 10.

Costley, D. (1996) Making pupils fit the framework: research into the implementation of the National Curriculum for pupils with moderate learning difficulties, focusing on key stage 4, *School Organisation*, 16(3): 341–54.

Croll, P. and Moses, D. (1985) *One in Five*. London: Routledge and Kegan Paul.

Crowther, D., Dyson, A. and Millward, A. (1998) *Costs and Outcomes for Pupils with Moderate Learning Difficulties in Special and Mainstream Schools*. Research Report 89. London: DfES.

Department for Education and Skills (2001) *The Special Educational Needs Code of Practice*. London: DfES.

Dyson, A., Millward, A. and Skidmore, D. (1994) Beyond the whole school approach: an emerging model of special needs practice and provision in mainstream secondary schools, *British Educational Research Journal*, 20(3): 301–17.

Farrell, P. (2000), Education inclusion and raising standards, *British Journal of Special Education*, 27(1): 35–8.

Fletcher-Campbell, F. (ed.) (2000) *Literacy and Special Educational Needs: A Review of the Literature*. Research Report RR227. London: DfEE.

Fletcher-Campbell, F. (forthcoming) *Provision for Pupils with Moderate Learning Difficulties in Northern Ireland*. A report for DENI and the Education and Library Boards.

Fletcher-Campbell, F. and Lee, B. (1996) *Small Steps of Progress in the National Curriculum: Final Report*. London: SCAA.

Goddard, A. (1997) The role of individual education plans/programmes in special education: a critique, *Support for Learning*, 12(4): 170–4.

Hegarty, S. (2001) Inclusion: the case against, *Journal of Moral Education*, 30(3): 229–34.

Hornby, G. and Kidd, R. (2001) Transfer from special to mainstream – ten years later, *British Journal of Special Education*, 28(1): 10–17.

Johnston, G. (1998) Students at risk: towards a new paradigm of mild educational disabilities, *School Psychology International*, 19(3): 221–37.

Kidd, R. and Hornby, G. (1993) Transfer from special to mainstream, *British Journal of Special Education*, 20(1): 17–19.

Lamb, S., Bibby, P. and Wood, D. (1997) Promoting the communication skills of children with moderate learning difficulties, *Child Language Teaching and Therapy*, 13(3): 261–78.

Lee, F. and Wright, J. (2001) Developing an emotional awareness programme for pupils with moderate learning difficulties at Durants School, *Emotional and Behavioural Difficulties*, 6(3): 186–99.

Lewis, A. and Norwich, B. (2001) A critical review of systematic evidence concerning distinctive pedagogies for pupils with difficulties in learning, *NASEN Journal of Research in Special Educational Needs*, 1(1) (http://www.nasen.uk.com/journal/000036_000122.php).

Meijer, C. (ed.) (2001) *Inclusive Education and Effective Classroom Practices: An Investigation into Classroom Practices across Europe* (http://www.european-agency.org/publications/agency_publications/ereports/erep2.html).

Nind, M. and Hewett, D. (1988) Interaction as curriculum, *British Journal of Special Education*, 15(2): 55–7.

Nind, M. and Hewett, D. (1994) *Access to Communication*. London: David Fulton.

Norwich, B. and Kelly, N. (2004) Pupils' views on inclusion: moderate learning difficulties and bullying in mainstream and special schools, *British Educational Research Journal*, 30(1): 43–65.

Organisation for Economic Coordination and Development (2001) *Special Needs Education: Statistics and Indicators*. Paris: OECD.

Ofsted (1993) *The Integration of Pupils with Moderate Learning Difficulties into Secondary Schools*. Report no 173/93. London: Ofsted.

Riddell, S., Baron, S. and Stalker, K. (1997) The concept of the learning society for adults with learning difficulties: human and social capital perspectives, *Education Policy*, 12(6): 473–83.

Riddell, S., Baron, S. and Wilkinson, H. (1998) Training from cradle to grace? Social justice and training for people with learning difficulties, *Education Policy*, 13(4): 531–44.

Riddell, S., Wilkinson, A. and Baron, S. (1999) Captured customers: people with learning difficulties in the social market, *British Educational Research Journal*, 25(4): 445–61.

Skrtic, T. (1999) Learning disabilities as organisational pathologies, in R. Sternberg and Spear-Swirling (eds) *Perspectives on Learning Disabilities*. New Haven, CT: Perseus Books.

Spillman, J. (1995) Teacher, tailor, differentiation, *Managing Schools Today*, 4(4): 12–14.

Stradling, R., Saunders, L. and Weston, P. (1991) *Differentiation in Action*. Slough: NFER.

Thomas, G., Walker, D. and Webb, J. (1997) *The Making of the Inclusive School*. London: Routledge.

Watson, J. (1999) Working in groups: social and cognitive effects in a special class, *British Journal of Special Education*, 26(2): 87–95.

Williams, P. (1993) Integration of students with moderate learning difficulties, *European Journal of Special Needs Education*, 8(3): 303–19.

CHAPTER FIFTEEN

Low attainment

Alan Dyson and Peter Hick

Who are the 'low attainers'?

Most education systems operate with the notion that there is a group of learners whose progress and attainments cause concern but whose apparent difficulties cannot be explained in terms of any evident impairment or under-lying condition. This group may not be categorized separately at all, but may be seen simply as part of the 'natural' continuum of attainments. There may be no special provisions in terms of funding arrangements, assessments and curricular or pedagogical approaches, and their teachers may teach them in much the same way as all other learners, though with less success. Elsewhere, a category is constructed that enables special provisions to be made, but that is clearly differentiated from the categories of special education. In the USA, for instance, such learners might be regarded as being 'at-risk' for educational failure (Franklin 1994), while in the Russian Federation they might fall into the 'compensatory' category (Beverton 2003). Elsewhere again – England being a prime example of this – such learners may fall within the ambit of special education, but special education may itself be defined in extremely wide terms so that it encompasses almost any learner who has difficulty in schooling (see, for instance, Gulliford 1971; DES 1978).

Even these categorizations prove to be extremely fluid. Not only are boundaries between 'low attainers', 'average attainers' and students with 'special educational needs' difficult to define, but the categories themselves shift over time. Franklin (1994), for instance, traces what he calls the move 'from backwardness to at-risk' in the USA as educators have struggled to categorize and recategorize children who do poorly in the education system. In England recently, large numbers of these children have (in principle at least) been removed from the special education system as a new 'code of practice' (DfES

2001) has effectively abolished the lowest level of special educational need. In its place, a primary national strategy has developed a series of 'wave two' interventions for children who need more than the good classroom teaching of 'wave one' but do not need the special educational interventions of 'wave three' (DfES 2003). Interestingly, across the border in Scotland, almost the reverse direction is being taken as moves are being made to develop a supercategory of 'additional support needs'. This seems likely to extend beyond a special educational needs category that is as broadly defined as England's and to encompass a wide range of what we are here calling 'low attainers' (Scottish Executive 2003).

This fluidity is not surprising. The defining characteristics of low attainers actually define very little. First, there is some evidence that the numbers and type of learners who do poorly vary from system to system (OECD 2001). They also change over time. The Scottish School Leavers Survey (Biggart 2000; SCRE 2000), to take just one example, traces how the proportion of boys failing to achieve the major national qualifications fell continuously in Scotland from 40 to 20 per cent between 1978 and 1996. At the same time, the proportion of girls, starting from a similar base line, fell to only 12 per cent. The assumption has, presumably, to be that changes in and differences between education systems or in societies more generally produce such differences in population. Second, what counts as 'doing poorly' varies likewise across systems and across time. As the Scottish example illustrates, the cut-off point may well be determined by the grades of a particular assessment or accreditation system, particularly in countries where grade-retention systems or (particularly at the current time) 'standards-based reform' and 'high-stakes testing' create hard-and-fast distinctions between success and failure.

Finally, even if the boundaries of a low-attaining group could be agreed, there is no reason to suppose that the members of the group share much in common beyond their low attainment. As anyone who has taught a 'low attainers' group knows, such groups frequently contain learners with a wide range of difficulties, not to mention those who appear to have no difficulty beyond a rejection of school and all that it entails. This, however, begs a huge question. If low attainers are so diverse as a group and if the category to which they are allocated is so fluid and variable, what explanation(s) can be offered for their poor educational outcomes and what sorts of interventions are necessary to bring about improvement? This question is made all the more difficult to answer by the absence of any defining impairment or condition. Whereas for other special educational needs categories there tend to be defining characteristics that exist outside the educational context, 'low attainment' is by definition an *educational* construct. Imputing shared non-educational characteristics to individuals within the low-attaining group is problematic and, even if it can be done, the relationship between those characteristics and low attainment may be far from clear.

This is particularly the case regarding the question of whether there is a 'distinctive' pedagogy for this group. Given the fluidity and diversity of the category, it is difficult to see how any single pedagogy could emerge as the most appropriate or most effective, other than in a very provisional and context-specific sense. Moreover, even within a narrow contextual framework, competing explanations of why learners do poorly would be likely to lead to very different pedagogies with very different objectives. Finally, some of these explanations might lead to interventions that are not pedagogical at all. They might, for instance, point to the nature of the curriculum, or the culture of schooling, or the family, community and social conditions within which learners live and argue for interventions in these spheres rather than in pedagogy *per se*.

In this context, any attempt to address the questions on which this book is focused has to consider the ways in which the group has been constructed over time, the sorts of explanations for their difficulties that have been developed and the sorts of interventions that have consequently been seen as appropriate. Given the range of such constructions and the number of education systems within which they have emerged, to do so comprehensively and historically would be impossible. What we propose to do, therefore, is to illustrate that range by reference to three approaches that are relatively clearly defined, that are well documented and that represent significantly different constructions. They are the 'Low Attaining Pupils Project' (LAPP) in England, 'Success for All' (SfA), which originated in the USA but has spread more widely, and 'Reading Recovery', which was developed by a New Zealand researcher but has likewise spread widely.

Constructions and responses

Reading Recovery

Reading Recovery is one of the most widely adopted and widely evaluated programmes for low attainers. Its originator, Marie Clay, describes it as a 'second chance, early intervention programme' (Clay 1993: 96) since its aim is to identify young children as soon as they begin to experience difficulties and provide them with an intensive intervention that will enable them to function at the same level as their classmates.

The programme targets children who, after one year of instruction, are the lowest attaining in literacy among their school peers. These children then receive individual tuition from a specially trained teacher on a regular and frequent basis (usually, daily for 30 minutes). The tuition starts with a diagnosis of the child's current reading skills (with a particular emphasis on her or his strengths) and then moves on to building those skills in line with a model of reading development formulated by Clay. This model allows for work on the 'sub-skills' of reading (phonological awareness, letter recognition, word recognition and so on), but also encourages the child to approach text strategically and to seek to make meaning from text, whether in reading or writing. Throughout the process, the approach is highly individualized, with careful record-keeping and individual planning on the part of the teacher. Once the child has made sufficient progress to function at the level of their peers (usually after 12–20 weeks), the programme is discontinued in the expectation that the child will make progress through good quality class teaching.

To the extent that the programme proposes an explicit model of reading development and an equally explicit view of what teachers should do to promote that development, Reading Recovery has a clear pedagogical basis. This pedagogical approach is indicated, *inter alia*, by the requirement for its teachers to undergo specialist training. However, there are two caveats. First, the models of reading development and teacher intervention are shared with all learners and to that extent are not distinctive. The assumption is that more and less fluent readers are both going through much the same processes and struggling with much the same difficulties, though with different degrees of success (Clay 1972, 1976). It is, therefore, simply the intensification and individualization of support for reading development that constitutes Reading Recovery's distinctive thrust. Second, whether the pedagogical implications of Reading Recovery are distinctive or not, they are narrowly focused on the acquisition of literacy. The approach adopted by the programme has not been developed so as to apply across the curriculum as a whole. How far it constitutes a pedagogy, therefore, and how far it is simply a collection of techniques, is a matter for debate.

This accords with the implicit model of low attainment on which the programme is based. Although Reading Recovery is very interested in identifying the technical difficulties that individual children experience in learning to read, there is no attempt to generalize this into a more wide ranging theoretical explanation of why some children do poorly in school. There is some evidence, for instance, that the programme is particularly effective for children from poorer families (Sylva and Hurry 1995) and that such children constitute the largest single group among its clientele (Douëtil 2002). However, children are not selected on the basis of family income and the programme does not attempt to intervene in what appears to be a risk factor for reading difficulties. On the contrary, the programme's basis in a universally applicable model of reading development leads it to play down an aetiological approach to understanding children's difficulties in favour of a functional one. Put simply, whatever the underlying causes of children's falling behind, the reading task remains the same and therefore the process with which the child needs to engage and the most effective forms of support are broadly similar for all. On this analysis, low attainment is seen as the consequence of functional failures in particular areas of skills mastery. This is why, of course, once those skills are mastered, the child can be expected to flourish in the ordinary classroom.

Reading Recovery is particularly significant from our point of view because it takes its place as one of a long line of 'remedial' approaches to low attainment (see, for instance, Sampson 1975; Tansley 1967; Westwood 1975, among many others). It is certainly one of the best evaluated and most consistently effective of such approaches and has some of the most robust theoretical and empirical grounding. None the less, as Woods and Henderson (2002) point out, it shares with other members of its family a resolutely individualized approach that focuses on how individuals function in relation to very specific aspects of the curriculum (the so-called 'basic skills') and advocates a somewhat technicist approach to intervention without considering more fundamental factors that might be implicated in low attainment.

Success for All

Success for All began as a programme of elementary school reform in the USA premised on the notion that there is no separate pedagogy for lower attaining students, and focusing instead on strategies for the prevention of learning failure. Most of the schools that have participated in the SfA programme have a majority of children living in economically disadvantaged circumstances.

The programme describes itself in the following terms:

> Success for All is a comprehensive approach to restructuring elementary schools to ensure the success of every child. The program emphasizes prevention and early intervention to anticipate and solve any learning problems ... Success for All provides schools with research-based curriculum materials; extensive professional development in proven strategies for instruction, assessment and classroom management; one-to-one tutoring for primary grade children who need it; and active family support approaches.
>
> (Success for All Foundation 2000)

Success for All aims to prevent difficulties, particularly in reading, where possible, or to provide intensive support at an early stage for those who experience difficulties. An essential component is a reading curriculum that claims to be based on research on effective practices, such as developing oral language skills, linking phonetic approaches with meaning and cooperative learning activities. The approach is focused on stories and children's literature – for example, with the use of 'big books' and 'shared stories' – and involves regular reading assessments. A range of support staff are trained to work with teachers to allow 'regrouping' into smaller classes for reading, based on children's reading levels. A further important element of SfA is individual 'reading tutors' for students who show signs of difficulty in progressing in line with their peers. Typically, this supports access to the same curriculum activities as the rest of the class or group through additional individual sessions.

To this extent, there are evident similarities between SfA and Reading Recovery. However, the former differs from the latter in some important respects. First, the approach has been extended from reading to other aspects of the elementary school curriculum – maths, science and social science – and into the middle years. Second, the SfA approach calls for the creation of a 'family support team' that aims to involve parents in the life of the school, and offers them training in reading with their children and in managing their behaviour. The family support team also intervenes with issues such as attendance or behaviour difficulties at school to prevent problems that have their origins in the home becoming barriers to learning. Third, and most important, SfA is conceptualized as a whole-school restructuring programme rather than simply as an approach to teaching this or that aspect of the curriculum.

For this reason, schools are expected to secure overwhelming support from their staff prior to adoption, to designate a trained facilitator and to agree to training for their teachers, while their principals are expected to participate in 'leadership academies'.

These differences reflect a distinctive conceptualization of low attainment. For instance, SfA's originator, Robert Slavin, characterizes the impact of reading failure in the following terms:

Students who have already failed in reading are likely to have an overlay of anxiety, poor motivation, poor behaviour, low self-esteem, and ineffective learning strategies that are likely to interfere with learning . . . In Success for All, the provision of research-based preschool, kindergarten, and first-grade reading; one-to-one tutoring; and family support services are likely to give the most at-risk students a good chance of developing enough reading skills to remain out of special education or to perform better in special education.

(Slavin and Madden 2001: 299)

The concept of 'risk' is important here, as in much American work on low attainment. In this context, risk refers to the sorts of family, community and wider social factors that are likely to generate early failure in school. This failure generates the sorts of secondary effects that turn children from learners with difficulties in some specific area to all-round low attainers. Like Reading Recovery, SfA uses research-based strategies to overcome failure quickly or, better still, to forestall it before the secondary effects emerge. However, the family support component of the programme also indicates an intention to intervene directly in the underlying risk factors. Moreover, whereas Reading Recovery is directed towards a small number of the lowest-attaining children, SfA is directed at the whole school on the grounds that, in 'high poverty' areas, most or all children are likely to be subject to risk.

This raises questions about the extent to which Success for All is an essentially pedagogical approach or, indeed, whether it contains any genuinely pedagogical elements. It belongs to a family of approaches emerging out of the school effectiveness and improvement movements, which have emphasized the key role of institutional and teacher characteristics in supporting or inhibiting children's learning (Teddlie and Reynolds 2000). On this view, if schools are well organized and well led and if teachers with good skills adopt research-based approaches, low attainment can be significantly reduced or, indeed, eradicated (see, for instance, Reynolds and Farrell 1996). This has two implications. First, it minimizes the role that is to be played by any 'distinctive' pedagogies for different groups of learners. Slavin, for instance, talks about 'neverstreaming' (Slavin *et al.* 1996) – the reduction of placements in special programmes – as a goal of SfA. He likewise plays down the differences between the programme's approach for learners identified as having special educational needs and their peers:

students who have IEPs [individualized education programs] indicating learning disabilities or related problems are typically treated the same as other students in Success for All. That is, they receive tutoring if they need it, participate in reading classes appropriate to their reading levels and spend the rest of the day in age-appropriate heterogenous homerooms. Their tutors or reading teachers are likely to be special education teachers, but otherwise they are not treated differently.

(Slavin and Madden 2001: 299)

Second, the focus on teacher and school effectiveness to all intents and purposes locates the response to low attainment outside the domain of pedagogy. Not only are teaching strategies only part of the SfA approach, but it is not clear that a collection of such approaches, proven by research to 'work', actually constitutes a pedagogy as such. Indeed, while similar questions arise in respect of Reading Recovery, Success for All does not even have the explicit model of reading development that characterizes Marie Clay's programme.

The Lower Attaining Pupils Programme

The Lower Attaining Pupils Programme differs from the other two programmes in being aimed at older secondary-aged learners where low attainment and its secondary consequences are already well entrenched. When it was launched in 1982, it was the first curriculum development initiative in recent times to be funded directly from central government. It grew out of government concerns with the lowest attaining 40 per cent of secondary-aged students who were leaving school with few or no qualifications (DES 1989). The public examinations of the time (GCE O level and CSEs) were deemed inappropriate for this group, who were therefore left stranded in their final years of schooling with no targets to aim for and cut adrift from an academic subject-based curriculum in which they had already failed.

The stated aims of LAPP were:

i)   to improve the educational attainments of pupils mainly in years 4 and 5 [of their secondary schooling] for whom existing examinations at 16+ are not designed and who are not benefiting fully from school;

ii)   to do this by shifting their education away from narrowly-conceived or inappropriate curricular provision and teaching styles to approaches more suited to their needs and by giving a practical slant to much of what is taught; to prepare them better for the satisfactions and obligations of adult life and the world of work; and to improve their self-respect and motivation.

(DES 1986: 7)

The programme operated by directing national funding towards local education authorities, which in turn supported initiatives in their schools. Beyond the invitation to explore alternative, non-traditional ways of providing for low attainers, there was little central specification of what selection criteria schools should use to identify their target group or what, in particular, they

should do with them once identified. As HMI (the national schools inspectorate) found in its evaluation of LAPP, individual reasons for 'low attainment'
can include:

Specific learning difficulties, physical handicaps, behavioural problems,
unresponsive attitudes, poor relations with one or more teachers, low
expectations by teachers and pupils, or work that is inappropriate or
poorly planned, organised and taught.

(DES 1989: 2)

In practice, therefore, a very wide range of learners was involved in the
project. Some schools, HMI reported, simply redesignated their bottom stream
or remedial class as the LAPP project group; others asked teachers to identify
pupils in their third year of secondary schooling whom they expected to
have difficulty with 'existing external examination objectives' (DES 1986: 6).
Typically the number of pupils identified within a school for LAPP projects was
limited by resources rather than by any more purely educational considerations, though in some cases pupils of *all* abilities were offered the opportunity to participate. Significantly, boys outnumbered girls by around two to one,
perhaps reflecting differential rates of achievement, but perhaps also reflecting gender stereotyping in the range of activities typically offered. These
tended to include work experience, college placements and outdoor pursuits.
Likewise, a wide range of approaches emerged with varying degrees of
emphasis on out-of-school learning, personal and social development, prac
tically oriented approaches to 'academic' subjects, vocational education and
so on. In addition, there were some LEAs where the programme focused
primarily on out-of-school centres or on particular underlying skills, such
as 'thinking skills' or oracy (Wootten and Haywood 1987). As LAPP developed,
moreover, the focus shifted from 'attainment', narrowly defined in terms of
academic qualifications, towards 'achievement' in a broader sense, incorporating personal and social competence. HMI concluded that: 'There had been
significant gains in pupils' self-esteem and in the development of personal and
social qualities, but standards in "academic" work remained disappointingly
low' (DES 1989: 18).

To some extent, the diversity of the LAPP reflects an initial failure to theor-
ize clearly the nature and causes of low attainment. However, the common
factor throughout the programme was the assumption that there were some
learners for whom 'traditional' academic approaches were inappropriate. The
low attainment of this group certainly reflected their limited capacity to cope
with what schools typically had on offer. To this extent, LAPP grew out of
approaches to low-attaining students that had long been familiar in
'remedial' and special education (see, for instance, Schonell 1942; Tansley
and Gulliford 1960; Gulliford 1969; Brennan 1974, 1979) – approaches that
emphasized the cognitive limitations of this group and therefore the distinctive nature of the provision that should be made for them. The tradition, of
course, also reaches forward to the present day, with the Westminster government busily engaged in promoting vocational alternatives for young

people who do badly in a curriculum that remains resolutely examinations-oriented (DfES 2002).

However, LAPP equally grew out of a sense that low attainment was as much the consequence of schools' failure to break out of their 'inappropriate curricular provision and teaching styles' as of the limitations of low attaining students themselves. It is but a short step from this position to one that questions the appropriateness of what schools offer to *all* their students. It is no coincidence, therefore, that at the same time that LAPP was pushing for new approaches for low attainers, a Technical and Vocational Education Initiative (TVEI) was making similar arguments about the narrowness of the school curriculum for all. These arguments continue to be taken forward in England with the current development of General National Vocational Qualifications (GNVQs) as part of an attempt to raise the status of vocational education within the English system (Yeomans 2002).

The extent to which LAPP embodied a distinctive pedagogy for low attainers is, therefore, doubtful. It certainly was concerned with developing 'teaching styles' that were 'appropriate' for low attaining students, though it is not clear that the nature of these styles was ever fully articulated beyond a rather imprecise focus on the 'practical' and the 'vocational'. It also seems to be the case that the distinction between teaching style and curriculum is blurred in LAPP, as in all similar initiatives. Whether students learn the same things as their peers through different experiences or whether those experiences offer them different things to learn is far from clear. Moreover, the generalization from LAPP to critiques of the narrowness of what schools offer to all learners casts doubt on any claims for the distinctiveness of its pedagogical approach. The emergence of TVEI would seem to imply that LAPP was simply trailblazing a set of alternative curricular and pedagogical approaches that had applications well beyond the low-attaining group.

What is distinctive?

A number of conclusions can be drawn from this brief review:

- There is no single approach to provision for low-attaining students and, therefore, even if the approaches we have examined contain pedagogical elements, it is difficult to argue that there is a *single* distinctive pedagogy. Much depends on how the group is defined, what are understood to be the sources of their difficulties and what aspects of the curriculum are seen as priorities.
- Approaches tend to focus on other aspects of provision as much as (if not more than) on pedagogy. The quality of teaching, the effectiveness of the school as an organization, the nature of the curriculum on offer and the effectiveness of support by families all tend to figure to a greater or lesser extent in different approaches.
- Where approaches incorporate some apparently pedagogical elements, there are some doubts as to how far these amount to fully developed

pedagogies as such. They tend to take the form of collections of tech-niques that have been demonstrated empirically to 'work' in one or other curriculum area.

- Although approaches have been developed specifically for low-attaining students, they tend to be generalizable to all learners. Regardless of how far the difficulties experienced by low-attaining students are attributed to their characteristics as a group, they certainly reflect the failure of schools to respond adequately to those characteristics. Customized approaches, there-fore, tend to take the form of improving in some way the quality of what the school has on offer. This improved quality, of course, is then available to all students.

This last point is, perhaps, central to understanding where low attainers sit in relation to the questions that this book is seeking to address. Since this group's difficulties cannot be explained in terms of constitutional impair-ments or conditions, there is no reason for assuming that they cannot learn and be taught in much the same way as the majority of their peers. The issue, therefore, is not whether a 'special' pedagogy is needed, but why it is that 'common' pedagogies delivered in 'standard' ways prove ineffective with this group. The three programmes we have examined offer a range of (sometimes implicit) explanations – in terms of the inappropriateness and irrelevance of curricula, the failure of teachers to use research-based techniques, the lack of effective family support and so on. Insofar as these programmes try to find ways of delivering a 'regular' pedagogy more effectively, they lend weight to the hypothesis with which the editors of this book started: that there is no discernible 'special' pedagogy for children regarded as having special edu-cational needs, but that common pedagogies may be delivered under special conditions. For our three programmes, these conditions include individual tuition, strengthened family support, intensive teaching, relevant curricular content and so on.

However, there is no reason why the explanation of children's difficulties and interventions to overcome those difficulties should focus solely on what happens in the classroom. As we have seen, Success for All addresses issues of school leadership and organization and of family support for schooling. Other approaches look wider still. For instance, the substantial literature on edu-cational 'risk' associates low attainment not just with school, or even family factors, but also with wider community and socio-cultural factors. The impli-cation is that interventions have to take place across a broad front (see, for instance, Wang *et al.* 1997; Balfanz 2000; Franklin, 2000). Similarly, there is an argument among economists that low attainment is driven by, and is best addressed through a frontal assault on, poverty (Robinson 1997). Finally, there is a body of radical commentary that argues that low attainment is the con-sequence of the systematic oppression of disadvantaged social groups and can be overcome only by substantial political change. What is needed, therefore, is a 'pedagogy of the oppressed' (Freire 1972) that uses the processes of teaching and learning for explicitly political ends.

What all of this reminds us is that the learning-focused interactions between teacher and student that we call 'pedagogy' are actually part of a much wider network of educational and social processes that produce patterns of achievement and difficulty in schools. The development of special pedagogies or of special conditions for the delivery of pedagogies may or may not have a part to play in overcoming the difficulties experienced by other groups. However, in the case of low attainers at least, such developments cannot be disembedded from their wider social and educational contexts. The decision as to which learners to regard as 'low attainers', where in these contexts to focus attention and how fundamentally to tackle the processes that produce low attainment are decisions that have an inevitably political dimension. They cannot escape challenging or supporting a status quo that patently produces different outcomes for different groups. What is 'special' about pedagogy for low attainers, therefore, may not be that it develops technical approaches to teaching and learning that are different from those used with other groups. Instead, it may be this political dimension. Whether avowedly so or not, it is unavoidably a 'pedagogy of the oppressed'.

Summary

Nature of the group

- There are questions about whether this is category relevant to **special educational needs**.
- There are national differences in definition, including at-risk and additional support needs.
- There is uncertainty about the range of what counts as SEN.
- Differences in education systems affect population differences, e.g. accreditation systems.
- A fluid, diverse and variable group is counted as low attainers.
- Low attainment is an educational construct.

Pedagogy

- The uncertainty of the category implies that no single pedagogy could emerge.
- Differing explanations could lead to different interventions, even ones that are not educational.
- Three well known models are examined.
- Reading Recovery has a clear pedagogic approach, but is not distinctive to the identified group of low attainers. There is a question of intensification.
- Success for all separates pedagogy for low attainers. It has preventive aims and a broader focus than Reading Recovery, and uses cooperative learning and individual tutors. It focuses on family and whole school, and goes beyond pedagogy. It aims to intervene in underlying risk factors.
- The Lower Attaining Pupils Programme (LAPP) shifts away from narrow/inappropriate curricular provision, involves a wide range of pupils, including those with traditional impairments, and focuses on wider achievement, rather than on academic attainment.

Curriculum

- LAPP questions the appropriateness of traditional academic curriculum provision in Key Stage 4, linked to vocational approaches to this group.
- Success for all involves broader non-school interventions.

Knowledge

- This is not a significant aspect of the argument in this chapter.
- Understanding of the causes of lower attainment is relevant to the kind of interventions undertaken.

Unique versus general differences position as pedagogic base

- There is no single approach for lower attainers, no distinctive pedagogy. The author inclines to a unique differences position but within a wider contextual understanding of causes of lower attainment.
- Approaches tend to be relevant to other learners.

Notable aspects introduced

- Approaches for this fluid group focus on other non-pedagogic aspects of provision school and teaching quality and effectiveness.
- Approaches also tend to focus on beyond child causes, including non-educational interventions.
- Pedagogy is the wrong field in which to search for a response.

References

Balfanz, R. (2000) Why do so many urban public school students demonstrate so little academic achievement?, in M. G. Sanders (ed.) *Schooling Students Placed at Risk*. London: Lawrence Erlbaum Associates.

Beverton, S. (2003) A trans-national study of literacy policies for low attainers aged 11–14 years, in *Proceeding of the American Educational Research Association Annual Meeting*, Chicago, April.

Biggart, A. (2000) *Scottish School Leavers Survey Special Report No. 2. Gender and Low Achievement*. Edinburgh: Scottish Executive Education Department.

Brennan, W. K. (1974) *Shaping the Education of Slow Learners*. London: Routledge and Kegan Paul.

Brennan, W. K. (1979) *The Curricular Needs of Slow Learners: Report of the Schools Council Curricular Needs of Slow-learning Pupils Project*. Schools Council Working Paper 63. London: Evans/Methuen Educational.

Clay, M. M. (1972) *Reading: The Patterning of Complex Behaviour*. London: Heinemann Educational Books.

Clay, M. M. (1976) *Young Fluent Readers*. London: Heinemann Educational Books.

Clay, M. M. (1993) *Reading Recovery: A Guidebook for Teachers in Training*. Auckland: Heinemann.

Department of Education and Science (1978) *Special Educational Needs: Report of the*

Committee of Enquiry into the Education of Handicapped Children and Young People (The Warnock Report). London: HMSO.

Department of Education and Science (1986) *A Survey of the Lower Attaining Pupils Programme: The First Two Years*. London: DES.

Department of Education and Science (1989) *The Lower Attaining Pupils Programme, 1982–88. Education Observed 12*. London: DES.

Department for Education and Skills (2001) *Special Educational Needs Code of Practice*. London: DfES.

Department for Education and Skills (2002) *14–19: Extending Opportunities, Raising Standards: Consultation Document*. Cm5342. London: The Stationery Office.

Department for Education and Skills (2003) *Excellence and Enjoyment: A Strategy for Primary Schools*. London: DfES.

Douëtil, J. (2002) *Reading Recovery National Network: National Monitoring 2001–2: Annual Report*. London: Institute of Education (http://k1.ioe.ac.uk/schools/ecpe/pdfs/Nationalreport0102.pdf).

Franklin, B. M. (1994) *From 'Backwardness' to 'At-risk': Childhood Learning Difficulties and the Contradictions of School Reform*. Albany: State University of New York Press.

Franklin, W. (2000) Students at promise and resilient: a historical look at risk, in M. G. Sanders (ed.) *Schooling Students Placed at Risk: Research, Policy and Practice in the Education of Poor and Minority Adolescents*. London: Lawrence Erlbaum Associates.

Freire, P. (1972) *Pedagogy of the Oppressed*. Harmondsworth: Penguin Books.

Gulliford, R. (1969) *Backwardness and Educational Failure*. Windsor: NFER.

Gulliford, R. (1971) *Special Educational Needs*. London: Routledge and Kegan Paul.

OECD (2001) *Knowledge and Skills for Life: First results from the OECD Programme for International Student Assessment (PISA) 2000*. Paris: OECD.

Reynolds, D. and Farrell, S. (1996) *Worlds Apart? A Review of International Surveys of Educational Achievement Involving England*. London: Ofsted.

Robinson, P. (1997) *Literacy, Numeracy and Economic Performance*. London: Centre for Economic Performance, London School of Economics.

Sampson, O. (1975) *Remedial Education*. London: Routledge and Kegan Paul.

Schonell, F. J. (1942) *Backwardness in the Basic Subjects*. London: Oliver and Boyd.

Scottish Council for Research in Education (2000) The characteristics of low-attaining pupils, *Research in Education No 66*. Edinburgh: SCRE.

Scottish Executive (2003) *Draft Education (Additional Support for Learning) Bill (Scotland)*. Edinburgh: Scottish Executive (http://www.scotland.gov.uk/consultations/education/deasl02.pdf).

Slavin, R. and Madden, N. (2001) *One Million Children: Success for All*. Thousand Oaks, CA: Corwin.

Slavin, R. E., Madden, N. A., Dolan, L. J. and Wasik, B. A. (1996) *Every Child, Every School: Success for All*. Thousand Oaks, CA: Corwin.

Success for All Foundation (2000) *Success for All*. Baltimore: Success for All Foundation.

Sylva, K. and Hurry, J. (1995) *The Effectiveness of Reading Recovery and Phonological Training for Children with Reading Problems*. London: Schools Curriculum and Assessment Authority.

Tansley, A. E. (1967) *Reading and Remedial Reading*. London: Routledge and Kegan Paul.

Tansley, A. E. and Gulliford, R. (1960) *The Education of Slow Learning Children*. London: Routledge and Kegan Paul.

Teddlie, C. and Reynolds, D. (eds) (2000) *The International Handbook of School Effectiveness Research*. London: Falmer Press.

Wang, M. C., Haertel, G. D. and Walberg, H. J. (1997) Fostering educational resilience in inner-city schools, *Children and Youth*, 7: 119–40.

Westwood, P. (1975) *The Remedial Teacher's Handbook*. Edinburgh: Oliver and Boyd.

Woods, A. and Henderson, R. (2002) early intervention: narratives of learning, discipline and enculturation, *Journal of Early Childhood Literacy*, 2(3): 243–68.

Wootten, M. and Haywood, R. (1987) The Gateshead LAPP: pre-vocational education in a cold climate, *Forum*, 29(3): 82–7.

Yeomans, D. (2002) *Constructing Vocational Education: From TVEI to GNVQ*. Leeds: School of Education, University of Leeds (http://www.leeds.ac.uk/educol/documents/00002214.htm).

CHAPTER SIXTEEN

Overview and discussion: overall conclusions

Ann Lewis and Brahm Norwich

Early discussion about the nature of this book led us to place SEN-specific categories at the heart of the book's structure and focus. This was a direct result of the position at which we had arrived as a result of our review concerning the SEN specificity of teaching strategies in relation to children with learning difficulties (see Chapter 1). Interestingly, coincident with our work on this book the DfES issued category-based guidance about identifying individual pupils according to conventional special needs categories (including MLD) for the purposes of government planning, studying of trends and monitoring interventions concerning special educational needs (DfES 2003). This does not necessarily imply that those categories have relevance for teaching, although the DfES does see the categories as having significance for planning and policy development.

We note that although contributors to this book might have made claims for the usefulness of *other* category bases, none has done so. Our centralizing of special educational needs did not presume an acceptance of the usefulness of those categories for the planning of teaching and the contributors have taken contrasting positions about this.

The nature of the special educational needs groups

Defining the nature of each of the 'SEN groups' discussed in this book was not straightforward. For some writers, group definitions reflected the use of medical definitions and associated forms of causality (Down's syndrome, PMLD, deafness, deafblindness, visual impairment). In a sub-set of chapters important distinctions were made between early (natal) and later onset of difficulties (deafblindness) and between medical contrasted with functional definitions (visual impairment). For some, group definitions reflected presenting 'symptoms' or behaviours (ASD, PMLD, language difficulties, dyspraxia).

Environment, including social networks and systems, was a significant *defining* aspect of the group for writers focusing on low attainers and MLD. This is inevitably linked with wide differences over time and place in defining such groups, because as the context shifts, so do the perceived difficulties (or their absence). Thus, for these groups (at least for our contributors) resolving pedagogic issues is likely to be salient in avoiding the creation of exceptional learning needs.

Environmental factors were seen as *interacting* with biological and psychological factors in defining one group (AD/HD). Less strongly, environment was regarded as significantly *mediating* difficulties for those writing on autism, Down's syndrome, deafness, dyslexia and EBD. The implication is that for both these sets of groups (as for those noted above for whom environment was seen as a defining characteristic) school factors will play a significant role in determining the extent to which such pupils are perceived to have exceptional learning needs. This does not in itself necessarily suggest either a general or an individual differences position.

Virtually all writers, to varying degrees, referred to the potential, or likely, co-occurrence of difficulties (including, for some contributors, mental health problems). This recognition of co-occurring difficulties was emphasized particularly in the chapters on ASD, dyspraxia, deafblindness, deafness, MLD, SLD, PMLD and AD/HD. Thus it is unlikely that 'pure' group-specific pedagogical practices based on the nature of the group could be sustained. All contributors also linked the nature of the individual group with continua of effects or impacts on learning, implying that, even if hypothesized, group-related pedagogic strategies would need to be applied differentially. Thus even this position places individual needs at the centre of pedagogic decision-making.

Conceptual framework: curriculum, pedagogy and knowledge

The orientation of the book, set out in the introductory chapter, was that *teaching* is regarded in terms of the interconnections between curriculum, pedagogy and knowledge. Questions about specialization or distinctiveness can be asked about these three interrelated aspects. The term *teaching* is therefore being used here in a general sense to cover a range of issues concerned with:

- What: curriculum issues.
- How: pedagogy and knowledge issues.
- Where: setting issues including both location and social aspects.
- Why: the rationale for addressing the above issues in terms of wider political and socio-cultural values and commitments.

We are aware that terms like teaching and pedagogy are not always used in these ways, so it is important to draw attention to the ambiguities that are associated with these commonly used terms.

Curriculum

In the introductory chapter the relationship between curriculum and pedagogy is presented as one where curriculum questions can set the determining context for questions about the commonality – specialization of pedagogy. This view was supported in several of the chapters. In the first chapter we highlighted the potentially contested nature of how a common curriculum could be conceptualized and designed. This includes traditional issues about curriculum design, such as academic versus vocational orientations, process versus product design approaches and collected versus integrated approaches to curriculum areas. The latter aspect was not mentioned in the first chapter, but did emerge in the chapter on children with speech, language and communication needs (SLCN), as we discuss below. Curriculum design involves different levels of generality and specificity at which commonality–specialization questions can be addressed. If commonality is set at the general level of aims and goals, then this enables flexibility to be built in. Specialized programmes for some children (supplementary or remedial/therapeutic programmes) can be mixed with common ones. If commonality is set at the level of specific programmes in particular areas of the curriculum, then questions of appropriateness to children with unusual or exceptional needs come to be significant. In the starting framework we identified two broad forms of specialized curriculum areas and programmes: supplementary or additional ones and remedial or restorative ones.

The contributors to the book adopt positions about the curriculum relevant to their particular areas of special educational needs that address all these aspects of the starting framework. They do this in different styles, as would be expected. Some discuss and cover a range of curriculum approaches and highlight differences found in their area of special educational needs, others take up a particular position, not intending to show a range within their area of special educational needs. Both approaches are useful and make a contribution to the overall picture. However, the implication is that the book overall does not provide a definitive overview of all teaching approaches – it is more illustrative of issues and positions.

Several of the chapters indicate that there are internal differences about curriculum questions, some of which can be attributed to the diversity or heterogeneity of the needs within their area of special needs. In the chapter on deafness, differences in curriculum approach are presented in terms of the heterogeneity of the broad group and related to the deaf culture based on the use of signing. There are similarities between the deaf and visual impairment areas with respect to the heterogeneity of the groups. In the visual impairment area the relevance of additional curriculum programmes concerned with mobility, for example, depends on severity of impairment. By contrast, in the PMLD area, the chapter indicated some difference between programmes in terms of the adoption of a more process or a more product orientation to curriculum design. Two of the chapters also provided evidence of how the wider cultural context influences the curriculum approach. In the deafness area, different curriculum approaches reflect commitments to whether communication is in terms of an English, signed English or signed bilingual medium. By contrast, the chapter on low attainers showed how the school curriculum can be linked to wider interventions outside the school with families and the neighbourhood.

Several of the chapters indicated that curriculum commonality could only be at the broadest general level of common principles, as otherwise the diversity of educational needs would call for specialization. This was most explicitly argued in the chapter on ASD, which questioned the concept of a 'universal curriculum design'. Curriculum relevance was judged to be more important than curriculum breadth for this group. Programmes for this group, it was argued, also require a therapeutic or remedial model. The chapter on PMLD implied that the curriculum for this group had a focus on communication and covered fewer curriculum areas. This was another example of the priority being to relevance rather than breadth.

Four of the chapters suggested that their areas required a curriculum approach that departed from the current dominant curriculum practices in the UK, though these variations depended on the particular area of SEN. In the ASD chapter, it was argued that access and remedial orientations needed to be combined. The strong emphasis on access in special education was not enough. A similar approach was evident, though not explicitly stated, in the AD/HD chapter. There it was argued that in teaching children with AD/HD it was important to circumvent difficulties by working to strengths, while also focusing on programmes to reduce inattentiveness and impulsiveness. The AD/HD chapter also implied that curriculum programmes need to be more flexible and geared to pupil learning styles. This is based on the argument that the uniformity and product orientation of current curricula are involved in the causation of AD/HD. The curriculum variation for children with SLCN involved a move away from a collected to a more integrated approach to curriculum areas, in particular between subject learning and language learning. For the PMLD group the development of intensive interaction programmes can be seen as a departure from a more product- or target-based curriculum approach. The chapter on low attainers questioned the appropriateness of traditional academic curriculum provision for those aged 13–16 years (Key Stage 4).

It is interesting that there were no clear links between these different areas of special educational needs in which contributors call for variations from dominant curriculum practices. This contrasts with the two related areas of SEN, deafness and visual impairment (sensory impairments) where the chapters indicate the need for additional curriculum programmes. In the visual impairment area, there are programmes focusing on mobility, use of residual vision, maximum use of senses and special literacy routes. In the deafness area, there are distinctive communication routes, though only where communication is in terms of signed bilingual or signed English approaches. Though the chapter on deafblindness does not indicate the need for additional programmes for this group, tangible symbol systems were identified as important. Their use could be taken to imply that additional programmes are needed for this group too.

For most of the areas of special educational needs there was no indication of the need for specialized curriculum programmes, or departures from dominant curriculum practices. These chapters suggest the need for a greater emphasis on certain common curriculum areas, *continua of common curriculum approaches*, the curriculum version of continua of pedagogic strategies. In the chapter on MLD, it is suggested that some people advocate a particular emphasis on programmes focusing on problem-solving and social interaction. In the PMLD chapter, there is reference to a curriculum emphasis not only on communication but also on choice-making, while in the EBD chapter the emphasis is more on the area of personal and social/emotional development. The curriculum emphasis in two other chapters, deafblindness and Down's syndrome, is on sensory strengths; in deafblindness on tactile senses and in Down's syndrome on visual rather than auditory senses. By contrast, in the chapters on MLD and SLD, the emphasis is not on curriculum areas, but on the degree of structure of the progression and sequence of the programmes. The focus is on the sequencing of small steps in both MLD and SLD, though the chapter refers to criticism of this in the SLD area and moves to more naturalistic approaches.

Curriculum is not treated as a significant focus compared to pedagogy and knowledge in the chapters on dyslexia and dyspraxia, two related forms of specific learning difficulties. In two chapters, on deafblindness and PMLD, it is explained how curriculum programmes draw on early child development stages and process. In deafblindness the programmes focus on early developmental stages associated with theories of attachment, early socialization and language, while in PMLD the intensive interaction programmes are also based on theory about early adult–infant interactions.

In terms of the starting framework about curriculum, some chapters referred to curriculum approaches that aimed to reduce difficulties rather than circumvent or accept them: the ASD, AD/HD and low attainers chapters. However, there were no references to specialized programmes focusing on cognitive/intellectual difficulties, such as instrumental enrichment or thinking skills programmes, in the MLD or SLD chapters. This may be because of the scarcity of programme effectiveness evidence or possibly because an emphasis on these skills may be seen as relevant to a common programme subject to a variation of emphasis for these groups, as was suggested in the MLD chapter's reference to problem-solving skills.

Knowledge

Relevant knowledge has emerged more strongly in the chapters in this book than it did in our preceding review, which focused on learning difficulties only (see Chapter 1). The inclusion of knowledge in the model proposed in Chapter 1 arose in part from the responses to our initial review (Lewis and Norwich

2000; Norwich and Lewis 2001). A minority of contributors to this book (low attainers, MLD, EBD, SLCN, deafblindness) did not discuss the knowledge aspects outlined in Chapter 1. In some cases the omission was deliberate, in others the omission was justified, in discussion with us, as reflecting wordage constraints and the relative, not absolute, lack of importance of 'knowledge'. Some implied knowledge requirements can be extrapolated from the chapters. For the other contributors, the nature of required knowledge in relation to our identified groups can be seen as spanning four foci.

Knowledge 1: the nature of the special needs group

This is strongly apparent in the chapters on PMLD, visual impairment, deafness, Down's syndrome, dyspraxia, dyslexia, ASD and AD/HD. The position is that, regardless of pedagogic relevance, such knowledge is valuable in its own right as underpinning the learner's development. One illustration of a strong position in relation to knowledge of the special needs group is the position taken in relation to deaf children. Here the knowledge base is strongly distinctive (reflecting advocacy of deaf culture). Some writers in this book argue for the importance of group knowledge even when the nature of the group is contested (e.g. dyslexia), suggesting that uncertainties about the nature of the group may be rectified by the field over time, rather than seen as irrelevant or misplaced. The AD/HD chapter expresses most clearly a view about how knowledge 1 – of the nature of AD/HD – impacts on teachers' practical thinking and decision-making.

Some aspects of knowledge are not directly relevant in relation to teaching strategy (e.g. life expectancy for children with Down's syndrome), but may be indirectly relevant. For example, they may intensify the salience of specialized knowledge for the knower (see knowledge 2). However, not all contributors make a case for knowledge of the group. For some contributors, group-related knowledge is not relevant, as the group label is not seen as having a valid, unique identity with relevance for pedagogic decisions (low attainers, MLD). There the value of the group labels is in drawing attention to the wider context of learning and the need to address, for example, the range of economic, family and community factors that may, despite schools' best efforts, hamper school-based learning. This signalling function of the label is echoed by some writers (AD/HD, dyslexia), who see the group label as carrying both alerting or orienting and specific pedagogic functions.

Knowledge 2: relates to oneself as teacher

Three chapters in particular (EBD, autism, low attainers) indicate that a further relevant aspect of knowledge relates to oneself as a teacher. Self-knowledge and professional identity may be linked with particular value positions (for example, valuing a broad and learner-centred curriculum) that operate across all learners. In this context what seems to be masquerading as an SEN-specific approach may be concealing a position that (ideally) would be applied to all learners but, perhaps because of perceived system features, is articulated in relation to the less constrained special needs context. In contrast, self-knowledge as a professional in the field may, drawing on social identity theory, be linked with a very strong SEN-oriented identity and expressed through various group maintenance strategies, such as advocacy of highly specialized approaches (Lewis and Crisp 2004). In this position the special needs group label has relevance to allied professionals, rather than to pupils, in identifying interprofessional relationships.

Knowledge 3: relates to the psychology of learning

This reflects a unique differences position in that knowledge about the psychology of learning would be seen as required for effective teaching of all learners (see chapters on Down's syndrome, SLD, ASD). For example, one might extrapolate that a sound understanding of self-regulation and attendant processes is of value to the teacher whether working with children with AD/HD, sensory needs or a range of learning difficulties.

Knowledge 4: knowledge of curriculum areas and general pedagogic strategies

This also reflects a unique differences position in that knowledge about curriculum areas and general pedagogic strategies is assumed to be important in relation to all learners (see chapters on Down's syndrome, low attainment, MLD, AD/HD, SLCN).

These four aspects of knowledge may be integrated and linked to pedagogy by conceptualizing knowledge 1 as a filter through which the other forms of knowledge are seen, leading to curriculum and pedagogic decisions. Where knowledge 1 is strongly defined (i.e. acting as a powerful filter) the resultant teaching strategy will be perceived as appearing to be very different from practice elsewhere; where knowledge 1 is less clearly defined (weak filter) this will not be the case.

One can illustrate this with reference to chapters that reflect contrasting positions. The chapter on low attainment reflects a weak 'SEN' filter position (broader social and economic factors are seen as paramount) and so the label has no usefulness in terms of the knowledge base from which to plan teaching. In contrast, the chapters on visual impairment and AD/HD note the distinctiveness of these groups and therefore the associated knowledge base; running through to produce different forms of teaching (if only by degree). The 'strong filter' position concerning knowledge, in interaction with knowledge 3 and 4, can be related to points about access and the need for distinctiveness at this level (for example, the argument for specialized resources through which particular groups of learners may access a common curriculum).

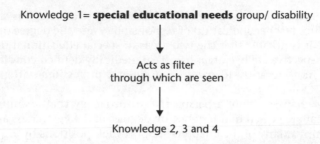

Knowledge 1= **special educational needs** group/ disability

Acts as filter
through which are seen

Knowledge 2, 3 and 4

LEADING TO PEDAGOGIC STRATEGIES FOR PARTICULAR LEARNER

Figure 16.1   Relationship between kinds of teaching knowledge

Pedagogy

The most widely made point in the chapters as regards pedagogy was the
scarcity of a researched evidence base about pedagogic strategies for the various special needs areas. Several of the chapters also commented that this was
partly due to the difficulties and complexities of undertaking systematic
evaluation and research studies. The assumed model here is one of comparative experimental or quasi-experimental evaluation studies. However, only the
AD/HD and EBD chapters approached the question of pedagogy in terms of
research into classroom pedagogy as involving teachers' thinking that lies
behind teacher actions. The analysis in the AD/HD chapter drew on research
into teaching as involving professional craft knowledge. Pedagogy when considered from this perspective is seen to be strongly influenced by teachers'
perceptions of pupil characteristics and to involve the use of ready-made categories, a 'typing' process. It was argued that typing can have negative or
positive potential, and that knowledge of conditions like AD/HD can sharpen
less sophisticated forms of the typing of children, and in so doing have a
positive impact on pedagogy. This perspective is very relevant to the main
themes of the book, because the argument about AD/HD might be applied to
other areas of SEN. It also illustrates how knowledge about the area of SEN, one
of the aspects of teaching examined in the book, comes to be relevant to
pedagogic matters.

This focus on typing in teachers' professional and pedagogic thinking also
presents a coherent way of introducing and supporting the notion of specific
group pedagogic needs. Yet only two chapters argue for the significance of
distinctive group pedagogy, ASD and AD/HD. It is argued that children with
ASD also have common pedagogic needs, but that their individual needs can
only be identified through a framework of group needs. As we discuss below,
this was the most coherent case made in the book for what we called in the
introductory chapter a group differences pedagogic position. In the AD/HD
chapter, the case is also made for a distinctive AD/HD pedagogy, though there
is no discussion of how these group pedagogic needs relate to common and

individual needs. The use of general AD/HD specific strategies, it is claimed, is likely to reduce teacher abdication of responsibility and the degree of need for medication. It is notable that the two areas of special educational needs that take this perspective are two areas based on medically defined conditions that have come more recently to parent, public and professional attention and interest.

The other chapters adopt a perspective to pedagogy that assumes generic strategies that are geared to difference by degrees of deliberateness and intensity of teaching. Many of the chapters support their positions by arguing that variations on the pedagogic strategies for their special needs area can also be useful for other children. The chapters on dyslexia, dyspraxia, MLD and SLD, for example, represent the pedagogic variations as reflecting deliberateness and intensity, in line with our original review of the learning difficulties literature (Norwich and Lewis 2001). In the SLD chapter, for example, it is argued that generic strategies, such as cuing, prompting, modelling and self-management strategies, are attuned to individual needs. In the sensory impairment areas, there is also reference to generic strategies, with more deliberate teaching for visual impairment and a continuum of strategies for deafness, when using an English approach. Two chapters that focus on broad areas, EBD and low attainers, point out that the diversity within these groups reduces any pedagogic significance of the category. In both areas it is also argued that the intensification of common pedagogic strategies required for these groups is not distinctive to the groups. In the case of EBD this is seen to be so even for the emotional and self-related aspects of pedagogy. In the case of low attainers, it is suggested that pedagogy is connected to wider interventions that involve whole schools and families and may be preventive in focusing on underlying at-risk factors outside schools. Though it is suggested that the different interventions relevant to this diverse group may be non-educational ones, all the examples used in this chapter involve some connection between classroom, school-wide and outside school interventions.

Though the starting model of teaching put pedagogy in the context of curriculum, it did not spell out how these aspects interacted. This is where some of the chapters have helped to advance this framework by showing the interrelationship between curriculum and pedagogic aspects. In the visual impairment chapter this is done through introducing the distinction between macro and micro pedagogic strategies. While the macro strategies are presented as generic, the micro strategies might be distinctive for those with visual impairment, where the modality of access might be different, e.g. through touch rather than sight. The interrelation between curriculum and pedagogy is also evident in the deafness area, where pedagogic strategies depend on curriculum orientation according to the use of English, signed English or signed bilingual communication approaches. The PMLD chapter also indicates the strong links between pedagogic strategies and curriculum approaches. In two other chapters there is reference to curriculum approaches that cannot be separated from pedagogic strategies. In the SLCN chapter, the pedagogic strategies are dependent on the integration of curriculum areas where subject and language learning are combined. In the EBD chapter there is reference to a pedagogic tradition that is integral to a learner-centred and process curriculum model.

As we noted in the above section on curriculum, the chapters on PMLD and deafblindness indicate that teaching is strongly informed by developmental psychology about typical development. It is also interesting that the two chapters that deal with the specific learning difficulties, dyslexia and dyspraxia, refer to background and related pedagogic factors that go beyond our focus on pedagogic strategies. In the dyslexia chapter it is suggested that there are other relevant factors, such as the general quality of teaching and the availability of teaching resources. In the dyspraxia chapter other pedagogic foci are indicated, such as the focus on language competencies and taking account of gender factors given the predominance of boys with the condition.

Individual versus general differences positions

What is represented in the introductory chapter as the difference between these two positions hinges on the significance of group-specific pedagogic strategies in informing pedagogic decisions and practices. It is important to clarify what is and is not involved in this distinction. The general differences position is not just about specific group needs, or, in other words, pedagogic implications do not flow just from group membership. This position also assumes that common needs inform decisions and practices and that these are attuned to individual needs. Nor is the individual differences position merely about individual needs. It assumes that decisions and practices are informed by a framework of general needs that are attuned to individual needs. The individual differences position can be seen as a default position; if we do not take account of specific group needs, then a reasonable alternative is to take account of common and individual needs and therefore adopt the individual differences position.

We might also expect that areas of SEN, where the group is more specifically defined, are more likely to adopt the general differences position. There is some evidence for this in the chapters on ASD and AD/HD. In the ASD chapter this group, despite its diversity, is presented as requiring different approaches, not just more of the same. In the AD/HD chapter the case is made for incorporating insights about AD/HD into teachers' practical theorizing and teaching. The ASD and AD/HD groups are defined more specifically than some of the others areas covered, such as EBD or MLD. The position taken in the ASD chapter is that needs are recognized through group differences, but not determined by them. It is also interesting that the area of EBD, which might be construed as including AD/HD and aspects of ASD, is a more general area that was not presented as supporting a general differences position.

The general difference position was also adopted in the chapter on deafness. As indicated in the previous section, where there is a commitment to signing as the form of communication, the use of a system such as BSL represents a strong version of the general differences position. The other area where a general differences position may be relevant is PMLD. It is noted in this chapter that the definition of this group implies a general differences position, but that the specialized teaching shares common characteristics with general teaching. Though pedagogy is presented as specialized techniques at the high intensity end of continua of pedagogic strategies, the degree of intensity may be seen as sufficient to count as difference of kind. This interpretation fits with a similar point made in the chapter on SLD, which is allied to the PMLD area (see below).

The other chapters incline towards the individual differences position, in line with the original literature review that we undertook several years ago. It is widely stated that there is no single or distinctive pedagogy and that strategies relevant to those identified in one kind of grouping are relevant to other learners too. However, a very important point is also made in the SLD chapter, which applies to other areas, that the presenting features of pedagogic strategies may appear different when the principles may still be the same. Strategies at the far end of intensity and deliberateness of the continuum of general strategies may at some point come to be seen to be different in kind and not degree. It is suggested that perceptions of difference in relation to pedagogic strategy may reflect the viewer's stance about learning and pupils.

Several general points can be made in summary. The areas where authors support the general differences position appear to be more clearly specified (ASD, AD/HD). General differences positions are also supported where pedagogic strategies interact with aspects of teaching access (visual impairment) and communication mode (deafness). The general differences position is also one that avoids simple stereotyping in terms of group-based pedagogic needs; it takes account of common and individual needs. However, the chapters that adopt the individual differences position show the limits of this position. High intensity along continua of general pedagogic strategies may come to be construed as no longer a matter of difference of degree, but of kind. However, a distinctive pedagogy for a child identified within, say, the PMLD group may not be relevant to another child within that diverse group.

Distinctiveness may be identified at an individual level, but this does not turn the individual differences position into a general differences position. The reason for this is that the general differences position requires a general relationship between a distinctive group, however defined, and a generalized and distinctive kind of pedagogy. The book illustrates how far we are from making these kinds of generalizations. It is crucial to be clear that when we discuss the distinction between individual and general difference positions, we are talking at the level of pedagogic principles, not about practical programmes with objectives and teaching procedures and materials. Teaching that embodies the same pedagogic principles adapted at different points along a continuum of intensity can be expected to involve different kinds of programmes at the levels of practical procedures and goals. To the teacher, the National Literacy Strategy will appear different from a programme like 'Alpha to Omega', designed for children with dyslexic type literacy difficulties. However, these programmes may share common pedagogic principles. This book is about the principles of teaching and their specialization.

Additional themes arising

Contributors have also made additional points that fall into three broad categories: intensification, research and professional training and education.

Intensification

Several contributors highlight aspects of pedagogic strategy (or of learning) in relation to a particular group and in so doing signal their wider research relevance. For example, sensory aspects of learning/teaching are noted as a relevant research focus for deafblind pupils. If one accepts our notion of continua of intensification (encompassing attentiveness and deliberation in teaching) then the sensory aspects of teaching that are so self-evidently important for deafblind pupils may be used in a less intense form for – say – low attainers or pupils with AD/HD. Because the research question has not been posed in this way, the evidence is not there to refute or support this hypothesis.

Research

All contributors note the serious dearth of research evidence (in terms of conceptually useful or valid approaches) on which to base their conclusions concerning the commonality or otherwise of pedagogic strategies. For many contributors the existing research evidence fails to address this question due to the repercussions of the problems with defining the special needs group. This is immediately apparent with those groups that are notoriously difficult to define (e.g. 'low attainers' or MLD) but, less expectedly, the same issue is noted with (superficially) more clear-cut groups such as deafblind or SLD. Thus, the research implications of the fuzziness of all the group labels in terms of unambiguous and relevant learner characteristics are for the adoption of research based on alternative dimensions (such as individual learner/teacher characteristics; or other, more categorical features, such as performance on standardized self-esteem or attainment measures). This points to a fine-grained and individual-learner centred approach.

This perceived absence of good research evidence has prompted our contributors to draw more heavily than we did in our original review on their expertise and professional experience in the selected field, to make hypotheses or claims for the importance of particular features of pedagogic strategy. How representative of their fields our contributors are is an open question. For some of the special educational needs groups in particular (notably deafness, ASD, dyslexia, AD/HD, emotional and behavioural difficulties, language) views within the field are polarized or diverse and personal value positions will shape strongly the frame within which questions about optimum teaching strategies are located. However, no research is value-free, so any attempt to research special educational needs and teaching strategy will reflect personal value positions; this is just more apparent in these hotly contested fields.

Some contributors make claims concerning the need for long time scales to show change, implying the need for longitudinal or possibly a series of cross-sectional designs. One response to this point is that the more fine grained the measure of change the more one would expect to be able to demonstrate change over a relatively short time scale (even for pupils with PMLD or SLD). In 'typically developing' populations one way round this problem might be to use analyses of secondary data, but the definitional problems noted earlier preclude this in the special educational needs context.

Professional training and education

A four-pronged approach to professional training and education in the special educational needs field can be adduced from a synthesis and critique of the chapters in this book.

First, the advocacy of a fine-grained approach to research in this field resonates with the stress on teaching as a craft, noted particularly in the chapters on AD/HD, emotional and behavioural difficulties and, less explicitly, ASD. In line with this point, several contributors note the unsatisfactory nature of 'packaged' programmes and the need to avoid 'quick fixes' in teaching children with SEN. An underlying theme, meshing with the notion of the *intensification of common pedagogic strategies*, is the skilfulness required to apply a common strategy differentially. This suggests that training in the special needs field needs to focus on this cultivation of craft knowledge, beginning with the 'commonality' position and moving through degrees of intensification and deliberation. Included in this may be the recognition of the value in borrowing and adapting approaches originating with one group to apply to another (noted in the language chapter).

Second, several contributors make a case for applying knowledge from child development and the psychology of learning to the context of special educational needs (SLD, Down's syndrome, PMLD, deafblindness). If one accepts this case (Norwich 2000), then professional education and training also need to address these areas. This developmental and psychological knowledge and understanding offers broad and holistic perspectives that can inform the processes of teaching and learning by opening up practical options. As the chapters have illustrated, this kind of knowledge and understanding can act as a cognitive resource for curriculum and pedagogic thinking, decision-making and practices.

Third, the broader social or cultural contexts are noted as significant in relation to curriculum and pedagogic strategies (low attainers, deafness, EBD). This indicates the need for professional education and training to be located as 'learning to teach children with SEN' within the immediate and wider social and cultural contexts of schooling and teaching. Finally, we would argue that a key aspect of professional education and training will include, but also go beyond, a competency model based on practical knowledge and skill. It will include an understanding of principles and concepts that underpin and help to make sense of competencies. This understanding can inform the development and deployment of competencies. We propose that the conceptual framework presented in this book – in terms of the interaction of knowledge, curriculum and pedagogy – the commonality–specialization continuum and the concepts of intensification and deliberateness have general relevance to preparing teachers to work with those with special educational needs in mainstream and separate settings. In the UK context, this means going beyond the approach used by the Teacher Training Agency in the National SEN Specialist standards (TTA 1999).

These standards are designed to assist identification of the specific training needs for those teaching children with 'severe and complex' SEN. There is reference to 'specialist teaching' in the Standards, though the language tends to be in terms of 'professional knowledge, understanding and skills common across the full range of severe and complex forms of SEN' (page 4.12a). 'Specialist' therefore comes to be associated with 'severe and complex SEN', the implication being of something distinctive in teaching compared with teaching those with less severe SEN and those without SEN. Who is included and excluded from the 'severe and complex' group is interesting – of the broad groups we have considered, those with specific learning difficulties are included, but moderate learning difficulties is excluded. There is no reference to degrees of differences within these groups, though the limited nature of these categories is noted.

One of the five aspects of the Core SEN Standards, which are common to all areas of severe and complex SEN, covers 'effective teaching, ensuring maximum access to the curriculum' (TTA, 1999 page 11). Teachers with specialist knowledge and skills are, for example, expected to:

iii. analyse complex sequences of learning and set smaller, but appropriate, achievable targets for pupils whose progress is not demonstrated when set solely against more conventional assessment criteria;
iv. identify individual learning outcomes and develop, implement and evaluate a range of approaches, including, for example, task analysis, skills analysis and target setting, to help pupils achieve those outcomes in a variety of settings;
v. explore ways of reducing barriers to learning.

What is specific about teaching those with special educational needs is absent in this formulation. The theme running through references to effective specialist teaching is the generalized phrase 'ensuring greater access to the curriculum'. These statements about effective teaching certainly apply to teaching pupils with less severe SEN and to low attainers not identified as having SEN. What is so notable about these National SEN Specialist Standards is the omission of a framework for conceptualizing the nature of specialist teaching and its relationship to teaching in general.

We propose the framework used in this book as a starting point for setting out a coherent and common framework of teaching that is inclusive, while making it possible for differences in the degree of intensity, attention and deliberateness in teaching to be recognized. However much research and development work is needed:

- to identify the different strands or dimensions along which teaching is intensified in curriculum and pedagogic terms;
- to analyse established and dependable teaching practices for the range of diverse special educational needs in terms of these strands.

It is unlikely that teaching standards that are relevant to pupils along the full continuum of need can be established without a more evidence-based and conceptual approach to their construction.

Concluding comments: implications for schools, services and policy

'What are the implications of this work for policy and practice?' is something we have been asked on many occasions over the past four years in which we have developed this work. As we note in the preface, this book does not aspire to be about specific 'tips for teachers', but aims to address fundamental conceptual questions concerning the specificity or otherwise of 'SEN teaching'. It has cleared some of the theoretical ground in making some key conceptual distinctions (individual versus general differences position), illustrating the interaction between aspects of teaching (curriculum, knowledge and pedagogy). It has also contributed by taking a position in relation to the question about commonality–specialization of teaching through highlighting the value of the *continuum* concept and how differentiation or specialization can be seen as a process of *intensification*.

Since our initial review of pedagogy for children with various forms of learning difficulties, we have wanted to extend our analyses to other areas of SEN, while responding to those who have shown us that we needed a broader framework for analysis. On the basis of the contributions about the range of areas of SEN in this book, we can conclude that the traditional special needs categories used in the UK, and internationally, have limited usefulness in the context of planning, or monitoring, teaching and learning in most areas. Where it is argued that they have usefulness, the categories operate as orienting concepts and inform decision-making about teaching as one of several other important elements. Special needs categories may have some administrative convenience in terms of additional resourcing, staffing, materials and equipment, but these are not issues we have addressed in this book.

Our conceptual framework also implies that teaching children with SEN has to be seen in terms of a many-levelled interacting system in which individual children are nested in the class group, whole school, local authority, regional and central government policies and practices. Classroom pedagogy is nested within teaching programmes that are determined by school and then ultimately national programmes and commitments. Practical pedagogies for those with special educational needs might look different from dominant mainstream pedagogies, but these are differences, we have argued, at the level of concrete programmes, materials and perhaps settings. They are not differences in the principles of curriculum design and pedagogic strategy.

We contend that a robust understanding of the debate embodied in this book should be part of the professional culture of all teachers, including those working predominantly with children with special educational needs. The book is presented as much as a start to this debate as a compilation and analyses of contemporary positions by a national group of experts in the field. The stance that we have taken calls for a response from others in the search for justifications for particular pedagogic practices. As such, the implications for policy and provision overlap with the earlier points concerning professional education and training.

References

DfES (2003) *Data Collection by Type of Special Educational Needs. Guidance*. London: DfES.

Lewis, A. and Crisp, R. J. (2004) Measuring social identity in the professional context of provision for pupils with special needs, *School Psychology International*, 25(3): 101–18.

Lewis, A. and Norwich, B. (2000) Is there a distinctive special educational needs pedagogy?, in *Specialist Teaching for Special Educational Needs*. Tamworth: NASEN.

Norwich, B. (2000) Educational psychology and special educational needs: how they relate and where is the relationship going?, *Educational and Child Psychology*, 16(2): 5–15.

Norwich, B. and Lewis, A. (2001) Mapping a pedagogy for special educational needs, *British Educational Research Journal*, 27(3): 313–31.

TTA (1999) *National SEN Specialist Standards*. London: TTA.

Index

Page references in italics refer to figures and diagrams. Special needs groups are referred to by initials, but the main entry gives the full description of the term in brackets.

Related books from Open University Press
Purchase from www.openup.co.uk or order through your local bookseller

ICT AND SPECIAL EDUCATIONAL NEEDS
A TOOL FOR INCLUSION

Lani Florian and John Hegarty (eds)

Information and Communications Technology (ICT) is indispensable to those who teach learners with special educational needs. This book gives the broader context for the use of ICT in special and inclusive settings. It gives a wide range of examples of ICT in use and considers the role of technology in overcoming barriers of access to the curriculum; includes in-depth examinations of the uses of ICT as a teaching tool to promote inclusion and raise standards for all; and features contributions from researchers and practitioners who explore the development of ICT, recent innovations, assessment, and specialist knowledge. This book will be invaluable to teachers on professional development courses and those preparing to teach learners with special educational needs, as well as experienced professionals seeking to update their knowledge and gain new inspiration in this rapidly developing area.

Contents
Introduction – ICT and SEN: issues and debates – ICT, SEN and schools: a historical perspective of government initiatives – From integration to inclusion: using ICT to support learners special educational needs in the ordinary classroom – Using computer-based assessment to identify learning problems – Integrated learning systems, literacy and self-esteem – ICT and SEN: a whole school approach – Innovations in ICT – Using virtual environments – Managing SEN provision with ICT – Service development and staff training – References – Index.

160pp   0 335 21195 X (Paperback)   0 335 21196 8 (Hardback)

SPECIAL EDUCATIONAL NEEDS, INCLUSION AND DIVERSITY
A TEXTBOOK

Norah Frederickson and Tony Cline

This book has the potential to become *the* textbook on special educational needs. Written specifically with the requirements of student teachers, trainee educational psychologists, SENCOs and SEN Specialist Teachers in mind, it provides a comprehensive and detailed discussion of the major issues in special education. Whilst recognising the complex and difficult nature of many special educational needs, the authors place a firm emphasis on inclusion and suggest practical strategies enabling professionals to maximise inclusion at the same time as recognising and supporting diversity.

Key features include:

• Takes full account of linguistic, cultural and ethnic diversity unlike many other texts in the field
• Addresses the new SEN Code of Practice and is completely up to date
• Recognises current concerns over literacy and numeracy and devotes two chapters to these areas of need
• Offers comprehensive and detailed coverage of major issues in special educational needs in one volume
• Accessibly written with the needs of the student and practitioner in mind

Contents
Introduction – Part one: Principles and concepts – Children, families, schools and the wider community: an integrated approach – Concepts of special educational needs – Inclusion – Special educational needs: pathways of development – Part two: Assessment in context – Identification and assessment – Reducing bias in assessment – Curriculum based assessment – Learning environments – Part three: Areas of need – Learning difficulties – Language – Literacy – Mathematics – Hearing impairment – Emotional and behaviour difficulties – Social skills – References – Index.

528pp   0 335 20402 3 (Paperback)   0 335 20973 4 (Hardback)